ETHICS AND COLLEGE STUDENT LIFE

Kenneth A. Strike
Cornell University

Pamela A. Moss
Cornell University

Allyn and Bacon
Boston • London • Toronto • Sydney • Tokyo • Singapore

Series Editor: Virginia Lanigan
Editorial Assistant: Nihad Farooq
Editorial-Production Service: Matrix Productions
Editorial-Production Administrator: Rosalie Briand
Cover Designer: Suzanne Harbison
Composition Buyer: Linda Cox
Manufacturing Buyer: Suzanne Lareau

Allyn & Bacon
A Viacom Company
160 Gould Street
Needham Heights, MA 02194
www.abacon.com

Library of Congress Cataloging-in-Publication Data

Strike, Kenneth A.
    Ethics and college student life / Kenneth A. Strike, Pamela Moss.
        p.   cm.
    Includes bibliographical references (p.).
    ISBN 0-205-17347-0
    1. College students—United States—Conduct of life.   2. Ethics—United States.
    3. Moral education—United States.   I. Moss, Pamela.   II Title.
    LA229.S665   1996
    378.1'981—dc20   96-12148
    CIP

Printed in the United States of America
10   9   8   7   6   5   4   3   2   1   01   00   99   98   97   96

*For Daniel and Janet, who survived college
and became fine people without the benefit of this book.*

*And for Madeleine and Cora,
who will be spared the necessity of doing so.*

CONTENTS

1

INTRODUCTION

SOME MORAL IDEALS

This book asks you to reflect on some of the ethical aspects of being a student. No doubt the very suggestion that you can think about ethics will raise questions. Some of them may be: "Aren't moral questions about values, and aren't values private things? Are you going to try to impose your values on us?" Or "Aren't ethics intimately related to religion? Can you really discuss ethics apart from religion, and can you really get anywhere discussing ethics in religiously diverse situations?" Perhaps you might even ask "Why should I be ethical? There may be occasions where I am better off if I'm not. I can get a better grade if I cautiously cheat on tests. If I can get away with it, why shouldn't I?"

We are going to say a few things about these questions later. We think, however, that our suggestions will make more sense if we start out by looking at an example of moral reflection and at some ethical principles that are important in thinking about moral issues. Thus we will first give you an example of ethically dubious conduct ("The File"). We will then describe various principles that often figure in moral reflection and try to illustrate how each of these principles might be used in thinking about why the conduct is unethical. In each of the subsequent sections of the book, we will provide a somewhat more complex case. There we will ask questions and suggest approaches to cases, but it will be your task to reflect on the case.

We have two broad goals we hope to accomplish in this book. It may help you to understand what they are. First, we want to help you learn to think clearly and powerfully about ethical issues, especially those that concern your life as a student. Thus, we will present some problems, mostly in the form of cases, and some ideas to help you think about these problems. We believe you will profit most from our work if you develop your own reactions to the cases with which we introduce each chapter before you read our discussion of them. It might be helpful if you make a few notes on your initial reactions to these cases and to the questions that follow them before you go on to read our discussion. You might even want to keep a journal.

Our second purpose is to help you to think of your college or university as a kind of moral community and to help you to make it one. Moral communities are places that take moral discussion seriously and try to achieve some shared understanding of what's right and wrong. Moral communities, we think, depend on *dialogue*, something about which we will have much to say later. For now you might think of dialogue as a special kind of discussion or conversation. Its purposes include mutual understanding and, when possible, moral consensus. It is an argumentative process that requires a kind of openness. It requires that you be willing to argue for your view and listen to the arguments of others. It requires that you be willing to persuade others and be open to being persuaded yourself. It means that you may have to hear people out patiently even if you sharply disagree with them. Moral community does not require that we always agree. But it does require that we be willing to listen to and consider the views of others.

Also, dialogue is more like a conversation between friends than a lecture or a sermon. When you discuss or debate with a friend, there may be both learning and edification, but there is not much teaching or preaching. In a dialogue, everyone is equal. No single authority dominates the conversation. If you are going to belong to a moral community, you have to be willing and able to participate in this kind of conversation. We hope this book will help you do that better.

Case 1.1: The File

The Co-op was a cooperative residence unit at Memorial College. Memorial was a commuter school. Most of its students were local and lived either with their families or in their own apartments. The Co-op had started as a way for students who had to rent to save a few dollars on rent and food. A large, somewhat decrepit old house near campus, it was owned and operated by its twenty-five current residents. It provided a social life for students who would otherwise have been disconnected; members often studied together and played together. New members were admitted only with the consent of a governing board, and many students wanted to join, not so much because they needed housing, but because they needed friends. Unfortunately, Co-op members were not known to be models of industry or studiousness. They were only occasionally successful athletes. While they usually managed to avoid failing outright in their academic work, some made it a matter of pride to get by with minimal effort. Few Co-op members permitted intellectual activity to interfere with the real work of having fun and making friends.

John wasn't entirely certain that he wanted to join the Co-op. He had been a reasonably serious student in high school, and he felt that academic work was important to his future. Nevertheless, his college experience so far had been lonely and joyless. He lived alone. He didn't have any place to belong, and he had only a few friends. Thus when one of those few friends decided to seek admission to the Co-op, John did, too. He was a little surprised that he was admitted, but he was pleased that his social life seemed secured.

Somewhere near the end of his first semester of membership, John began to get a new picture of his role in the Co-op. Carl, the Co-op's vice-president, introduced him to The File. The File contained A papers that members of the Co-op had collected from a wide range of large courses. The role of The File was to provide a database of successful papers that Co-op members could use in developing their own papers for various courses. What "developing" seemed to mean was that members were under strict instructions to modify any paper that they turned in sufficiently so that the plagiarism would not be obvious. The File even contained a meticulous record of when each paper had been used and to whom it had been submitted. Each paper was on disk so that adaptation was easy.

Carl explained to John that because he seemed academically talented, it was expected that he would be more of a provider than a user. Apparently each year the Co-op carefully selected a few providers to assist their less fortunate members. They would contribute their better papers to The File. Indeed, they were occasionally advised as to which courses needed additional contributions, and were expected to "seriously consider" enrolling for such courses. The providers, Carl assured John, were especially valued members of the Co-op, except for those selfish few who put their own interests ahead of the interests of the group. They often seemed to move out after a year or so because they just didn't fit in. Carl knew that John would fit in.

ISSUES

Consider some of the things we might ask about the ethical issues in this case. First, is anything wrong with the Co-op's maintaining The File? It seems intended to assist members in cheating or plagiarism. Why might cheating or plagiarism be wrong? Might The File have legitimate uses? Is it wrong for a student to get a grade that the student hasn't earned?

Is John being exploited? Carl seems to be offering John a trade of friendship for work. Is there anything wrong with such a trade? If so, what? Aren't many human relationships based on such exchanges? How does a trade of friendship for work differ from a trade of a salary for work? Is John being coerced?

What are the effects of The File on the college community? Is the community being harmed? Does the college community have purposes that are undermined by The File? Does the Co-op have any responsibility for the welfare of the college community? Are the students of this college even members of a community, or are they just customers paying a fee for a service?

We are now going to suggest a few ethical principles or concepts that might be used in examining this and other cases. We will explain the basic idea of the principle and then give an argument about the case that appeals to this principle. Consider whether you agree with these arguments and whether there are other applications of these principles that we haven't developed. Note that sometimes our comments about these principles may seem redundant. This might suggest that these concepts aren't mutually exclusive; perhaps some of the principles are just applications of others. Some philosophers, for example, would argue that what we call the *principle of benefit maximization* is the only principle required and that the others can be derived from it if they are useful at all. We don't plan to take a position on these issues of abstract philosophy, although you might enjoy discussing them. Instead, we want to sketch a variety of perspectives from which one can make ethical judgments. Our purpose is not to develop an abstract ethical theory. It is to help you to understand some ideas that may be useful in moral reflection. We will appeal to these principles frequently throughout the book, and their meaning should become clearer as we progress.

SOME ETHICAL PRINCIPLES

1. Benefit Maximization. The principle of benefit maximization evaluates actions by looking at their consequences. It says that the best actions are those that have the best outcomes. Thus if we want to compare action A to action B, we need to know the consequences of A and of B, whether these consequences are good or bad, and whether A or B has the best overall consequences for those affected. The principle of benefit maximization requires that we seek the greatest good for the greatest number (a philosophy sometimes referred to as *utilitarianism*).

In examining the case of The File, we might apply the principle of benefit maximization by thinking about the consequences of plagiarism or cheating. There are some benefits to cheating, especially for those who are not caught. But it seems likely that there are also many negative consequences. First, when students cheat, they do not learn. Thus they deny themselves the benefit of learning. Second, when some students cheat and others do not, cheating distorts the value of the cheater's grade in comparison to the grades of those who do not cheat. Honest students are denied the benefit of their work. Thus they are harmed by cheating. Indeed, if cheating were so commonplace that students' grades came to be viewed as unreliable, everyone would be harmed. For example, no one would believe college transcripts. (See Chapter 2.) Finally, students who cheat may do themselves some long-term harm. They may damage their own characters. They might become dishonest persons who will not be trusted by others and whose lack of integrity may be a source of pain to themselves.

2. Equal Respect for Persons and **Consistency.** The principle of equal respect begins with the assumption that every human being is an object of intrinsic worth and thus deserves to be treated with dignity and respect. Another way of saying this is that because people have intrinsic worth, they cannot be treated as though they are merely means to someone else's ends. Because everyone is of equal worth, we must treat everyone fairly. This principle might be behind the argument that Carl was exploiting John. Carl does not seem to care about John. He treats John as though he were valuable only insofar as John served Carl's goals. Thus he treats John as a means to his own ends, but not as someone who is worthy of dignity and respect.

One way to decide whether we are showing respect for people is to apply the Golden Rule to the situation ("Do unto others as you would have others do unto you"). The Golden Rule asks us to treat others as we would like to be treated by them. It thus asks us to judge our actions by their consistency. Could we approve a given action if we were in the other person's shoes? Would Carl approve of The File and of recruiting some bright but friendless person to provide for it if he were the person being exploited? Quite likely Carl would not be willing to be used in such a way. If not, Carl is being inconsistent. This kind of inconsistency is a measure of whether people are being treated with equal respect.

3. Relationship. One of the things that adds value to our lives is the relationships we form with others. We don't mean only that it is a good thing to form connections that may be useful in advancing our careers or that it is worth knowing people who will do things for us. Instead, we mean that we find relationships such as friendship, companionship, caring, love, and affection intrinsically worthwhile. Sports events and concerts are more enjoyable when we have someone to share them with us. We enjoy a good conversation. Loving and being loved in turn help make life worthwhile. However, it is difficult to maintain such relationships while also treating the people unfairly and exploitatively. It seems likely that Carl couldn't have recruited John to the Co-op if he had been honest about the role he expected John to perform. Because Carl means to exploit John, he must also deceive him, and meaningful relationships can't be built on a foundation of deceit and exploitation. John is outside the circle of friends in the Co-op. Perhaps its members cannot be his friends, because they do not care for his welfare.

4. Community. We might think of community in two ways. First, a community is a network of relationships. In healthy communities, people can form non-exploitative and beneficial relationships. However, communities are often formed to pursue certain goods or values: religious communities may exist to serve God or to save souls; tennis clubs exist to further a sport and allow members of the community to play it while enjoying each other's company; sororities and fraternities are created to provide friendship. Given this, some activities can be regarded as unethical because they disrupt community. This might mean that they destroy the personal relationships on which the community depends. It might also mean that they are inconsistent with the values that the community serves. A member of the tennis club who consistently called shots by his or her opponent "out" when they were in would do both. It is unlikely that someone who consistently cheats will retain many friends in the tennis club. Moreover, by cheating, such a person undermines the fairness of the competition. Fair scoring is essential to the game. A player will not long maintain interest in playing with someone who wins by cheating.

Colleges and universities are also communities. They serve values such as the pursuit of truth and the dissemination of knowledge. Here, as in the tennis club, dishonesty disrupts the community. When some people are intellectually dishonest, learning cannot thrive, and friendships cannot form around the collective pursuit of shared values. Maintaining The File thus seems to disrupt the college community.

5. Character Growth. Finally, our actions not only produce consequences that we seek; they also contribute to making us a certain sort of person. People who behave dishonestly become dishonest people. People who exploit others become exploitative. Thus we can judge our actions in terms of our ideal of the kind of person we would like to be and whether this kind of action makes us more or less like this person. What kind of person is Carl becoming? It seems that he is becoming deceitful and exploitative and that he will not want to think of himself in this way. How will he avoid it? He might justify his conduct to himself by rationalizing, saying that he is not really damaging John. He might even claim to be benefitting him. Or he might say that John deserves his treatment, attaching a disparaging name to John such as "nerd" or "dork" and persuading himself that somehow it is all right to exploit someone with such unfavorable traits. If John is a member of a different race, Carl might use this as a justification. Such reasoning would suggest that Carl's moral damage to himself is even greater than we had supposed. Not only is he becoming deceitful and exploitative, but to continue to think of himself as a good person, he must engage in rationalization and self-delusion. He must lie to himself, both about himself and about John. Thus he increases the damage both to John and to himself. We thus suggest that unethical conduct eventually does harm to the doer. Perhaps the ultimate harm is to turn oneself into the sort of person who is no longer moved by a concern for one's own character.

Are other principles involved in this case? Of course. In fact, in developing these we have hinted at others, such as privacy, due process, and democracy. Our reasons for selecting these principles are that we believe that they are broad enough to allow you to reflect seriously about most ethical problems, and that using them to discuss issues will eventually lead you to other important ethical concepts. It is also significant that many thinkers throughout the history of philosophy have viewed these concepts as among those most central to ethical reflection.

In the chapters that follow, we are going to provide you with a set of cases that seem to us to represent a reasonable range of ethical issues that are especially important to students. We are not going to attempt any deep or detailed analysis of these cases. We will, however, follow each case with some questions that will point to possible applications of some of the principles sketched above. When we have finished, we will return to some of the questions asked in the first paragraph of this introduction.

QUESTIONS

Usually we will follow our cases and discussions with questions that deal specifically with issues raised there. Here we want to raise some questions that are more general. Since we will discuss responses to a few of them in our last chapter, think of them as questions to keep in mind as you work through the book.

1. In our discussion of various ethical concepts, we have assumed that each of the five moral principles we sketched has a role in ethical reflection. Yet in academic philosophy, these concepts often seem to be aligned with competing views. How do you see the relationship between the various concepts? Should we try to decide which are central? Should we try to show that some are merely applications of others? Should we try to choose between them? Or should we appeal to those that seem most reasonable in light of the requirements of the case or issue at hand?

2. Some people in our society believe that moral truths are revealed by God and are absolute. Others consider ethical ideas relative, varying from culture to culture. Note that we have not used either the word "absolute" or the word "relative" in our discussion. However, we have assumed that

there is a point to thinking and arguing about ethical ideas. We assume this because we consider some ethical views more reasonable than others. We also think that sometimes it is possible to know whether an action is right or wrong. Even when this is not possible, it may be possible to show that some choices have more going for them than others. Does this make us absolutists or relativists? In fact, we think we are neither, and that these words serve more to confuse and disrupt discussion than anything else. What do the words "absolute" and "relative" actually mean?

3. Are religious views necessarily absolutist and secular ones relativist? Kant thought that when we judged ethical concepts by the Golden Rule we would find that such moral maxims as "Don't kill" or "Don't lie" are true without exception. Was Kant an absolutist? Saint Augustine said "Love and do what you will." Was he a relativist?

4. Are any of the moral concepts we discussed above required by, or inconsistent with, various religions?

5. Ours is a pluralistic society. It consists of people of different religions, races, genders, cultural backgrounds, social classes, and sexual orientations. What relevance do these and other differences have for ethical reflection? Must we disagree because we are different? Do some of the concepts discussed above provide a framework for ethical reflection that can allow us to discuss ethical issues despite our differences?

6. One response to moral disagreements is "Let's talk about it." Why is this important? Should we treat dialogue as one of our central moral principles?

After we discuss a variety of ethical issues in chapters two through eight, we will return to discuss these questions in chapter nine. If you're curious now, there's no harm in looking ahead.

FOR FURTHER INQUIRY

While the concepts discussed above have been chosen primarily because they can illuminate the kinds of ethical issues we will sketch, they also have been important in the history of philosophy and in contemporary discussions of ethical issues. Following are a few sources that may be especially useful if you wish to pursue some of these ideas in more depth or to read the concepts of some of the thinkers who have been central in developing them.

Benefit Maximization.   Utilitarianism, the idea that the best or most just society is the one that produces the greatest good for the greatest number, is represented in two works by the English philosopher John Stuart Mill

(1806–73). In *Utilitarianism,* Mill lays out the basic principles of utilitarianism; *On Liberty* provides a utilitarian argument for individuality (freedom of lifestyle) and freedom of opinion. Mill's arguments are, perhaps, the best source for understanding the commitments required for a free society.

Equal Respect for Persons and Consistency.   In the modern era, the main philosophical competitor for utilitarianism has been the ethics of German thinker Immanuel Kant (1724–1804). Kant resisted the view that actions should be judged primarily by the desirability of their consequences, and argued instead that actions should be evaluated according to whether or not they show consistency and respect for persons. These views are developed in Kant's central ethical works, *Critique of Practical Reason* and *Groundwork of the Metaphysics of Morals.*

Mill's and Kant's Enlightenment philosophies have had a profound impact not only on how we understand our own ethical choices, but also on how we evaluate the morality of liberal democratic institutions. For a contemporary classic that takes a Kantian rather than a utilitarian approach to political philosophy, see American philosopher John Rawls' *A Theory of Justice.* Rawls argues that utilitarianism is defective, in part, because it permits some to benefit at the expense of others so long as the average welfare is increased. He insists that justice consists not in the greatest good for the greatest number, but in a scheme of social cooperation that all can accept under conditions of equality and impartiality.

Community, Relationships, and Personal Growth.   Some contemporary philosophers have argued that both of these Enlightenment philosophies fail to take into account the centrality of community in human life. One important source of this argument is Scottish philosopher Alaisdair MacIntyre. In his book *After Virtue,* MacIntyre argues that our sense of self and our moral beliefs are necessarily shaped by our family backgrounds and the communities that form us. Thus our ethical choices are not purely rational, as Mill or Kant believe, but deeply influenced by our personal and cultural histories, which we must try to understand.

Many communitarians consider themselves influenced by the works of Greek philosopher and scientist Aristotle (384–322 B.C.), who tries to show how community, relationships, and personal growth are linked. Aristotle argues that human beings are social and political animals who live best only in well-ordered communities that sustain the virtues, such as contemplation and friendship, necessary for both good lives and good communities. Aristotle also argues a point that we will frequently echo: in judging conduct it is important to remember that moral virtues or habits are formed by engaging in moral acts. Aristotle's major works include *Politics,* which contains his philosophical theory of the state, a detailed study of the forms and methods of government, and a vision of the ideal state; and *Nicomachean Ethics*, which summarizes his ethical views at the end of his life.

Some contemporary religious ethicists have also argued for the centrality of community. An illustrative work is *A Community of Character: Toward a Constructive Christian Social Ethic* by Stanley Hauerwas.

Some feminist philosophers have recently developed an ethic that emphasizes relationships and growth in opposition to the more abstract concerns involved in ethics emphasizing justice. Two examples are *Caring: A Feminine Approach to Ethics and Moral Education* by American philosopher Nel Noddings and *In a Different Voice* by American Carol Gilligan. Noddings sets out "an ethic of caring" in which caring for others and being cared for by them, rather than principles or rules, form the basis of our moral responses; ethical judgments should be particular to each situation, rather than universally applicable. Gilligan's work contrasts women's moral reasoning, in which relationships are central, to the more typically male emphasis on justice, described in Lawrence Kohlberg's developmental theory of moral reasoning.

Finally, there are two works that specifically discuss the character of university communities: *The Idea of a University* by John Henry Cardinal Newman (1801–90) and *The Ideal of the University* by contemporary thinker Robert Paul Wolff.

REFERENCES

1. Aristotle. *Nicomachean Ethics*. Translated from the Greek and with an introduction by David Ross; revised by J.L. Ackrill and J.O. Urmson. New York: Oxford University Press, 1980.
2. ———. *Politics*. Translated from the Greek and with an introduction, notes, and glossary by Carnes Lord. Chicago: University of Chicago Press, 1984.
3. Gilligan, Carol. *In a Different Voice: Psychological Theory and Women's Development*. Cambridge, Mass.: Harvard University Press, 1982.
4. Hauerwas, Stanley. *A Community of Character: Toward a Constructive Christian Social Ethic*. Notre Dame, Ind.: University of Notre Dame Press, 1981.
5. Kant, Immanuel. *Critique of Practical Reason*. 1790. Translated from the German and with an introduction by Lewis White Beck. Indianapolis, Ind.: Bobbs-Merril, 1986.
6. ———. *The Moral Law; or, Kant's Groundwork of the Metaphysics of Morals*. 1794. A translation from the German with analysis and notes by H.J. Paton. London: Hutchinson University Library, 1961.
7. MacIntyre, Alaisdair. *After Virtue: A Study in Moral Theory*. Notre Dame, Ind.: University of Notre Dame Press, 1984.
8. Mill, John Stuart. *On Liberty*. 1859. Edited and with an introduction by Gertrude Himmelfarb. New York: Viking Penguin Inc., 1987.
9. ———. *Utilitarianism*. 1863. Indianapolis, Ind.: Hackett Publishing Co., 1979.

10. Newman, John Henry. *The Idea of a University Defined and Illustrated: I. In Nine Discourses Delivered to the Catholics of Dublin. II. In Occasional Lectures and Essays Addressed to the Members of Catholic University*. Edited and with an introduction and notes by I.T. Ker. Oxford: Clarendon Press, 1976.
11. Noddings, Nel. *Caring: A Feminine Approach to Ethics and Moral Education*. Berkeley, Calif.: University of California Press, 1984.
12. Rawls, John. *A Theory of Justice*. Cambridge, Mass.: Belknap Press of Harvard University Press, 1971.
13. Wolff, Robert Paul. *The Ideal of the University*. Boston, Mass.: Beacon Press, 1969.

2

ACADEMIC INTEGRITY, GRADING, AND CHEATING

Case 2.1: Cheating

Terri Benson was a senior in the engineering program of Andersonville College. She had been a marginal student since she entered Andersonville. She had been on probation twice, and had had to take one semester off. She was still in danger of not finishing. In addition to her marginal grade point average, she still had two required courses to complete in her major. She was currently enrolled in one of these, Physics for Engineers, which was offered only during the fall semester. She was not doing well.

Not only that, but she had been accused of cheating on the midterm exam. There seemed little doubt that she was guilty. The responses on her answer sheet, even the wrong answers, exactly matched those of the person who was seated directly in front of her. The probability that two students could produce an identical set of incorrect answers on ten different items was close to zero. Moreover, given their positions in the room, it was virtually impossible that the other student could have copied from Terri.

Professor Ames, the instructor, prided himself on his firm sense of academic honesty. He thus decided to charge Terri with violating the college's academic integrity code, although he wasn't required to do so. Because Terri wasn't exactly a model student, it also seemed important to him to protect the engineering profession from someone who wouldn't bring credit to it.

Andersonville College had a committee on academic integrity. A student accused of cheating had to be charged before that committee by the instructor of the course in which the alleged cheating took place. The committee would then consider the evidence, make a judgment, and, if the student was found guilty, decide on a penalty. This semester, the academic integrity committee was chaired by Professor Bloom, who had a reputation for fairness unburdened by mercy.

Professor Ames made a persuasive case against Terri. She admitted her guilt and excused herself by saying that she had panicked because she was afraid that if she failed the exam she wouldn't be able to complete the program. She still hoped to enter the Master of Engineering program at Andersonville. She was afraid that failing Ames' course would doom her admission. The committee then sent her out of the room while they discussed their verdict.

The verdict was that Terri was to be suspended for the rest of the academic year, after which she could reapply for admission. In announcing the verdict, Professor Bloom delivered a sermon on the importance of intellectual honesty to the academic community. He explained that the college's central values included the pursuit of truth and excellence in one's work, and that absolute honesty was required by these goals. He concluded, "thus you have violated the central moral principle of an academic community, intellectual integrity, and we have no choice but to protect the college against such behavior. However, we have also decided that after you have undergone your punishment and learned your lesson, you may have another chance to complete the program."

Terri didn't say much, and that seemed to be the end of it. She left, and the committee members started to leave, too. However, some of Terri's friends had waited for her outside the hearing room; they were commiserating with her when the committee was leaving. Unhappily, Professor Bloom overheard Terri say, "I wish the old fart would apply those standards about 'community integrity' to his colleagues. Maybe then I wouldn't have had to cheat."

Professor Bloom was irate. He called the committee back into the room and demanded an explanation and an apology from Terri. He got neither. Instead, through angry tears, Terri gave an indictment of the education she had received. It went something like this:

"You talk about the integrity of the academic community. There has never been a community here for me! When I came here you made me take 'screening' classes that felt more like boot camp than education. My faculty 'advisor' has never even learned my name. When I tried to get involved in research, I was told that research opportunities were only for students who could 'really contribute.' Professor Ames barely prepares for his class, and that seems the norm here, not the exception. So far as I can see, you people stole the tuition money I paid, refused to teach me, refused to treat me as a member of any community, and used my money to pursue your own consulting careers. If I cheated, I did nothing but copy your example. The only moral principle teachers at this college seem to follow is 'do whatever is necessary to further your career.' *That's* one thing you taught me well!"

Questions

1. Professor Bloom says that intellectual honesty is the central value sustaining a college community. Why might this be? What are some other values that might be similarly important?

2. If Terri's description of her education is accurate, has the engineering faculty of Andersonville also failed to show academic integrity? Do you think this is how students are treated in your college or university? What could be done to create a stronger sense of community?

3. Some institutions have an honor code in which students promise not to cheat and also promise not to tolerate cheating in others. Would such a code work at your school? Why or why not? Is it possible to create an academic moral climate that would make students not want to cheat? How? What values would be essential?

4. Many students often sympathize with those who cheat. Even if they don't exactly approve of cheating, students rarely turn in or even criticize those who cheat. Should they? In many situations, loyalty to friends or solidarity with members of one's group are important virtues. Are they in cases of cheating? How do you see your responsibilities here?

5. Terri's last reaction to Professor Bloom seems common in real-life ethical discussion. She accused him of inconsistency because he and his colleagues seem to violate the same values they blame her for violating. Is Terri's claim that she just copied the faculty's example plausible? If it is, does it justify her cheating? Is "and you're another" or "everybody does it" ever a reasonable defense of unethical conduct?

6. Another common defense for some kinds of unethical behavior is that it doesn't really hurt anyone. Does cheating harm anyone? If so, whom, and how?

7. If teachers' salaries are substantially paid by students' tuition, do teachers have a stronger obligation to perform conscientiously than they would if their money came from somewhere else, such as an endowment? Is their failure to teach students the same as theft? Might it be a breach of an implied contract?

ISSUES

Why shouldn't Terri Benson cheat? Let's consider the possibility that there's really nothing wrong with what she did. Suppose we say that cheating is a kind of victimless crime because no one is hurt. Had Terri succeeded, she would have gotten a passing grade. Professor Ames wouldn't have been damaged by this. Neither would the other students. Their grades would have been the same. Who, then, is hurt? If nobody is hurt, can cheating be wrong? When we say that some action is wrong, don't we mean in part that it harms someone?

There are a number of approaches you might take to this problem. We'll first note some that you might consider, but that we won't explore here:

One approach appeals to the idea of character growth. Perhaps one result of Terri's cheating will be that she'll find it easier to cheat the next time. She is developing a habit of dishonesty; that is, she is not only doing something dishonest, but she is also becoming a dishonest person. Does this argument seem believable? If it does, how might cheating on this test affect Terri's life? How is integrity or trustworthiness valuable?

Another possibility is to look at Terri's actions in light of the principle of consistency. How might Terri feel if her role and Professor Ames' role were reversed? Would she be willing to allow cheating?

A third argument might claim that Terri erodes her relationships with other students by cheating. After all, they worked hard for their grades. How would they feel about someone who got a good grade by cheating when they had to study hard for theirs?

You might want to see whether you can develop some arguments about cheating along some of these lines. We'll show you what we mean by "develop some arguments" as we explore two different approaches in more detail. First, we'll use the principle of benefit maximization to think about whether, in fact, someone is hurt by Terri's cheating. Second, we'll ask about how intellectual integrity might be required to make an academic community work.

Benefit maximization suggests that we should prefer practices that make a society more efficient in its use of human resources. A society that hires the people who are best able to do a particular job is more efficient than one that does not. Similarly, a society that provides educational opportunities and career training to those who are most able to profit from such training can make better use of its resources than one that does not. If a society is to be efficient in these ways, it needs to measure ability to perform a job and ability to profit from an education. One measure of these capacities is grades. Moreover, if grades are used to award jobs or further education, students who want these positions will compete for grades. Cheating might then have the following consequences: it would make it harder to award positions on the basis of merit, and it would give cheaters an unfair advantage over those who don't cheat.

Who is hurt? One answer is that people who confer benefits on the basis of grades are hurt. An employer who hires Terri, believing that she is a capable engineer, might be hurt because she isn't competent. A university that admits Terri to graduate school might be injured because it would believe, erroneously, that it was investing its limited resources in a competent student. Had Terri not been caught cheating, these people would have been lied to and injured.

Other possible victims of cheating are other students. In many cases, students compete with one another for jobs or for admission to further education. If Terri were to succeed in cheating, she would appear more qualified in relation to other students than she really is, and thus unfairly improve her competitive advantage with them. Her position would be similar to that of someone who had bought something with counterfeit money.

Surely it's in everyone's best interest for employers and universities to hire or admit the best qualified people. Better qualified employees are likely to do better work. Their employer will benefit, and so will those who buy the employer's product or service. Similarly, if universities admit the most qualified students, these students can be expected to do better work. This means that eventually we all benefit from having better trained people. Thus, everyone in society is hurt by cheating.

The arguments presented demonstrate the use of the benefit maximization principle: in short, cheating ultimately undermines society's ability to use human resources efficiently. When that happens, everyone is worse off. Can you think of other examples in which everyone suffers when some people cheat? Are there any cases in which cheating is genuinely victimless?

Applying the principle of benefit maximization usually requires that we make some assumptions about the consequences of our actions. These assumptions may be arguable. In this case, our argument assumes that grades are a reasonable measure of the ability to perform on a job or to profit from further education. Are they? If these assumptions are incorrect, is cheating acceptable?

Note that these arguments about why cheating is wrong seem to view what is learned as a kind of commodity—something that has economic value and that can be exchanged or used to get other valued things. Is this how you think of your education? Are you a student primarily because you believe that education has economic benefits? What other reasons might there be for getting an education? (See Chapter 8.) In these other views of the purpose of learning, is cheating still harmful? For whom?

Suppose that the course in which Terri cheated was unrelated to her engineering major and her intended profession, such as a literature course. Could Terri argue that it was acceptable for her to cheat in this course because her knowledge of literature has nothing to do with her professional credentials?

Another way of examining why cheating is wrong is to consider the nature of the academic community and intellectual integrity. Colleges and universities are not simply employment agencies; they are places where ideas are important, and where, ideally, new knowledge is sought and ideas are debated and evaluated. This process of seeking truth by argument and judging evidence is most important to higher education, and it is a process in which honesty is absolutely central. Any form of intellectual dishonesty is thus inconsistent with the nature of an academic community. Professor Bloom's lecture to Terri seems to express this view. He believes that cheating violates the academic community's central commitment to intellectual honesty. Is he right?

What would life be like in a college or university that couldn't count on the intellectual honesty of its members? For example, consider professors' research. If scholars were not routinely honest in reporting data and in making arguments, we couldn't rely on the results of their research; immense effort would have to be put into policing and checking everything they did. Under these conditions, the academic community couldn't accomplish its purpose of seeking and communicating results that are as fair and accurate as researchers can make them.

A similar argument might be made about teaching. Suppose you couldn't rely on the honesty of your professors in teaching their subjects. Suppose they were willing to misrepresent their own fields to advance their careers or to defend their pet theories. Suppose that instead of relying on arguments and persuasion in class, they relied on lying, misrepresentation, or even coercion to win arguments. What would your education be like? Would its value for you change?

We think that Professor Bloom's view that intellectual integrity is essential to academic communities is clearly right, but we're less sure that it applies clearly to Terri's case. To examine why, let's consider some distinctions among three ways of judging students' work:

1. *Criticism* emphasizes discussing the merits of an argument or problem-solving approach, the quality of students' writing or calculations, and so on. It is feedback, usually provided in comments on papers or tests. Criticism is crucial to learning because it helps us see how to improve.
2. *Grading* involves putting a performance or an object into a category. It may involve a judgment of quality, such as when a paper is judged as good, bad, or average. Colleges and universities often grade because they want to know whether students have achieved minimum competence in a subject, or whether they have passed enough courses to earn a degree. However, grading need not involve such quality judgments. We don't judge the worth of eggs, for example, when we grade them into size or color groups.
3. *Ranking* involves a comparative judgment. We rank when we order a series of examples according to our judgment of how good each is compared to the others.[1]

---

[1] Our description of these three ways to judge students' work follows Wolff, *The Ideal of the University*, p. 59.

What we call "grading" in most educational settings may involve all of these ways. If colleges were interested only in the pursuit of truth and in initiating students into the processes of scholarship, they would probably use only criticism. Instead, they use grading or ranking for their own administrative convenience, so that they can award credit and grant degrees, and because they view grades as commodities. Grading and ranking have little to do with evaluating arguments or with scholarship. They have much to do with an attempt to communicate students' comparative levels of success to other colleges and employers.

What does this have to do with Terri? We think it suggests that the argument that Terri has implicitly lied to future employers or to other colleges or universities to which she might apply is stronger than the argument that she has violated the essential intellectual honesty of an academic community. Why do we think this?

First, we suspect that the kind of test on which Terri cheated was intended to grade or rank students more than to criticize them. We suspect that this is often, if not always, the case with tests and that it is especially true of tests on which it is possible to cheat by copying the right answer from another student, as Terri did. Such a test has not been designed to allow students to present arguments or evaluate claims, both of which would be hard to copy and perhaps reveal more of what students understand. However, professors give multiple-choice and fill-in-the-blank tests because they are asked to grade and rank their students.

Second, Terri has not been accused of falsifying data or misrepresenting a bad argument as a good one. She has not plagiarized ideas, or "cooked" data. She has copied test answers. Our point isn't that Terri's cheating is acceptable or even that it is less bad than these types of dishonesty. However, we suggest that Terri hasn't violated the central value of an academic community, because intellectual honesty isn't really involved here. Tests of the sort that Professor Ames gives don't ask students to engage in any academic process other than showing that they have learned required material. Such tests are usually graded merely by noting right and wrong answers, and their primary purpose is to grade and rank students, not critique them. Terri's dishonesty is thus more like a case of theft—in this case, of credentials or ranking—than like a case of misleading others about her ideas or research. It is more like stealing than lying.

However, even if Terri's cheating is more similar to stealing than to intellectual dishonesty, it still may have serious consequences for Andersonville and for Terri. In cheating, Terri may have helped to create a climate at Andersonville in which other students will also find it easier to cheat. At some point, if students come to believe that a lot of cheating is going on, they may feel pressure to cheat in order to keep up. Or they may rationalize cheating by telling themselves that everyone is doing it. What are some of the things that influence how you feel about cheating?

Terri may also have injured herself. Cheating may substitute for learning. Terri's willingness to cheat may also result in her working less diligently and thus losing the most important benefit of college, a good education. She also may have taken a step that shapes her own character. She may be making herself into a dishonest person.

In summary, our two arguments about cheating assume two different pictures of higher education. With *benefit maximization*, knowledge is viewed as a commodity. Scholars produce it and provide it to various consumers, such as governments, industries, and students who, in turn, can exchange it for jobs and income. In this image, cheating seems most like a form of theft because the cheater gets an undeserved benefit and deprives others of this benefit. The other view, expressed by Professor Bloom, sees a college or university as an intellectual *community* engaged in a shared project of inquiry. In this picture, cheating undermines the assumption of intellectual integrity that is essential to serious inquiry. It's more like lying. These pictures are different. Are they incompatible? How do you see your own education? Does the answer to these questions affect the way you view cheating? In either case, cheating can undermine the climate in which colleges and universities attempt to accomplish their purposes. Does your college have a climate that encourages honesty or cheating? How do you think this affects the quality of your education?

EXAMPLES OF COLLEGE AND UNIVERSITY CODES ON ACADEMIC DISHONESTY

1. *Excerpt from the* Code of Academic Integrity *of the University of Maryland*[2]

Introduction

The University is an academic community. Its fundamental purpose is the pursuit of knowledge. Like all other communities, the University can function properly only if its members adhere to clearly established goals and values. Essential to the fundamental purpose of the University is the commitment to the principles of truth and academic honesty. Accordingly, the *Code of Academic Integrity* is designed to ensure that the principle of academic honesty is upheld. While all members of the University share this responsibility, the *Code of Academic Integrity* is designed so that special responsibility for upholding the principle of academic responsibility lies with the students.

---

[2] *Code of Academic Integrity*, University of Maryland at College Park (Gary Pavela, Director of Judicial Programs).

Definitions

ACADEMIC DISHONESTY: any of the following acts, when committed by a student, shall constitute academic dishonesty:

a. CHEATING: intentionally using or attempting to use unauthorized materials, information, or study aids in any academic exercise.

b. FABRICATION: intentional or unauthorized falsification or invention of any information or citation in an academic exercise.

c. FACILITATING ACADEMIC DISHONESTY: intentionally or knowingly helping or attempting to help another violate any provisions of this *Code*.

d. PLAGIARISM: intentionally or knowingly representing the words or ideas of another as one's own in any academic exercise.

Responsibility to Report Academic Dishonesty

Academic dishonesty is a corrosive force in the academic life of a university. It jeopardizes the quality of education and depreciates the genuine achievements of others. It is, without reservation, a responsibility of all members of the campus community to actively deter it. Apathy or acquiescence in the presence of academic dishonesty is not a neutral act. Histories of institutions demonstrate that a laissez-faire response will reinforce, perpetuate, and enlarge the scope of such misconduct. Institutional reputations for academic dishonesty are regrettable aspects of modern education. These reputations become self-fulfilling and grow, unless vigorously challenged by students and faculty alike.

All members of the University community—students, faculty, and staff—share the responsibility and authority to challenge and make known acts of apparent academic dishonesty.

2. *Excerpt from* **The Honor Code** *of Stanford University*[3]

A. The Honor Code is an undertaking of the students, individually and collectively:

(1) that they will not give or receive aid in examinations; that they will not give or receive unpermitted aid in class work, in the preparation of reports, or in any other work that is to be used by the instructor as a basis for grading;

(2) that they will do their share and take an active part in seeing to it that others as well as themselves uphold the spirit and the letter of the Honor Code.

---

[3] *The Honor Code,* Stanford University (Student Legislative Council, 1977).

B. The Faculty on its part manifests its confidence in the honor of its students by refraining from proctoring examinations and from taking unusual and unreasonable precautions to prevent the forms of dishonesty mentioned above. The faculty will also avoid, as far as practicable, academic procedures that create temptations to violate the Honor Code.

C. While the faculty alone has the right and obligation to set academic requirements, the students and faculty will work together to establish optimal conditions for honorable academic work.

3. *Excerpt from the student handbook of Tompkins Cortland Community College[4]*

A. Plagiarism

Plagiarism is the dishonest use of the work of others.

[. . .] Plagiarism means presenting, as one's own, the words, the work, or the opinions of someone else. It is dishonest, since the plagiarist offers, as his or her own, for credit, the language, or information, or thought for which he or she deserved no credit. It is unproductive, since it defeats the purpose of the course—improvement of the student's own powers of thinking and communication. It is also dangerous, since the penalties for plagiarism are severe. [. . .]

Examples of plagiarism as it might occur in term papers, research papers, laboratory reports, and other written assignments are listed below:

- Failure to use quotation marks: All work which is quoted from a source should be enclosed in quotation marks and followed by a proper reference giving the exact page or pages from which the quote is taken. Failure to use the quotation marks, even if a footnote source is provided, is plagiarism.
- Failure to document ideas: When a student uses one or more ideas from and/or paraphrases a source, he or she must give the exact page or pages from which the ideas or paraphrasing were taken. [. . .]
- False documentation: Falsifying or inventing sources or page references is plagiarism. [. . .]
- Ideas which are part of the general fund of human knowledge (e.g., George Washington was the first President of the United States, Albert Einstein developed the Theory of Relativity, etc.) need not be documented in papers.

[4] "Statement of Academic Integrity" in *The 1992–93 Student Handbook*, Tompkins Cortland Community College (Dryden, NY), pp. 40–41.

ADDITIONAL CASES

Case 2.2: *The Tutor*

David was having a lot of trouble writing the paper for his English 200 course, and he was beginning to panic—there was only one week left until it was due. Then one evening he noticed an ad on the library bulletin board: "English grad student, experienced editor, offers tutoring and paper-writing assistance." He called the listed number and found that for a not unreasonable fee, the tutor would work intensively with him in the upcoming week and help him write "a good paper." He ended up spending many hours with the tutor in the next few days, going over ideas and drafts. He was happy to spend a lot of time on the paper because this was an important course for him, and it didn't hurt that the tutor turned out to be a friendly, attractive young woman named Maria.

At last the paper was done—just in the nick of time. David was quite proud of it. He recognized that Maria had helped him tremendously: she explained the assignment more clearly than the professor had and helped him clarify his paper topic, she talked through his ideas (adding many good ones of her own), she edited and rewrote the two drafts he prepared for her, and she showed him how he could reorganize his argument to make it much clearer and more forceful. David was happy to pay Maria's fee. In fact, he gratefully realized that this paper was far better than anything he could write on his own, and he'd learned a lot from working with her. When the paper got an A– instead of the C– he'd gotten on his first paper, David was elated. "Too bad I can't afford to pay you to tutor me in all my classes!" he said wistfully.

Questions

1. Maria seems to have done a substantial amount of David's work, and he knows he couldn't have done as well by himself. When does "help" become "cheating," or getting credit for someone else's work?
2. Is there a problem with relying heavily on someone else to do your work if you are also learning a lot at the same time?
3. Is the outside tutoring David got fair to other students in the class? What if David had gotten all this extra help from the professor?
4. Would your reactions to this case differ if Maria had been David's girlfriend rather than a paid tutor? In other words, does it matter whether the helper is paid in cash or in something less tangible, such as friendship or sexual favors? (See Case 1.1 in Chapter 1.)

Case 2.3: *Time Crunch*

Roxanne has been working extra hours at her part-time job in a clothing store. The store needs her help because the holiday rush is starting, and she needs the money to pay next semester's tuition and to fix her car so that she can drive home for the holidays. The coming holiday season also means the end of the semester and, unfortunately, final exams. Roxanne simply doesn't have time to study for all of her exams and also work the extra hours she needs.

Something has to give, and she decides to fake being sick on the day of her Biology exam so that she can take the make-up exam the next week and have more time to study. She knows that it won't be hard to get a note from the busy school health clinic saying that she's too sick to take the exam; her friend Debbie works there and can "borrow" a page of their letterhead stationary. "Even if I have to lie, it's fair that I get extra time to study," Roxanne tells herself, "because I have to work, and I can't study all the time like students who get mommy and daddy to pay for everything."

Questions

1. Roxanne seems to see her lie as a simple case of manipulating an unfair system. Is there anything wrong with manipulating the system? Is her strategy fair to the other students in her Biology class?
2. She seems to justify her behavior with a vague idea that "unfair" differences between people that have nothing to do with effort or intelligence, such as wealth, should not be reflected in their grades. What do you think about her claim that she deserves more time to study than other students because they don't have to earn money? Are there similarities between this argument and programs that officially give advantages (such as quotas, financial aid, or special remedial classes) to ethnically under-represented students?

Case 2.4: *TakeNote: Help or Hindrance?*

Many introductory and low-level courses at Cornell University have a service offered by a private company called TakeNote. For about $50 per course, students can purchase a complete set of class notes, taken at every lecture by a graduate student in that field. In fact sometimes the notes are taken by one of the T.A.'s for the class. The detailed notes are printed on red paper so that they can't be photocopied by students unwilling or unable to buy the service. Graduate students are happy to earn extra money by taking notes, and TakeNote's customers are happy to have class notes that are usually more complete and accurate than those they take on their own. TakeNote's satisfied customer comments include "having TakeNote lets me just concentrate on listening to the professor!" "Now if I have to miss a class I don't get so anxious!" "With TakeNote, I know that when I study for the exams, I have all the material and didn't miss any important points!"

The only people unhappy with the service seem to be some students who can't pay for it and some of the professors of the courses for which it's offered. These teachers feel that buying class notes encourages students to skip class and keeps them from learning to take their own good notes. (One teacher said, "Learning to take notes is an important skill; when you take notes, you're processing and organizing information, and connecting it to things you already know, in a way that you can't do with someone else's notes. Taking good notes really helps you learn.") Of course, professors can refuse to allow TakeNote in their classes, but there is considerable pressure from students to have the service. Instructors also have no choice about who takes the notes, and some feel that poor note takers have misled students ("I know who's buying TakeNote when I get the same wrong answer on 40 percent of the exams").

Questions

1. Do you think that paying someone else for class notes keeps students from learning how to take good notes, or encourages them to skip class?
2. Do TakeNote customers have an unfair advantage over students who can't or won't pay for the service?
3. Could TakeNote be considered a form of cheating? If so, who is being cheated?
4. What are the implications of Cornell University's implicit, if not official, sanctioning of TakeNote? Should TakeNote customers have any (legal?) redress against note-takers who supply them with wrong or misleading information?
5. Would there be any problem with such class notes if they were given out by the professor to all students?

Case 2.5: A Question of Plagiarism

Frank Llewelyn sighed as he examined the student's paper, and then he looked back to the neatly-typed title page: The Rise of the Modern Nation-State, by Steven Johnson. "I'm sorry, Steven, whoever you are," he thought to himself, "but not only are you going to fail this paper, I'm also going to report you for plagiarism to the Honor Board. This is just too blatant." Frank recognized the source on which Steven had, to put it politely, modelled his paper; and Steven did not credit this work even once. In fact, Steven seemed oblivious to the need for footnotes and a bibliography in a research paper. Not only did the argument of Steven's paper closely follow a single source, but many of the ideas also came from this work, and numerous phrases in the paper were lifted directly from it. The copied phrases were mostly in quotation marks, it was true; however, no references were given, and Steven had been careless about including end-quote marks. Quite a few were missing, so that one had to guess exactly where the quotation ended and Steven's words (or those of some other source) began. With a sigh, Frank wrote a big red "F—See Me!" on the title page.

Steven did go to see Frank right after the papers were handed back. He turned out to be a tall, raw-boned young man, who was red with anger and close to tears. Frank carefully explained why the paper was unacceptable and said that he would have to report Steven for plagiarism. Steven sullenly claimed that he hadn't realized his paper plagiarized anything; he hadn't had many chances to write papers before, and he thought this was the way to do it. He added heatedly that it wasn't fair to punish him for not knowing how to do something he hadn't been taught; he certainly wasn't a liar, but wasn't that what Frank was calling him?

Questions

1. Consider the fact that because of his large class size, Frank Llewelyn did not even know who Steven was when he was reading his paper. Do Frank, other instructors at the college, or the college administration bear responsibility for Steven's ignorance about how to write an acceptable research paper? Is it plagiarism if a student does not intentionally cheat but apparently doesn't know how to write an acceptable paper? Would the problem be resolved if Steven added appropriate footnotes to the paper?
2. Steven's paper did seem to contain a few ideas of his own. Is plagiarism involved if *all* of the ideas in a paper are someone else's, but credit is given? In other words, is there a moral and intellectual difference between misrepresenting someone else's work, and complete reliance on someone else's work?
3. Because much academic work involves learning from others' arguments and ideas, exactly what is wrong with plagiarism?

Case 2.6: *There Isn't Enough to Go Around*

Bruce's parents have been going over his financial aid application very carefully. In fact they have had him rewrite some sections to hide their true assets. Bruce feels a little funny about this, but his parents have explained several facts to him. First, without at least some financial aid in addition to Bruce's student loans, they cannot pay for four years of college for both him and his two siblings. Second, they feel that colleges reward middle-class people who don't save money by giving them financial aid, rather than rewarding people who've saved all they can. His mother gives him a long speech on the subject:

"We've scrimped and saved for years, putting all of our savings in a college fund for you kids since you were infants. But that money will just barely cover your educations because tuition costs have gotten way out of line! And it just kills me when I hear that our neighbors the Joneses got financial aid for Samantha. I happen to know that their income is very similar to ours, but they've never saved anything. They've always lived high off the hog, taking fancy vacations and living the good life. So of course they have no liquid assets at all now, which is exactly why Samantha qualifies for financial aid. You should get financial aid, too; if anything, we deserve it more than the Joneses because we've been planning for the future and saving as much as we could, while they spent everything."

Bruce's father adds that given the excessive cost of tuition today and shrinking government support for students, large numbers of middle-class students are unable to finish college, or they go into enormous debt to get their degrees. "When I was in school, we had the G.I. bill to help us pay for college. It was our country's way of investing in the future. But no more! Now each individual is fighting against all the others for the limited money out there. You've got to do whatever you can to get ahead because a college degree is more important than ever today. It's all the fault of the current political climate, and those crazy Republicans. They—"

"O.K., Dad, I get your point," Bruce hastily interrupts. He hates it when his father gets into one of his long-winded political tirades. And anyway, his parents have convinced him that it's fine to fudge a bit on his financial aid application.

Questions

1. Are you convinced by Bruce's parents' arguments that lying on his financial aid application is acceptable? If not, why not?
2. What ethical principles might apply to this case? How could you use them to argue for or against the morality of cheating or lying in this way?
3. Is there something unethical about the basis on which colleges award financial aid? If so, how might they assign financial aid more fairly?
4. Are there other ways that financing a college education (through loans, grants, aid, or savings) might have moral implications?

BACKGROUND READING

Several recent newspaper stories have looked at cheating on campus: Rudy Abramson, "A Matter of Honor" in *The Los Angeles Times*, 3 April 1994, sec. E, p. 1, col. 2, talks about the movement (often initiated by students) to make honor codes a fixture on more campuses. Jeff Prugh, "Extent of Cheating Isn't Easily Measured" in *The Los Angeles Times*, 3 April 1994, sec, E, p. 2, col. 2, discusses the difficulty of measuring cheating on campus and various ways in which schools are trying to deal with the problem. And Reagan Walker, "Tech Students, Faculty Consider New Honor Code to Cut Cheating" in *The Atlanta Journal and Atlanta Constitution*, 15 November 1994, sec. E, p. 2, col. 1, describes the apparently increasing frequency of cheating at colleges and the methods that one school (Georgia Tech) is considering to combat it.

For a different perspective on cheating, see "Abigail Witherspoon" (a pseudonym), "This Pen for Hire: On Grinding Out Papers for College Students" in *Harper's Magazine*, June 1995, vol. 290, no. 1741, pp. 49–57. This slightly humorous, slightly bitter piece describes the life and moral dilemmas of a woman who writes college students' "term papers, book reports, senior theses, take-home exams" for a living.

ADDITIONAL MATERIALS

1. For articles that discuss grading practices, see "At Stanford, a Rebellion on Grades" in *The New York Times*, 31 May 1994, sec. A, p. 14, col. 6; David Margolick, "Stanford U. Decides to Make Courses Harder to Drop But Easier to Fail" in *The New York Times*, 4 June 1994, sec. A, p. 7, col. 1; Donald Kennedy, "What Grade Inflation?" in *The New York Times*, 13 June 1994, sec. A, p. 15, col. 2; and "Editorial: Making the Grade" in *The New York Times*, 5 June 1994, sec. 4, p. 16, col. 1.

Recently Stanford University reinstated the grade of F. For about two decades, Stanford students could not fail a course. They merely did not get credit. Moreover, if they did not pass, the fact that they were enrolled in the course was not noted on their transcripts. Additionally, most students got A's and B's in their courses. Do such grading practices erode the information available in a student's transcript? Are they a form of lying by professors? Similarly, in some institutions it is rare for a professor to write a negative recommendation. What consequences might this have for the value of recommendations? Is it a form of lying?

For more information on grade inflation generally, see Carol Jouzaitis, "Easy College 'A's Become Rampant" in *The Chicago Tribune*, 4 May 1994, sec. 1, p. 1, col. 1; Anthony Flint, "Grade Inflation Losing Air at Some Colleges" in *The Boston Globe*, 4 June 1994, p. 1, col. 2.; Laurel Shaper Walters, "Attention College Students: The Easy 'A' May Disappear" in *The Christian Science Monitor*, 18 October 1994, p. 1, col. 3; Gary M. Galles, "Math-Ignorant Americans Play Games with Numbers in Order to Distort Reality" in *The Atlanta Journal*, 17 November 1994, sec. A, p. 19, col. 1; and Toby Jackson, "In the War Against Grade Inflation, Dartmouth Scores a Hit" in *The Wall Street Journal*, 8 September 1994, sec. A, p. 18, col. 3.

2. The following information appeared in a letter written on December 1, 1994, by Kuan Wong and Gary Pavela, Office of Judicial Programs, University of Maryland at College Park, to all faculty members:

"In 1993, Professor Donald L. McCabe at the Graduate School of Management at Rutgers University studied the extent of self-reported cheating by 1,800 students at nine medium-to-large state universities. He found that 52% of the students admitted cheating on an examination at least once. 38% admitted to examination cheating on *three or more occasions*."

Do these figures seem consistent with what you know of students at your school? It has been found that the major predictor for the amount of cheating on a campus is the "cheating culture" at the campus, that is, how common and acceptable cheating seems to be among students there. How would you characterize your campus's "cheating culture"? Who primarily benefits from reduced cheating, and whose responsibility should it be to discourage and punish cheating—college administrators, students, professors, honor boards, or some other group? What steps might students and faculty members take to reduce the incidence of exam cheating at your school?

3

TOLERANCE, DIVERSITY, AND HATE SPEECH

Case 3.1: Hate Speech

Percy was a white male sophomore at Pinecrest College. He was viewed by his friends as a nice guy when he was sober, which was most of the time. However, when he got drunk he often embarrassed his friends, and some of them simply refused to go out drinking with him. He was not a violent drunk, but alcohol certainly weakened his normal verbal inhibitions. After a few beers he often became belligerent and offensive to friends and strangers alike.

Saturday night Percy went out drinking with a few friends after a basketball game. Pinecrest had won, which was a rare occasion this year, and a celebration seemed in order. The celebration lasted for several hours, and Percy lost count of the number of beers he had consumed. The mood was light until Percy and his friends headed back to their dorm. On the way there, they passed a group of African American students walking in the other direction.

Percy, rather unsteady on his feet, didn't seem to notice the other students until they passed by. But as their conversation faded behind Percy and his friends, he started off on a tirade against blacks that grew gradually louder and more offensive; it culminated in a stream of racial insults shouted at no one in particular. Percy's friends tried to quiet him down, without much success. Finally they steered him to his room and left him there.

Percy didn't stay. He seemed to need an audience for his drunken harangue. After stewing for a few minutes, he went out to find one. Unfortunately, he succeeded.

The police report read as follows:

"At approximately 2 A.M. Sunday, I received a call that there was someone standing outside the African-American Study Center, screaming racial abuse. When I arrived, I found Percy Miller, 18, standing in the center of a small crowd, arguing with several minority students. Apparently these students were still at the center studying for a Monday exam. A number of other students, on their way home from Saturday night partying, had stopped to watch. Miller was clearly drunk and was yelling obscenities and racial epithets in a very loud voice. His main target seemed to be the minority students who had been in the center, but he had also made loud and vulgar remarks about gays and several other groups. While no violence had occurred, it was clear that the situation was volatile. Some students were responding to Miller in kind, and others were urging him on. I arrested Miller for disturbing the peace. Once I had him in custody, the other students quieted down and left, so I saw no reason for further action."

The arresting officer was a patrolman on the municipal police force of the town surrounding Pinecrest College. Percy had been charged by the town with disturbing the peace. It seemed likely that he would plead guilty and receive a suspended sentence. However, Percy had also been charged by the college with hate speech, which could carry a much stiffer penalty.

Pinecrest College's official Code of Conduct contains the following statement:

Pinecrest College attempts to create an educational environment that is open to the widest possible range of ideas. However, it believes that speech that serves primarily to denigrate the dignity or worth of other members of the community serves no intellectual purpose, functions to silence the voices of minority groups, and undermines the climate of civility, openness, and respect that is required for free discussion and the pursuit of truth. Therefore, speech that denigrates members of the Pinecrest community on account of their race, religion, ethnicity, gender, national origin, or sexual orientation is forbidden. Members of the community who engage in such speech may be punished by community service, suspension, probation, or expulsion.

Later in the week, an African American student wrote home:

Dear Mom and Dad,

When I come home for break, I want to talk with you about transferring to another school. I don't think I can stand to be at this place another semester. The racism is just overwhelming.

Earlier this week, while I was studying at the center, some white drunk started yelling racial insults in the courtyard. Some of my friends went out and yelled back. I'm glad they did. Somebody needed to respond, but I couldn't. Fighting back just takes too much energy. I can't live where I have to be angry all of the time.

This is the third incident I know about this year. Earlier someone spray-painted some stuff on the wall of the center, and one of my friends had a note that said "Kill the Niggers" tacked to her dorm door.

What makes it worse is the reaction of the whites. My white friends usually tell me that I shouldn't care what a few jerks say and insist that most white people aren't racists. Maybe, but I wonder how they'd feel if someone threatened to kill them because of their race? The university seems to think that this is an issue about free speech. All they want to talk about is "how the First Amendment protects even offensive speech." They don't want to talk about racism. The prof in my government class is the worst. He made this incident a discussion topic in class. I don't remember exactly what he said. He was his usual confusing self. What I do remember is how white people were "US" and black people were "THEM" and how everything was about how "WE" should treat "THEM." The prof singled me out after class (there's only one other black kid in the class) to ask why I was so quiet. "Don't you have some thoughts on the topic?" he wanted to know. Well, I do have more than a few. But I didn't feel like either telling him or representing "THEM" to all the whites in the class. If anyone's free speech here needs protecting, I think it's mine. How can I talk in the climate of racism here, and why should I have to be the voice of "THEM"?

Mom and Dad, I'm tired of being "THEM." Everything that happens here makes me feel as though I don't belong. I need to consider going someplace where I can be "US" for a while.

Love,
Malcolm

Questions

1. There is a child's saying: "Sticks and stones may break my bones, but names will never hurt me." It is almost certainly false. How do names hurt?

2. Words not only can hurt, they can exclude. How does hate speech exclude?

3. What issues of free speech are raised by regulations prohibiting hate speech? Does hate speech act to deny a voice to those it targets?

4. How can "US versus THEM" assumptions be avoided in classroom discussions? Should they always be avoided?

ISSUES

We hope that most of our readers will believe that there is something immoral or unethical about Percy Miller's conduct. Perhaps, however, it is less clear what this something is. The statement about hate speech in Pinecrest's Code of Conduct makes two suggestions. One of them is that hate speech is inconsistent with recognizing the dignity and worth of those people against whom the speech is directed. Here the argument is that hate speech is immoral because it is racist. Racism is objectionable because it denies equal respect to some on the basis of race. The second objection is that hate speech excludes, and that this exclusion is inconsistent with the values of an academic community. Such exclusion can be viewed as racism, too. But it can also be seen as undermining the university's commitment to free and open debate. Hate speech excludes some people from the community, in part by denying its targets a voice in the community's life and deliberations. Malcolm's letter to his parents expresses this feeling of being excluded and denied a voice. Thus hate speech seems inconsistent with both *respect for persons* and *community.*

American society has been very reluctant to regulate speech of any sort. It has tended to think that the benefits of free speech are great enough to outweigh the occasional harm that can result from unlimited free speech. This is especially true of academic communities, which are inclined to believe that truth is best discovered in free and open debate. Colleges and universities have thus been very reluctant to limit the expression of unpopular views.

John Stuart Mill described the idea that the pursuit of truth requires free and open discussion in a classic statement:

> *We have now recognized the necessity to the mental well-being of mankind (on which all their other well-being depends) of freedom of opinion, and freedom of expression of opinion, on four distinct grounds, which we will now briefly recapitulate:*
>
> *First, if any opinion is compelled to silence, that opinion may, for aught we can certainly know, be true. To deny this is to assume our own infallibility.*
>
> *Second, though the silenced opinion be an error, it may, and very commonly does, contain a portion of truth; and since the general or prevailing opinion on any subject is rarely or never the whole truth, it is only by the collision of adverse opinions that the remainder of the truth has any chance of being supplied.*
>
> *Thirdly, even if the received opinion be not only true, but the whole truth; unless it is suffered to be, and actually is, vigorously and earnestly contested, it will, by most of those who receive it, be held in the manner of a*

prejudice, with little comprehension or feeling of its rational grounds. And not only this, but, fourthly, the meaning of the doctrine itself will be in danger of being lost or enfeebled, and deprived of its vital effect on the character and conduct: the dogma becoming a mere formal profession, inefficacious for good, but cumbering the ground and preventing the growth of any real and heartfelt conviction from reason or personal experience. (Mill, On Liberty, *p. 64).*

Pinecrest College's hate speech regulation, however, suggests another perspective about free speech. While the college, along with Mill, values free and open debate, it also assumes that hate speech undermines the conditions that allow free and open debate. Hate speech does this because it tends to exclude its targets from meaningful debates and because it undermines the climate of civility required for a fruitful exchange of ideas. Pinecrest College seems to believe that in order to have a real academic community and truly open dialogue, it is necessary to limit some kinds of speech. In effect, Pinecrest's hate speech regulations assume that in order to have a free and open debate, some voices might have to be excluded from the debate, and that steps should be taken to ensure that other voices are not intimidated.

Is the college right? If so, it is important to remember that the question is not simply how to balance free speech against the expression of racism. There are other views of what is meant by a genuinely free discussion. One view holds that free speech is unregulated speech. The second holds that discussion can be made more open and more equitable if intimidating or racist speech is forbidden. Are there other alternatives? These are the central questions we will pose in this chapter.

Consider how the principles of *respect for persons* and *community* might be applied to this case:

Pinecrest University's Code of Conduct seems to claim that hate speech violates the idea of respect for persons. It says that hate speech denigrates the dignity and worth of its victims. Is this true? Why? What harm does hate speech do?

One idea here may be that people have intrinsic worth, dependent only on the fact that they are human beings, but independent of such personal characteristics as race, religion, or ethnicity. It is sometimes held that however people may differ, as persons they are of equal worth. Can one view hate speech as speech that seems to deny the equal worth of persons on the basis of characteristics such as race, religion, or ethnicity? Might other kinds of behavior also have this interpretation?

The Code of Conduct also implies that speech that denigrates people because of their race, religion, ethnicity, gender, national origin, or sexual orientation is particularly harmful. Is it? Consider other characteristics that might be employed in hurtful speech. Obesity, baldness, intelligence, height, and wealth are some. Is it less offensive to insult someone because of their weight than because of their race? Why or why not?

Consider that some types of hateful speech are true. People who are attacked because of their weight are often obese. Can asserting the truth count as hate speech? Does it violate the idea of respect for persons? How do words do harm?

The Code of Conduct also suggests that hate speech violates the principle of *community*. It does this by undermining the conditions essential to the purposes of a college community, namely civility, openness, respect, free discussion, and the pursuit of truth. Are these requirements really essential to a college or university community? Why? How might some kinds of speech undermine these conditions and not others?

The code also suggests that hate speech tends to silence the voice of its targets and exclude them from the community. Does it? Are you willing to participate in a discussion with a group that seems to devalue you or your contribution? How does racism exclude people from free and open discussion?

Consider the idea that one purpose of an academic community is to pursue truth and that colleges do this by free and open debate. It might be useful here to distinguish between a debate, in which the purpose is to discover truth, and an argument, in which each side attempts to seek its own interests. In the first case, each party might be expected to decide what to believe on the basis of the evidence put forward by everyone in the debate. Here debate is a form of inquiry. Some of the following qualities might be important in a "debate-as-inquiry": listening and trying to understand, willingness to change one's views on the basis of evidence, and openness to the views of people from outside one's group. Does hate speech undermine these conditions of debate-as-inquiry? If so, how? Are civility and inclusiveness requirements of debate-as-inquiry? (See Chapter 9.)

Is it disruptive of a feeling of community to argue that someone is wrong about something? How would you feel about criticism of someone's religion, or claims that certain kinds of behavior associated with the culture of a particular group are somehow wrong? Would a hate speech prohibition forbid these kinds of activities?

Might there be cases in which a seemingly open debate actually serves the interests of one group over another? Can you think of ways, other than hate speech, in which people can be prevented from contributing their views to a discussion?

Free and open debate may be important to academic communities, but there are many bases for community. Is it wrong to feel closer bonds with people who are like ourselves? When does identification with people like "US" become racism? In an academic community, might there be some occasions when it is acceptable for people to associate on the basis of such commonalities as race, religion, or ethnicity, but other cases in which this is inconsistent with the central purposes of a college or university? If so, how might we distinguish between these cases? (See "Additional Cases" 3.4 and 3.6 in this chapter.)

In his letter to his parents, Malcolm claims that hate speech is only one example of patterns of speech and behavior that exclude African Americans from the college community and define him as "Other." Is he right? Is "US versus THEM" talk racist? Why? Always? What other kinds of speech or behavior tend to exclude people from the community? What might Pinecrest College do to create a more inclusive community?

Malcolm also suggests that he feels excluded by much of what goes on in his classes. Are there teaching practices that tend to exclude on the basis of race? What might some examples be? What kinds of teaching practices are more inclusive?

Not every evil is punishable. Sometimes we may feel that a certain action is wrong, but also that there are reasons why it would be inappropriate or undesirable to seek to punish a person for doing it. Perhaps not everything that is immoral should also be illegal. Can you think of some reasons for this view? Should hate speech be regulated?

We do not doubt that hate speech is immoral. However, it is less clear that it should be regulated. We are going to suggest an argument that concludes that Percy should not be punished for his behavior. We do not necessarily agree with this argument. However, reflecting on it might help you to understand the ethical issues involved more clearly.

One problem with penalizing hate speech is that it attaches penalties to the content of speech. However, free societies and especially college communities must strongly protect freedom of speech. They cannot say that truth is sought by free and open debate and that it is important to protect the right of people to make unpopular arguments, and also say that some kinds of speech are too hateful to be tolerated. The boundaries between arguing an unpopular opinion and hate speech are too vague. Lack of clarity about what is forbidden has a chilling effect on all controversial speech. If colleges are to be places in which free and open debate is possible, they must also tolerate hateful speech. This is a cost of intellectual freedom.

This argument, like the position taken in Pinecrest College's Code of Conduct, accepts the view that free and open debate is essential to the pursuit of truth. It defends what may be the conventional view (such as Mill's) about what is required in order to maintain the climate of openness. Can you state clearly the assumption it makes? Can other positions be taken?

Are members of minority groups more likely to be harmed by hate speech than are whites, or white males? If so, does the argument against prosecuting hate speech unfairly prefer the interests of white males to the interests of minorities?

Following are a few examples of unpopular views that have been argued in recent years:

> People of European descent are "ice people." They are morally and intellectually inferior to darker-skinned "sun people" because of a deficiency of melanin.

> Catholics cannot be good Americans because they owe allegiance to a foreign potentate, the Pope.

> Blacks are not poor because of white racism. They are poor because of their high rate of illegitimacy.

> Homosexuality is a sin and a perversion, not a lifestyle choice or an innate orientation.

Would you classify any of these statements as instances of hate speech? Might they be under some circumstances? Would any of these be punishable under Pinecrest College's policy? Should they be?

Could the college deal with hate speech in some other way than by punishing it? Some religious communities deal with members whom they see as having engaged in sinful behavior by shunning them. Should Percy be shunned? Are there educational solutions to hate speech? Can you think of alternatives to punishment that are preferable? What are they? What makes them better? Can you explain why they are better by appealing to some of the moral principles we have described in the introduction?

Some colleges that have tried to ban hate speech have written codes distinguishing between the content of speech and the manner of the speech. They assume that what is important isn't what is said, but how it is said. What are the merits and liabilities of this approach?

How do the following examples of college and university codes about hate speech differ? Do any of them succeed in resolving the tension between banning hate speech and protecting free speech? How do they reflect the principles of *community* and *respect for persons*?

EXAMPLES OF COLLEGE AND UNIVERSITY CODES ABOUT HATE SPEECH

1. Excerpt from the code of student conduct of *The University of Pennsylvania*[1]

---

[1] *The PennBook 1994–95: Policies and Procedures Handbook*, University of Pennsylvania (Office of the President, 1994), p. 16.

I. Preamble

The University of Pennsylvania is a community in which intellectual growth, learning from others, mutual tolerance, and respect for freedom of thought and expression are principles of paramount importance. In an environment that promotes the free exchange of ideas, cultural and intellectual diversity, and a wealth of social opportunities, Penn students take advantage of the academic and non-academic opportunities available to them. [. . .]

II. Rights of Student Citizenship

Membership in the University of Pennsylvania community affords every student certain rights that are essential to the University's educational mission and its character as a community:

[. . .]

(b) The right to freedom of expression.

(c) The right to be free of discrimination on the basis of race, color, gender, sexual orientation, religion, national or ethnic origin, age, disability, or status as a disabled or Vietnam Era veteran. [. . .]

III. Responsibilities of Student Citizenship

Students are expected to exhibit responsible behavior regardless of time or place. Failure to do so may result in disciplinary action by the University. Responsible behavior is a standard of conduct which reflects higher expectations than may be prevalent outside the University community. Responsible behavior includes but is not limited to the following obligations:

[. . .]

(c) To respect the right of fellow students to participate in university organizations and in relationships with other students without fear, threat, or act of hazing.

(d) To refrain from conduct towards other students that infringes upon the Rights of Student Citizenship. The University condemns hate speech, epithets, and racial, ethnic, sexual and religious slurs. However, the content of student speech or expression is not by itself a basis for disciplinary action. Student speech may be subject to discipline when it violates applicable laws or University regulations or policies."

(A National Public Radio broadcast on 11/18/94 focused on reactions to this controversial policy. A transcript ($10) or tape ($12) of the program is available from National Public Radio Tapes and Transcripts, Washington DC 20036, or (202) 822-2323.)

2. Excerpt from the UNH policy on nonsexist language of the University of New Hampshire[2]

[2] "Administrative Policies and Regulation" from the *1994–1995 University of New Hampshire Student Rights, Rules and Responsibilities* (Division of Student Affairs), p. 35.

The University of New Hampshire, as an equal opportunity educational institution, is committed both to academic freedom and the fair treatment of all individuals. It therefore discourages the use of language and illustrations that reinforce inappropriate and demeaning attitudes, assumptions, and stereotypes about sex roles. Accordingly, all official University communications, whether delivered orally or in writing, shall be free of sexist language."

ADDITIONAL CASES

Case 3.2: The Canon

Columbia College has long required all freshmen to take a Great Books course that has a reading list made up of canonical western writers. Recently, critics have noted that the required readings are, without exception, from "dead white males," and they are arguing for a more inclusive list that would include works by white women and male and female writers of color. In the Tuesday morning section of the Great Books course, Professor Smith (a not-quite-dead, middle-aged white male) is arguing with Simone (an articulate and outspoken female African American student) about the choice of books in the course. The atmosphere is charged, and the other students are listening intently.

Simone heatedly asks, "What about *my* people while all this was going on? We were here in America, too, but you'd never know it from what we've been reading!" Professor Smith responds that "they *were* here, and they played a big role in actually building the country and in creating its folk culture, popular speech, humor, and music. But they just didn't influence major American political, legal, and economic institutions. That's what this course is about: studying the major works in the western tradition that influenced our national institutions."

Simone, however, refuses to back down in the face of Professor Smith's calm explanation. "I know there have been important black writers, such as W.E.B. Dubois, who did influence things. How come we just ignore them? I feel that this course is trying to say that black people, including me, just don't count."

A white student sitting near Simone adds, "The same thing is true about women in general! How are we supposed to feel good about ourselves if everything we read suggests that women have made no contributions?"

Questions

1. Professor Smith argues for sticking to the (white male) classics on the basis of their supposed historical influence, while his students argue

against them because of the damage they supposedly do to nonrepresented students' self-esteem. Are minority and women students "oppressed" by being made to read works that don't "represent" them?
2. Does this logic discourage them from reading the same masterpieces that their parents and grandparents had no chance to read because overt racism and sexism kept them from higher education?
3. Should teaching primarily build students' self-esteem or impart "facts"?
4. Would reading works by women and minorities mainly benefit students with the same backgrounds, or would it benefit all students, including white males? Why or why not?

Case 3.3: Self-Segregation

Like many college campuses across the country, North Carolina State has had a Black Cultural Center since the early 1970s. N.C. State's recent decision to move the center from a suite in the Student Annex to a new, freestanding building has sparked debate among students and faculty. Seniors Kevin and Tony each wrote editorials to the student newspaper, arguing opposite sides of the issue. Their comments are excerpted here.[3]

Kevin's Piece:

> *On the surface, the Black Cultural Center (BCC) sounds like a good idea. Why shouldn't our Black students have a place to fraternize and study, and our African-American program have a place to hold classes? [. . . .] Dig a little deeper, however, and you will find that not only is it a bad idea, it goes against the beliefs of those who fought for civil rights. Furthermore, such a center would tear at the seams of cultural unity.*
>
> *Why should North Carolina's students be separated on the basis of race? Martin Luther King, Andrew Young, and others who fought in the South wanted to insure that this generation would not be segregated. [. . . .] The debate is reminiscent of the separate but equal status of Blacks in the 1950s and '60s, but now it is Blacks arguing for segregation, not whites. [. . . .]*
>
> *[. . .] I understand that the BCC will serve as an educational resource for the campus at large. But will the BCC actually strive for equality and education or will it further segregation? [. . . .]*
>
> *[. . .] [A]ny person who opposes the building of the new Center is labelled a racist. In a time when students have to deal with crowded dining halls, cancelled classes and journals, and the loss of good professors to more affluent institutions, why should we pay for a duplication of services? In*

---

[3] Excerpted from Kevin Ryan and Tony Williamson, "A Difference of Opinion," in *The Cornell Political Forum*, December 1993, vol. VIII, no. 2, pp. 25–26.

other words, we do not need a second student center when there are already libraries, auditoriums, and office space on campus.

Tony's piece:

> *Before we can all "get along," we have to know and appreciate each other's differences. The African-American Cultural Center is a place where everyone can learn about the rich African-American heritage. [. . . .]*
>
> *[. . .] Thus, the Center provides a foundation for something that is sorely missing not only on college campuses, but in society as a whole—racial harmony.*
>
> *African-Americans, who have to face the daily pressures of being a minority and the frustrations of being excluded from the history and culture of America, need an outlet for self-identity and assurance. A cultural center provides such an outlet [. . . .] Since it has been proven that high self-confidence contributes to a student's academic success, the African-American Cultural Center also enhances academic performance. [. . . .]*
>
> *[. . .] People who are ignorant of cultural centers' functions within universities believe that they are merely havens of segregation and racism. These people fail to understand African-Americans' severe need for self-identity. After all, no other race in American history has had to suffer through slavery. Some of the results of slavery (deprivation of self-knowledge, separation of family, self-hatred) still affect the African-American community. The cultural center is a place where African-Americans can redefine themselves through self knowledge and expression. In essence, the African-American Cultural Center is a reflection of African-Americans' struggle for equality. It has nothing to do with racism. The presence of a cultural center on campus contributes to social equality. [. . . .]*
>
> *[. . .] There should be an African-American Cultural Center at every school in the United States; not because America owes something to African-Americans, but because it has an obligation to provide all students with the chance to learn about and appreciate other cultures. [. . . .]*

Questions

1. Evaluate Kevin's and Tony's arguments on the basis of the ethical principles discussed in Chapter 1. Do the two students' arguments appeal to different principles?
2. Does racial segregation on campus protect minority identity, build self-worth, raise achievement levels, and give students the support they need in a hostile world (as proponents of separate student centers or dorms, like Tony, argue)? Or does it destroy minority students' self-worth, lower

their achievement levels, make their entry into mainstream society difficult, and cause them to feel like pariahs, as the Supreme Court's 1954 arguments against educational segregation in *Brown v. Board of Education*
insisted?

3. How might self-segregation differ from imposed segregation? Does
   white students' self-segregation differ in its causes or effects from self-
   segregation practiced by minority students? How?
4. Historically black and female colleges were expected to disappear in the
   1970s and '80s. Instead many seem to have gained new support and
   vigor (for example, see "Black Colleges in Demand as Never Before" in
   The New York Times, 2 January 1993, p.1). At the same time, historically
   all-white and all-male colleges seem to have desegregated or gone co-
   ed. How might you explain these different results of the civil rights and
   women's movements? Do minorities and women somehow have more
   "right" (or more need) to self-segregate than white males?
5. How is sexual self-segregation (such as all-women dorms, centers, or colleges) different from racial self-segregation, if it is?
6. Construct your own case about a separate dorm for gay students. Would
   your analysis of this case differ from your analysis of the African-
   American students' "Self-segregation" case above?

Case 3.4: Cross-Racial Dating

Monica and LaVerne are good friends despite their differences: Monica, who is white and petite, was raised in the big city, while tall La-
Verne is African American and comes from the suburbs. That is, they
were good friends until Monica started dating Dexter, a good-looking
black student she met in one of her classes. LaVerne has been avoiding
Monica ever since she saw the couple at a movie. Monica can't figure
out why LaVerne is shunning her, and she feels hurt. Finally, she decides to leave LaVerne a note, after trying to see her several times without success.

Hey LaVerne—
   *What gives? I never see you anymore, and I get the strong feeling
you've been avoiding me ever since you saw me with my new boyfriend at
the movies. Since you don't even know him (I asked him), I can't figure out
what's bugging you. Did I do something? Let's talk.*   *— M.*

LaVerne calls her up later that same day. "Listen, Monica," she says.
"I thought I could trust you, that you understood how things are. But
you should know better than to go out with a black man! After all I've

talked to you about how hard it is to find a good black man, you've got some nerve stealing one. There aren't enough brothers around for us as it is! It's not like you don't have plenty of white guys you could date. This campus doesn't have many black men, in case you haven't noticed, and a lot of *them* come slobbering after any white girl who's available, ignoring their black sisters. They don't need any help from you! And I sure don't either."

Questions

1. Interracial couples face many kinds of pressure in a society uncomfortable with mixed-race relationships. How should Monica (and Dexter) respond to LaVerne's attempt at peer pressure?
2. Can Monica nurture her friendships with both LaVerne and Dexter?
3. Should Monica and Dexter respond differently if their parents, rather than a peer, try to discourage their relationship?
4. The basic facts behind LaVerne's worries are correct: roughly half as many African-American males as females graduate from college, whereas the proportion of graduating Caucasian males to females is roughly the same.[4] LaVerne's attitude seems to be that Monica is stealing a scarce resource (educated African-American males) that Monica (a) has no right to and (b) doesn't need, because she presumably could "take" one of the large number of white males on campus (something LaVerne seems to feel is not an option for her). Does Monica have a duty to a wider community (African American women, some of whom are her friends) in choosing a partner, or is her choice of a boyfriend purely a private affair?
5. What if Monica were being pressured not sell her car to Dexter on account of his race, not to rent her house to him, or not to hire him as a tutor, rather than to stop dating him? Might some kinds of private choices an individual makes be the legitimate concern of others?
6. Does it matter who is pressuring whom? That is, would the pressure have a different moral force if Monica's white friends tried to get her to break up with Dexter, or to get Dexter to break up with her, or if LaVerne pressured Dexter instead of Monica?

Case 3.5: Cafeteria Friendships

Mary King, Director of Student Affairs at Jefferson County Community College, has noticed something that disturbs her every time she

---

[4] In 1991, the latest year for which figures are available, 24,601 African-American males and 41,622 African-American females received B.A.'s. In comparison, male and female Caucasians graduated in roughly similar numbers: 415,506 men to 488,555 women. (*The Almanac of Higher Education*, 1994, p. 36.)

eats in the student dining hall. Unlike most of her fellow staff members (who avoid the student cafeteria), Mary enjoys mingling socially with students and trying to get to know them outside of office hours, and she thinks this is part of her job. When she takes her tray from the serving line and looks for students to join for lunch, she tries to scan the entire cafeteria first, to see who might need a friend or want to talk to her.

Over the loud clatter of silverware and even louder babble of talking, she sees a striking pattern: every table seems to be made up of students from the same racial group, and usually the same age group as well. Whites and blacks, Asians and Hispanics, older students and younger students—each group has its own table or tables, which might as well have "reserved for young Hispanics" or "reserved for older white students" on them. All of the students seem to sit consistently with people just like themselves. The groups even seem to dress similarly, such as the table of funky, neo-grunge young white students to her left, and the conservatively dressed Asian students at the table to her right.

Mary feels that segregated seating and segregated friendships are almost as harmful to students' personal growth and the promotion of a sense of unity and harmony on campus as official segregation would be. She explains her observations to the dean: "The cafeteria is only the most obvious place to see this segregation. If you look at students walking around campus or at sport events, the groups are just as separate. I'm told they even tend to sit in different parts of the same classroom! Just because no one's officially *keeping* students apart doesn't mean that racism and mutual distrust aren't being promoted by this pervasive unofficial segregation. If Jefferson really wants to promote tolerance and equal opportunity for all, the way we say we do, we have to do something about this situation."

Questions

1. Is de facto ("in fact" or unofficial) segregation similar in its harmful effects to de jure ("by right" or legalized) segregation?
2. Should institutions such as Jefferson County Community College intervene in what seem to be students' natural friendship patterns? If they should, what could Jefferson College (or Mary) do? When, if ever, do private choices like whom to sit next to, or date, become the business of the college community?
3. When does feeling closer to people like yourself become racism?
4. If Jefferson College, and the county itself, have a history of serious racial and ethnic tension, would mixing student groups and trying to promote intergroup friendships be more necessary (as well as more difficult)?

Case 3.6: *Long-Lost Friend*

Carol and Greg hadn't seen each other since eighth grade, when they went to different schools. Carol still remembered Greg vividly, though. He was her best buddy from ages nine to thirteen, the person who made her laugh the hardest and think the deepest. They told each other secrets that they had never told anyone else. And Greg's family always seemed warmer and more open than her own. She used to wonder whether all black families were like his, and all white families like hers; secretly she thought it would be nicer to be black. When Greg went out of her life, Carol had gone through a big change—whether because of not having him around any more or because of just growing up, she wasn't sure. At any rate, she stopped climbing trees, fishing in the creek, playing softball, and generally being what her parents disapprovingly called a tomboy. It was funny, but Carol had also never had a close black friend again. However, she still thought of those years with Greg as the happiest and most carefree of her life.

Why hadn't they kept in touch, she wondered? They had lived in the same suburb all those years between eighth grade and now. She was feeling nostalgic after her first year away from home, and she suddenly thought, "I should just write and tell him to come visit me here at college!"

Now she was waiting at the bus station. Greg's bus was due any minute, and Carol found herself surprisingly nervous. Maybe she hadn't visited Greg or his family all those years because she'd started to realize that white girls weren't supposed to be best friends with black boys. Maybe she'd unconsciously started to feel that as she got closer to dating age, she should stick to her own kind. Maybe she and Greg wouldn't even recognize each other—what if he'd turned into some kind of scary dude who resented her and her white privileges? And what would her (all white) friends think of him? It might be so awkward! On the other hand, what if he were still Greg and they could take up where they left off? Maybe he could help her deal with her guilty feelings about race and lost innocence. Or maybe he would think it was racist of her to want to talk to him about race . . . With Carol's thoughts in this confused muddle, Greg's bus finally arrived.

Questions

1. Carol seems to blame herself for the fact that she and Greg have drifted apart; however, despite years of official desegregation, most Americans draw most of their friends from their own racial group. What kinds of external pressures might have pushed Greg and Carol apart?

2. Do individuals of good will have a duty to try to establish or maintain friendships across racial lines? Is it racist to value a friendship (largely, or in part) *because* it is with a person of another race?

3. Is it appropriate for Carol to try to sort out her "white guilt" with Greg because he's African-American, or is it her job to do this work on her own (or with a therapist, minister or rabbi)?

Case 3.7: Consciousness-Raising

Because of past tensions on campus, Northlake University recently instituted a required week-long orientation program for all prospective dorm students. The program featured a variety of activities, from noncompetitive games and evening dances to workshops on racism, sexism, and homophobia, and presentations about multiculturalism. The university designed the program "to promote tolerance and acceptance of difference among the diverse population of students who share dorm life," but it did not seem to be having this effect with some students. In fact, midway through the week, a sensitivity-training workshop brought on a heated argument between two students.

Jerry, who sensed that his conservative religious views were not shared by many other students, saw the whole program as indoctrination into bizarre left-liberal views, amounting to reverse discrimination against religious white males like himself. "It seems to me that the main point of all this 'consciousness-raising' is to make white guys feel as humiliated and oppressed as minorities and gays and women say they are," he said angrily. "It's not *my* fault they've had a hard time. I feel as though I'm supposed to apologize for being male, heterosexual, and white, if I want to live in the dorms!"

Isabella, a Latina psychology major, saw the workshops as personally empowering and valuable for building up empathy and esprit de corps among diverse dorm students. "You seem to feel threatened by people different from yourself," she replied in her best therapeutic manner. "If you want to get along in the dorm you have to accept the truth about your privileged position in society, and work to be less racist, homophobic, and sexist, and more empathetic."

Jerry blew up at what he saw as her condescension and insults. "Oh, right! Being persecuted is supposed to make me more empathetic. I don't *want* to get along with people who call me racist and sexist when they don't even know me! You and your politically correct friends can keep the dorms. I'm going to live off campus!" And with that, he stalked out of the room.

After a moment of shocked silence among the remaining students, Isabella said, "Well, it's too bad he can't handle it, but he probably couldn't handle living with diverse people in the dorm either."

Questions

1. Is there anything Northlake University can do to improve the orientation program so that it really does "promote tolerance and acceptance of dif-

ference" of all students? Or is Isabella right that some straight white males will inevitably feel threatened when previously disenfranchised groups assert their right to equal participation?

2. Consider the situation if Jerry's religious beliefs require that he not tolerate some other students. For example, if Jerry believes the Bible teaches that homosexuality is sinful and homosexuals should be shunned, is the university unlawfully discriminating against his religion if it requires that he accept gay students as the price of living in the dorms?

3. What if his antigay (or antiblack, or antiwoman) beliefs were based on personal feelings and fears instead of on religion—would the school have more, or less, reason to try to change them?

4. Are students entitled to hold racist, sexist, homophobic, or otherwise offensive beliefs, so long as they don't seem to be hurting anyone? Or might these attitudes cause pain and division even if they are not expressed in hate speech or violence? Does an educational institution have a duty to try to uproot intolerance and to promote mutual understanding in an increasingly diverse society? (See Chapter 9.)

Case 3.8: The Christmas Party

Beth thought she was the only student living in Rockwell Hall who felt excluded by the dorm's upcoming annual Christmas party. Brightly printed fliers had been up for weeks advertising the fun: "Christmas caroling, Santa Claus, tree trimming, hot chocolate and cookies, and other holiday cheer." She had tried to explain to her roommate that she didn't feel comfortable going but also was sorry to miss out on the dorm's biggest party of the year. "Well, why don't you come then?" her roommate had asked. "It doesn't matter if you don't know any carols—I'm sure everyone will be glad to teach them to you. It'll be fun!"

Beth didn't know how to explain to her well-meaning roommate that that wasn't the problem. She'd certainly heard carols before, but it felt wrong for her as a Jew (even a rather unobservant one) to sing about "Jesus the Son of God." She felt uneasy listening to everyone else sing praises to "Christ the Lord," too. And the presence of someone dressed as Santa Claus would be an unhappy reminder of the pained looks on her parents' faces when, as a child, she'd come home from school crying and asked why they couldn't be Christians so that Santa would visit them too.

Now Beth discovered someone else who felt upset by Rockwell's Christmas party plans. Fatima, a Muslim student on the second floor, agreed that the dorm's holiday festivities inadvertently made non-Christians feel slighted and left out. "My friends have told me that there won't be anything especially Christian about the party—no crosses or nativity scenes or anything. They just don't get it. There's no way a Christmas party won't be Christian, and uncomfortable for me, even if they don't mean it to be. And what's even worse," Fatima added angrily, "this Christmas party is blowing a major chunk of the dorm's activities fund for the whole semester! *Our* money is helping to pay for a party that leaves us out."

Questions

1. Should Beth and Fatima lighten up and go to the party, ignoring aspects of it that displease them, or are they right to feel hurt and excluded?
2. If their grievance seems legitimate, what should they do—find some other entertainment by themselves the night of the party, go to the party and protest the aspects of it that offend them, or do something else to raise others' consciousness of the problem?
3. Which ethical principles are at stake in this case, and how might Beth and Fatima appeal to them in arguing for a more inclusive party?
4. Do the Rockwell Hall party planners have a responsibility to make the holiday party feel inclusive to everyone? If so, should they try to make the affair combine elements of different religious traditions, or make sure that it completely avoids references to any particular religion? Are there other options?
5. Is it possible to have a "holiday party" that doesn't offend any group?
6. Would the problem be alleviated if the money for the party came not from common funds, but privately from the pockets of a few wealthy students who invited all the rest?

BACKGROUND READING

David Denby, Annals of Education: "Does Homer Have Legs?" in *The New Yorker*, 6 September 1993, vol. LXIX, no. 28, pp. 52–69. A self-described "middle-aged, middle-class white male" goes back to Columbia University to attend a Great Books class and see how the traditional Western canon is taught and justified. He also ruminates about how the books in the course affect him and the other students in the class (who are a young, ethnically diverse group). For examples of the controversy surrounding the canon and more background on the debate, see Dinesh D'Souza, *Illiberal Education: The Politics of Race and Sex on Campus* (New York: The Free Press/Macmillan, 1991), especially Chapter 6 pp. 157–193, and pp. 246–247.

Louis Menard, "The Culture Wars: A Review of *Dictatorship of Virtue: Multiculturalism and the Battle for America's Future* by Richard Bernstein (Knopf, 1994)" in *The New York Review of Books*, 6 October 1994, pp. 16–21. This lengthy and largely negative review discusses a number of recent college and university cases of hate speech, "political correctness," criticisms of multiculturalism, and attempts at gender equity on campus, some of which are mentioned below under "Additional Materials." It also presents an argument against speech codes and even the use of "multiculturalist categories like race, gender, and sexual orientation" on campus (p. 18).

Paul Berman (editor), *Debating P.C.: The Controversy Over Political Correctness on College Campuses.* (New York: Dell/Bantam Doubleday Dell, 1992). This book is a collection of excerpts from writers who cover the political and cultural spectrum of opinions about ``political correctness.'' The excerpts are arranged into six sections: debating political correctness; politics and the canon; free speech and speech codes; the "Texas Shoot-Out" (see "Additional Materials" item 2 below); the public schools; and diverse views. Berman describes the background of the debate in his "Introduction: The Debate and Its Origins" (pp. 1–26), and also precedes each excerpt with a paragraph summarizing its context.

Jean J. Schensul and Thomas G. Carroll, "Vision of America in the 1990s and Beyond: Negotiating Cultural Diversity and Educational Change," in *Education and Urban Society*, August 1990, vol. 22, no. 4, pp. 339–345.

This issue of *Education and Urban Society* focuses on cultural diversity on campus. Schensul and Carroll's article introduces three other articles discussing the background of the current campus debate between advocates of multicultural studies and the traditional Western canon. Schensul and Carroll also summarize various responses American schools have taken to student diversity in the past, and they suggest a program of cultural pluralism and cultural transformation for the future.

George Will, "A Kind of Compulsory Chapel: Multiculturalism is a Campaign to Lower America's Moral Status," in *Newsweek*, 14 November 1994, vol. 124, no. 20, p. 84. This work is an analysis of a list of "multicultural horror stories" that the conservative columnist culled from Richard Bernstein's *Dictatorship of Virtue: Multiculturalism and the Battle for America's Future.* Readers should be aware that others have challenged the accuracy of the facts in some of Will's descriptions. Will also favorably reviews Bernstein's book.

Paul Berman, "Reflections: The Other and Almost the Same," in *The New Yorker*, 28 February 1994, pp. 61–66, 68–71. This article is a detailed analysis of the historical roots and meaning of tensions between black and Jewish Americans. It begins with a discussion of a Kean College, New Jersey speech by a representative of Minister Louis Farrakhan and the Nation of Islam. It goes on to suggest the wider cultural implications of this campus event, which was seen by many as an example of hate speech.

For more in the same vein, see John Blake, "When Friends Feud," in *The Atlanta Journal and Atlanta Constitution*, 5 June 1994, sec. G, p. 1, col. 2. This is the text of a round-table discussion on relations between blacks and Jews that involved three participants (including a college student) from each group.

Lena Williams, "Growing Black Debate on Racism: When Is It Real, When an Excuse?" in *The New York Times*, 5 April 1992, sec. 1, p. 1, col. 1. This article examines an emotionally-charged debate among African-Americans today. An increasing number of black Americans have become openly critical of the actions of black public figures such as Mike Tyson, Leonard Jeffries (see "Additional Materials" item 5 in this chapter), and Marion S. Barry, suggesting that the communal psychology that has long bound black Americans in unanimity is slowly dissolving. Such criticisms are being countered by other groups claiming that Tyson, Jeffries, and Barry are victims of the white establishment.

A number of Supreme Court case rulings have affected the desegregation of colleges. In *Missouri ex. rel. Gaines v. Canada* (1938), the Court ruled that if a state provides a graduate education in law to white students, it must, under the equal protection guarantee of the Fifteenth Amendment to the Constitution, offer a substantially similar education to blacks. Similarly, *Sweatt v. Painter* (1950) affirmed that a qualified black student has a constitutional right to a state-provided legal education equal to that offered to qualified white students. *McLaurin v. Oklahoma State Regents for Higher Education* (1950) ruled that a black student admitted to an all-white university as a Ph.D. candidate cannot be assigned to separate seating in the classroom, library, and cafeteria. And although the landmark case of *Brown v. Board of Education* (1954) applied specifically to elementary schools, the ruling was taken broadly to mean that all segregated education is inherently unequal and thus unconstitutional. Later, amid concerns about the effect of "reverse discrimination" on white students, the Court rather confusingly decided in *University of California Regents v. Bakke* (1978) that colleges and universities cannot use racial quotas in admissions decisions, but they can consider the race of applicants.

Judith Lichtenberg, "Racism in the Head, Racism in the World" and Alaka Wali, "Multiculturalism: An Anthropological Perspective," in *The Report from The Institute for Philosophy and Public Policy*, Spring/Summer 1992, vol. 12, no. 1, pp. 3–5 and 6–8.[5] This entire special issue of *The Report* is devoted to discussions of ethical issues involved in "Race, Discrimination, and Group Identity." Lichtenberg analyzes the differences between individual racism, racist institutions, and racist societies, and argues that even if "racism in the head" disappeared, "racism in the world" would not. Wali discusses the "virtual meaninglessness" of the biological category of race and examines the reasons for and implications of racial and ethnic identification, particularly in current debates about multiculturalism.

Gerald Early, "Understanding Afrocentrism: Why Blacks Dream of a World Without Whites" in *Civilization, the Magazine of the Library of Congress*, July/August 1995, vol. 2, no. 4, pp. 31–39. This cover story seeks to explain why a growing number of African Americans reject the pro-integration stance of many blacks during the Civil Rights movement in the 1960s. It also defines the doctrine of Afrocentrism and explores its historical and psychological roots.

William A. Kaplan, "A Proposed Process for Managing the First Amendment Aspects of Campus Hate Speech," in *The Journal of Higher Education*, September–October 1992, vol. 63, no. 5. This lengthy article provides a legal overview of the subject of hate speech. Specifically, it defines "the character and harms of hate speech," ex-

---

[5] *The Report* is available from The Institute for Philosophy and Public Policy, School of Public Affairs, University of Maryland, College Park MD 20742 (301) 405-4759.

plores the first amendment (freedom of speech) aspects of the topic, reviews judicial rulings touching on hate speech, and recommends a process for colleges and universities to follow in dealing with hate speech.

ADDITIONAL MATERIALS

1. Bernard Malamud, a Jewish novelist, has written a powerful novel, *The Fixer* (New York: Dell Publishing, 1968), about anti-Semitism in Russia. Many of his characters are anti-Semites who say things that should be viewed as hate speech, if anything should be. Is he guilty of hate speech? What does this tell us about the importance of context in making judgments about the meaning of speech?

2. For further information about the following case, see Louis Menard, "The Culture Wars: A Review of *Dictatorship of Virtue: Multiculturalism and the Battle for America's Future*" by Richard Bernstein (New York: Knopf, 1994), in *The New York Review of Books*, 6 October 1994, p. 20. See also section 4 of "The Texas Shoot-Out" in *Debating P.C.: The Controversy Over Political Correctness on College Campuses* (New York: Dell/Bantam Doubleday Dell, 1992). A controversy arose at the University of Texas at Austin over a proposal to force all sections of the required composition course to use readings on racial and sexual discrimination. Adherents saw the change as a needed counterbalance to racist and sexist undertones on campus and in society at large. Critics saw the proposal as an attempt to impose "thought control" on the 40 percent of Texas students forced to take the course. After increasing furor led to national attention, the proposal was eventually dropped.

Do you think the proposed course change would have closed down or opened up campus discussions? Why would you or wouldn't you want to take such a course? How might the principles of community and respect for persons be applied to both the course proposal and the controversy that followed it?

3. For further information about the following case, see Michael deCourcy, "No Penalties for Black Students Who Took Magazines at Penn," in *The New York Times*, 16 September 1993, sec. B, p. 9, col. 4; and "Panel Says Penn Police Overreacted," in *The New York Times*, 28 July 1993, sec. A, p. 15, col. 1. A group of African American students at the University of Pennsylvania were long angered by a conservative student newspaper that they considered racist. Finally they confiscated all copies of one issue of the newspaper to protest a columnist's criticisms of Martin Luther King Jr. and claims that the university gives preferential treatment to African Americans in admissions and disciplinary procedures. Campus police could identify only nine of the sixty students involved in confiscating the newspaper, and the university at length dismissed all disciplinary proceedings against them. The newspaper staff felt that although the university talked forcefully about protecting freedom of speech, it refused to punish those who violated it, or to guarantee police protection against the papers being stolen again.

Is confiscation of offensive material a legitimate or effective way to deal with it? Does it matter who does the confiscating, who the audience is, or whom the offensive material targets? You might think here of additional examples, such as pornography, or notoriously "dangerous" books such as Hitler's *Mein Kampf.* What other options might the African American students have had? Are the kinds of opinions expressed by the conservative columnist really examples of hate speech? How would you evaluate the university administration's response to this incident, in terms of finding a balance between banning hate speech and protecting free speech?

4. For more information about the following, see Terry Wilson, "New Support Group Seeks to Offer Help to Gay Teachers," in *The Chicago Tribune,* 29 December 1994, sec. 2C, p. 7, col. 1. Some people believe that homosexuality is somehow contagious. At least, that seems to be the reasoning behind a number of laws and social practices affecting gays. For example, teachers, professors, and college students studying to be teachers often fear being fired (or not hired) if they admit that they are gay, or if they present positive gay and lesbian role models to students. Do you think that gay teachers should be kept away from students (of particular ages)? Why? In the same vein, should the influence of gay student groups be limited by not allowing them to use campus facilities? University of South Alabama sophomore George Hite Wilson is pushing to overturn an Alabama law banning gay student groups from using public funds or facilities because they "promote a lifestyle" outlawed in Alabama's anti-sodomy statute. (For more information see Judy Sheppard, "Gays Need Not Apply" in *The Atlanta Constitution,* 16 August 1994, sec. A, p. 3, col. 2.)

A recent survey found pronounced differences between the numbers of gay men and women who have college educations, and those who do not (David W. Dunlap, "Gay Survey Raises a New Question," in *The New York Times,* 18 October 1994, sec. B, p. 8, col. 4.). Do these figures suggest that homosexual teachers influence students to become gay (as some fear), that people with homosexual orientations tend to go to college proportionally more than their nonhomosexual peers, or that college raises gay students' consciousnesses and makes them more willing to openly identify themselves as homosexual? Can you think of other explanations for this difference? Should a purpose of the college experience be to help students discover or explore their sexual orientations? (See also Chapter 8.)

5. "Watching Dr. Jeffries Self-Destruct," in *The New York Times,* 25 August 1991, sec. 4, p. 14, col. 1. Leonard Jeffries Jr., Chairman of the Black Studies

Department at the City University of New York, has had a highly controversial career. He advocates a radical form of Afrocentric education that many critics see as racially divisive, hate-filled, and based on "misinformation." Among Jeffries' contentious theories are his assertions that Jews financed the African slave trade, that American Jews and Italian Americans conspired to denigrate and destroy African Americans in the movies, and that African Americans are morally and genetically superior to European Americans. However, Jeffries has gathered strong support among his black students and many in the African American community, who feel that he restores their sense of self-worth and pride in their ancestry (see Jacques Steinberg, "Jeffries Misses Brooklyn Rally on Racial Issues," in *The New York Times*, 16 August 1991, sec. B, p. 3, col. 1; Steven Lee Myers, "500 Rally to Support Controversial Professor," in *The New York Times*, 12 August 1991, sec. B, p. 3, col. 3; Ellen Whitford, "Jeffries Stresses Heritage," in *The Atlanta Constitution*, 2 April 1992, sec. B, p. 4, col. 4; and "Professor's Remarks Reported as Bigoted," in *The New York Times*, 28 November 1994, sec. B, p. 5, col. 2).

The controversy over Jeffries began when he made an angry speech attacking Jews at the state-sponsored Empire State Black Arts and Cultural Festival on July 20, 1991. Then-Governor Mario Cuomo, other state officials, some top CUNY administrators, and many faculty members quickly assailed Jeffries' "anti-Semitism" and urged CUNY to take disciplinary action against him. But the CUNY Faculty Senate declined to censure Jeffries, and the university trustees merely put Jeffries on one-year probation as chairman of the Black Studies Department because they were "hesitant to dismiss him for fear of adding to racial tensions already high on campus" (Joseph Berger, "CUNY Board Votes to Keep Jeffries in Post," in *The New York Times*, 29 October 1991, sec. B, p. 1, col. 5).

Next, a student reporter from the *Harvard Crimson* claimed that Jeffries threatened his life if he used statements Jeffries made about two black scholars during an interview, and he ordered a bodyguard to seize his tape recording of the interview, which Jeffries had permitted, after Jeffries turned hostile. Jeffries continued to make contentious statements, and then on March 23, 1992, the CUNY Trustees replaced him with a far less controversial figure as Black Studies Department chair. Jeffries promptly sued CUNY for reinstatement, testifying that his academic freedom and right to free expression had been violated by the school. He also warned that his demotion would spark community resistance (Maria Newman, "Jeffries Warned of Unrest if Demoted, Official Recalls" in *The New York Times*, 24 April 1993, sec. A, p. 26, col. 5). A federal court ruled in Jeffries' favor on August 4, 1993, saying that CUNY violated his free speech rights. The judge further ordered the university to pay Jeffries $400,000 in damages and to reinstate him as head of the Black Studies Department. On November 14, 1994, the Supreme Court took on the case, although the Court has not decided it as of this writing (mid-1995).

How can a college ensure a civil, nonintimidating atmosphere while also protecting students' and faculty members' right to free speech? Should colleges even try to curb or censure racist or other hate speech, or only teach students how to respond to it? Are Jeffries' statements examples of (properly censured) hate speech, or of bigoted remarks that nonetheless might serve an important purpose in bolstering minority students' self-esteem? If his theories are false, what implications might this have for his students' raised self-esteem? Why should (or shouldn't) increasing self-esteem be a purpose of education?

For more information, see Edwin M. Yoder, Jr., "A First Amendment With Footnotes: Is the Supreme Court Preparing to Broaden Exceptions to Free Speech?" in *The Washington Post*, 18 December 1994, sec. C, p. 4, col 1; "Editorial: Professor Jeffries' Speech," in *The Washington Post*, 16 November 1994, sec. A, p. 24, col. 1; "Editorial: Pity His Students," in *The Washington Post*, 9 August 1993, sec. A, p. 16, col. 1; Nathan Glazer, "Academic Freedom? Academic Farce," in *The New York Times*, 21 May 1993, sec. A, p. 27, col. 2; Lynne Duke, "Colliding Racial Beliefs Test Speech Limits at CUNY," in *The Washington Post*, 9 November 1991, sec. A, p. 1, col. 1 (interviews Jeffries and another professor); "Editorial: Words That Provoke," in *USA Today*, 19 August 1991, sec. A, p. 8, col. 1; and Roger E. Hernandez, "The New Racism," in *The Washington Post*, 16 August 1991, sec. A, p. 29, col. 1.

6. Until 1995, the University of Maryland offered the Benjamin Banneker scholarship to high-achieving black students. The program set aside scholarship money for about thirty such students each year. In these financially-strapped times, white students have complained that race-based scholarships are unfair, and in fact the Supreme Court recently let stand a lower court ruling that such scholarships violate the equal protection clause of the 14th Amendment to the Constitution. However, a study by the NAACP Legal Defense Fund indicates that "nationwide there is a plethora of scholarship programs that give financial aid exclusively to members of specific groups and that they have not been the subject of legal challenges." The scholarships are offered to groups such as "Jews, Chinese Americans, Italian Americans, foreign students, women, Greek Americans, men, Christians, lineal descendents of Confederate soldiers, Baptists," and so on (Steven A. Holmes, "Minority Scholarship Plans Are Dealt Setback by Court: Decision On Maryland Program Is Let Stand," in *The New York Times*, 23 May 1995, p. B9). Indeed, many scholarships and preferential admissions policies exclusively benefit two relatively privileged groups: student athletes, and alumni sons and daughters. Is there any reason race-based policies should be thought of differently?

Are such affirmative-action scholarships ethical? Why or why not? What moral principles might be useful in analyzing this issue, and how would you apply them? Are minority-specific scholarships in the best interest of the country as a whole, or only in the interest of the particular minority group be-ing helped? Do colleges owe blacks or other racial or ethnic minority stu-dents some sort of compensation for past discrimination? For more information, see Holmes, "Minority Scholarship Plans Are Dealt Setback by Court"; and a transcript of the March 19, 1995 *All Things Considered* broadcast on National Public Radio, which aired a debate between Banneker scholar Miesha Harris (a senior at the university) and a male freshman there.[6]

7. Ralph Frammolino, "Getting Grades for Diversity?" in *The Los Angeles Times*, 23 February 1994, sec. A, p. 1, col. 1. The Western Association of Schools and Colleges proposed to hold its member colleges accountable for fostering cultural diversity on campus, using accreditation as a tool for en-forcing compliance. In other words, schools that did not meet the Associa-tion's diversity standards would not be accredited even though they met all other accreditation standards, and they would thus lose students and per-haps professors, and become ineligible for crucial government and founda-tion grants and private donations. Is bureaucratic enforcement of school diversity (either privately sponsored, as in the association, or publicly man-dated, as in federal or state prohibitions against segregated schools) an ap-propriate way to ensure better education for minority students? Various university presidents reacted angrily to the association's proposal. But what differences, if any, are there between the association's plan to enforce diver-sity and federal and state statutes that refuse tax-exempt status to racially segregated schools? Should schools be punished for being unwilling (or per-haps even unable) to attract and keep traditionally under-represented stu-dents? Why or why not?

8. Dinesh D'Souza, *Illiberal Education: The Politics of Race and Sex on Campus* (New York: The Free Press/Macmillan, 1991). Chapter 5 describes the case of Reynolds Farley, who was "acknowledged as America's leading demogra-pher in the field of race relations," a self-proclaimed liberal democrat, author of widely assigned sociology textbooks, and a popular professor on the Michigan State campus, when he was criticized in the student newspaper for remarks he made during a Sociology 303 class on racial and cultural contacts in the fall of 1988 (p. 148). Professor Farley was accused of showing "insensi-tivity" to Malcolm X and Marcus Garvey because he mentioned less-than-flattering facts about these black leaders. He was also castigated for quoting "prejudicial statements to the class," although he claimed that he used these to "help describe the history of race relations" (p. 149). A student in the class wrote that "Farley is insensitive to issues of racism and sexism" and "perpet-uates a racism that's in the university as a whole." The student called for the

---

[6] Available as a transcript ($10) or tape ($12) from "National Public Radio Tapes and Tran-scripts," Washington DC 20036, or (202) 822-2323.

course to have a different instructor in the future, "someone who's sensitive—preferably a person of color" (p. 150).

The Department chairman convened a faculty executive committee to meet with students and discuss their grievances. At the meeting, other faculty who defended Farley were themselves denounced for insensitivity. However, no action was taken, and eventually the whole affair subsided. Farley nevertheless felt that his reputation had been "gravely damaged" by unsubstantiated, irresponsible charges. He was angry that the university hadn't stood up for academic freedom and open expression, and he decided never to teach the course again.

Farley's student critic seems to assume that only a person of color can be sensitive to issues of race, and thus that only a nonwhite professor should teach about subjects touching on race. Do you accept this reasoning? Why or why not? If you do, does this also imply, for example, that only women should write novels about female characters? Does it mean that black professors are never prejudiced against black students, or that female professors can't be sexist? If you don't agree, do you think that professors (of whatever color or sex) should still be evaluated at least partly on whether or not they bring a minority viewpoint to the classroom? Do colleges and universities have a duty to counter the dominant culture's racism and sexism in what and how they teach? If so, how can they best go about doing this? How might the principles of benefit maximization, respect for persons, and community apply to this case?

4

PRIVACY AND DIALOGUE

Two Cases: Invading Personal Space

Case 4.1: Incompatibility

Bill remembered the form he had filled out for Residence Life. It had asked him to indicate the qualities he wanted in a roommate. Because he had been on the cross-country team in high school and liked classical music, he checked off athletics and music as his interests, and he asked for a nonsmoking roommate. He had gone three for three. Fred was into sports—boxing, which he watched religiously on his TV. And he loved music—he played riffs on his electric guitar at high decibels. At least he didn't smoke.

Although at first Bill didn't altogether hate Fred's feeble imitations of Tom Petty, his idea of music to study by ran more toward Mozart. Fred seemed to have no opinion about suitable studying music, because he appeared not to study. However, he was disciplined about practicing his guitar regularly, at high volumes, often until the wee hours of the morning. Maybe all that loud music had done something to his hearing, because it seemed that everything Fred did was loud: he always turned the volume up high when a match was on TV or when he played his stereo, and he even talked loudly. Fred had turned their room into a dormitory version of a nightclub. Fred's friends felt free to walk in anytime and hold a jam session or play a new tape they'd gotten. The loud music and conversation often went on until two or three in the morning. Because Fred usually slept until noon, he didn't seem overly deprived of sleep, but Bill had an 8:00 A.M. lab. He could escape his room to study, but he had nowhere else to sleep.

At first Bill tried polite requests, but these seemed lost on Fred and his friends. They just invited him to join in and have a drink. Fred pointed out that "this is my room, too. There's nowhere else we can play. And who are you to tell me when I can practice or what I can listen to?" When Bill asked if they could play more quietly, Fred responded simply that "this music's got to be loud," and turned up his amp.

Finally Bill yelled, "couldn't we at least talk about this?" Fred just ignored him. That was when Bill decided to ask for a new roommate, but the college was short on rooms. They said they'd see what they could do for him next semester.

In desperation Bill tried being a little more aggressive with Fred. He told him that he had had it with the loud music and that Fred and his friends should find a practice room somewhere. Unfortunately, this seemed to be a mistake. Up until this point, Fred had tolerated Bill. But now Fred seemed to think that Bill had challenged him, and he had to defend his honor before his friends. Now Bill became the butt of increasingly nasty jokes. Fred often "accidentally" knocked Bill's books and papers over or spilled soda on his things, and a couple of times he roughly shoved him. Bill was in no hurry to get into a fight with a bunch of guys at once, so he always backed down, much to his humiliation.

By the end of the semester, Fred and his friends had turned Bill-baiting into an art form. Bill decided that if he couldn't get out of that room for the next semester, he would drop out.

Questions

1. Does Bill have a right to tell Fred how Fred can use their room? How would you justify such a right?
2. Suppose that Bill simply disliked the kind of music that Fred played and took the position that Fred should not play it whenever Bill was in the room. Does Bill have a right to demand this? Suppose that Bill used the room only to study or sleep and insisted that Fred maintain complete silence whenever he was in the room. At what point would Bill's demands for Fred's silence become unreasonable?
3. How could Bill and Fred settle a disagreement about the use of the room? What should Bill do if Fred won't discuss it?

Case 4.2: *Different Strokes*

Rachel and Judy shared a lot of interests and enjoyed one another's company, despite a noteworthy difference in their backgrounds: Rachel was a Jew from New York City and Judy was the quintessential suburban WASP. They had learned to live together well. Neither was a neat freak, and neither was a slob. They had worked out a study schedule. They managed to know when to exit when the other was entertaining, and neither abused the privilege. Everything was great—until Rachel's parents invited Judy to visit them in Brooklyn for a weekend.

There was much that Judy enjoyed: new foods, fascinating places to visit, and the parade of friends and relatives who wandered in and out of Rachel's house at all hours. Rachel's mother held court in the kitchen, serving food and gossip to all who came. By late Saturday, Judy knew more about Rachel's family and her neighbors than she did about her own. All of the weddings, divorces, child rearing problems, and operations were constantly discussed and debated. Judy was astonished when Rachel's mother told her how much she and Rachel's father earned and how much they had paid for their house and various items in it. Advice was freely given by all to each, and hugs and kisses seemed to be offered equally generously. Judy found it all quite wonderful until it was her turn.

Judy's family honored their Scottish ancestors by making much of the virtue of privacy. They never gossiped; it was understood that the affairs of each member of her family were their own business. People could discuss their private lives if they wished, but "Don't ask, don't tell" seemed the rule. In Judy's family, prying was a major sin. And hugging, kissing, and displays of emotion in general were simply not done—she had not been hugged by her parents (or seen them hug anyone else) since she was a small child.

Judy didn't have much trouble with the first question asked of her, although it was accompanied by squeeze of her hand (Rachel's mother seemed to touch other people constantly as they talked). She answered that her father worked for an insurance company and her mother was a chemistry teacher. However, she was uncomfortable about being asked how much her parents earned. Rachel's mother clearly couldn't believe that Judy didn't know, and because this was obviously an important fact about Judy's family, she pressed before reluctantly going on to other subjects.

Judy tried not to be impolite, but in fact there was much that Rachel's mother asked that she couldn't answer, and much about which she said less than she could have. And she couldn't help shrinking away from all the touching and hugging with people she barely knew; they even sat closer together than she liked. By the end of the weekend, Rachel's mother had once referred to her as "my Rachel's mute friend" and intimated that there must be something suspicious about a family with so many secrets.

Judy was embarrassed for Rachel. She felt that she ought to reassure her that everything was still all right between them, and that she hadn't really minded her mother too much, but she hadn't quite found a tactful way to broach the subject. Rachel beat her to it. Soon after they got back to the dorm, she said, "Judy, how could you treat my mother that way? She really put out for you this weekend. She treated you like her own daughter, and you just clammed up every time she asked you a question! And you hurt her feelings when you tried to shake hands instead of hugging her goodbye. How could you be so rude?"

Questions

1. Having written this case, we worried that the character of Rachel's mother might seem like a negative Jewish stereotype. Do you think it is?
2. Does it make a difference that one author of this case has a Jewish background, and the other has Celtic ancestry?
3. Why would it be unlikely for anyone to complain that Judy is a negative Scottish stereotype? What makes a stereotype?
4. Judy and Rachel come from families with different expectations about physical and emotional openness and the disclosure of personal information. Is there any reason to believe that either view is right?
5. Was Judy rude to Rachel's mother? Because she accepted the invitation of a family with different expectations, should she have been willing to accommodate them? Or should Rachel's mother been willing to accept Judy's reluctance to discuss her family?
6. Would Judy violate any trust or obligation she has to her family by discussing family matters with Rachel's family?
7. Does a reluctance to talk about yourself suggest that you have something to hide?

ISSUES

Universities feel entitled to do something that would not be tolerated anywhere else (except prison and the military): they assign people to live in the most intimate of arrangements with total strangers. Not only that, they fill large buildings with people condemned to such an existence. For students living in dorms with roommates, a little time to oneself, a little space of one's own, can be hard to find. Even apart from living arrangements, college life is often more "groupish" than life elsewhere. Students are frequently herded together in classes where they are expected to talk even if they do not wish to. Sometimes they are asked to talk about sensitive or personal matters. Perhaps this book has been a vehicle for such expectations. Is it reasonable for you to be expected to discuss your views on ethical questions of the sort we raise here, in a group situation with people you don't know?

College often subjects students to several kinds of intrusiveness. There is the kind Bill was the victim of—overt and heavy handed. Fred simply behaved as though Bill's views about the use of the room didn't count, and as though Bill had no right to either privacy or a say about the use of the room. The tension between Judy and Rachel is more subtle. They come from families with quite different views about privacy and intrusiveness. Questions and touching that Judy finds invasive are meant by Rachel's family as an offer of friendship, trust, and inclusion. What Judy sees as protecting her privacy, Rachel's family sees as rejection, coldness, and unsociability.

Somehow privacy seems important in both cases. What is privacy? Should we value it? Why? How does it fit into each case? Is there anything common to the two cases?

Perhaps what is common to the two cases is that both Bill and Judy have a sense of their own space and feel that someone else has intruded into this space. Bill's space is in one sense physical—a room. But it is more than that. It is control over space, time, sound, and conversation. Bill isn't free to arrange the circumstances of his life even in his own room. For Judy the space is not so much physical as psychological. Judy has inhibitions about sharing personal information and being touched. While there is nothing wrong with her sharing personal information and hugging if she wishes to do so, she doesn't want to, and she feels pressured by Rachel's mother to do so. She is especially reluctant to talk about her family, knowing they would not wish it. Thus in both cases what seems at issue is control over personal space.

Perhaps you found the case of Bill and Fred to be clear-cut. We hope that it is at least obvious that Fred has not treated Bill very well. Nevertheless, some things may not be very clear. Let's see if we can make the case a little more ambiguous.

First, consider that we might make a case for Fred, not Bill, by appealing to the principle of *benefit maximization*. Fred shares his room with many of his friends. Their ability to use it is a significant convenience to them. After all, there is no other handy place for them to practice their music: there are few available empty rooms on campus, and these must be reserved well in advance. Spontaneous jamming would not be possible without using Fred's and Bill's room. Playing music builds a sense of camaraderie, provides a healthy outlet for tension, and satisfies the need for creative self-expression. Bill could study in the library. Maybe he could get himself some ear plugs for the noise. All in all, isn't it possible that Fred and his friends derive more benefit from playing music in the room than Bill loses? Doesn't the principle of benefit maximization suggest that if this is so, Bill should give way to Fred and his friends?

These questions can be raised in a more general way. Suppose that people have rights, such as a right to privacy. This would mean that people have a right to some control over their personal space. Although we don't quite know what this means yet, let's grant the point for the sake of discussion. Suppose also that privacy or some other right turns out, under some circumstances, to be inconsistent with benefit maximization. What then? Do people continue to have these rights even if more overall benefit might result from rejecting their claims? Fred might back up his claim to use the room as he wished with the belief that "the needs of the many outweigh the needs of the few or the one." That certainly seems logical. But wouldn't this result in Fred's having unlimited control over Bill's space, so long as he continued to share it in a way that he and his friends benefitted more than Bill was harmed? Was Bill just being selfish?

We can also look at this case from the perspective of *community*. Fred and his friends are forging bonds of loyalty, friendship, and good fellowship. They are enjoying a shared creative activity. Aren't these good things? They have offered to include Bill. Even if he has a right to continue being an outsider, does he have a right to be selfish about the use of the room when so much good seems to result?

It is far from clear that some ethical principle helps determine what counts as a good way to share the room. Perhaps Fred has been unreasonable. We might very well have written the case to make Bill seem unreasonable. Suppose that Bill insisted that there be no noise at all in the room while he was there, or suppose that he was a "neat freak." Does Bill have a right to expect Fred to make his bed? Does he have a right to expect Fred to dress "tastefully"? How far can Bill push his right to control his personal space? Must Fred accommodate any request?

Here, too, we can put the question broadly. What are the bounds of Bill's personal space? How far can he extend his personal space when doing so affects Fred? If we claim a right to control our own space, and if we understand what counts as our space broadly enough, at some point we begin to control others. Are there principles to which we can appeal to decide the boundaries of our personal space?

Let's look at Rachel and Judy. What Judy seems to want is some right to control information about herself and her family. But why shouldn't she share this information? Rachel's mother has offered Judy friendship and inclusion. Moreover, Judy is on Rachel's family's home turf. Aren't there good reasons for Judy to accommodate Rachel's mother? Judy has accepted her hospitality. Isn't she being rude to her? Isn't she asserting her own cultural assumptions against those of Judy's family? Because she is in Rachel's home, shouldn't the assumptions that apply there govern her? It is unlikely that Judy would be harmed by being more forthcoming. In fact, much good might result. Her inclusion into Rachel's family might grow in a way that could become quite important to Judy. Why should she reject friendship and inclusion? Can she bring her right to control her personal space into Rachel's home?

So far we have suggested two ideas that we need to explore. The first is that the idea of privacy involves control over personal space. The second is that the boundaries of personal space are not always clear.

We can begin to explore these ideas a bit more by inventing a theory of privacy. Consider one claim that we hope everyone will agree with: people own themselves. We do not belong to anyone but ourselves. People are not property. Children are not the property of their parents. Husbands do not own their wives, nor wives their husbands. Slavery is wrong. (Question: Perhaps self-ownership is a consequence or a corollary of the idea of *respect for persons*. Can you explain why this might be?)

So far so good. Self-ownership is inconsistent with evils such as slavery. But once we get past these obvious consequences, what follows? How does it help us with the cases of Bill or Judy?

Exactly what does it mean to claim ownership over something? Usually it means that the owner (in preference to others) has the right to use or dispose of the object as he or she sees fit. Because I own my car, I can decide who is allowed to drive it. Because I own my house, I can decide who lives in it. Property confers the right to control.

To own myself thus means to have the right to control myself. But what does this mean? If we define this idea too broadly, we might conclude that no one ever has the right to tell anyone else what to do. That would be too broad, and inconsistent with the very ideas of law and government. Philosophers (such as John Locke[1]) who emphasize self-ownership as central to a free society mean to object to monarchy or slavery and to insist on democratic and limited government. They do not mean to reject the very idea of government.

How then can we affirm self-ownership, but not end up rejecting the very idea of government? Or, to put the question differently, how can we tell legitimate authority from slavery?

One approach is to note that while we have said that people own themselves, perhaps owning yourself doesn't mean that you must have absolute control over all aspects of your life. Try thinking of it this way: What do you believe is central to your self? What are those areas of your life that, when they are intruded into, when others claim the right to control them, make you feel most violated?

We do not want to provide an exhaustive response to this question, but we do want to suggest five things:

First, self-ownership requires that we respect those things that seem important to people's self-definitions or self-understanding. The best examples here are people's religions and cultures. Because these things tend to make us the people we are, to define us, to be the basis of our deepest understandings of life, they are part of us. Self-ownership means that we have a right to our own religions and cultures. If we are to respect people, we must respect their choices about such things.

Second, most people have aspirations that we will describe as their projects. They want to be something, to do something, to be like someone. They

---

[1] John Locke, *Two Treatises of Government.* Introduction by Peter Laslett. (New York: Cambridge University Press, 1960). Original work published 1690.

want to be philosophers, carpenters, photographers, saints, or athletes. They may belong to a group or be committed to a cause. Such projects may be close to the center of their sense of self. People have a right to their projects.

Third, self-respect is important to people. We deny people their self-respect when we subject them to circumstances that are degrading or humiliating, when we do not respect their basic dignity.

Fourth, self-ownership requires that people have a large degree of control over their bodies—with whom and when they will be sexual, when they will submit to physical pain at the hands of others (such as a doctor or coach), by whom and how they will allow themselves to be touched, how they will use their bodies in work and play. People obviously cannot control everything that happens to their bodies (illness, accidents, and death come to mind), but they should be able to say no to others' unwanted intrusions on their bodies, the most personal space of all.

Finally, it is often important to people that they be able to control information about themselves. Disclosing something about myself to another frequently makes me vulnerable to that person. It risks my self-respect. If I know something about someone else, I'm in a position to damage her self-respect by criticizing or rejecting who she is. People thus have good reason to want to control information about themselves and to reveal themselves only under circumstances they choose.

None of this suggests that privacy in these areas is absolute. Respecting people's religion does not require that we permit human sacrifice. Respecting their projects does not require that society find jobs for those who wish to make items nobody wants, or purchase the output of inept workers. But because privacy is a right, we should have compelling reasons for asserting any control over people's lives in such matters. (However, not only do most poor people have few material possessions, they also cannot be said to own themselves in the way we have described. Their right to privacy is effectively denied by bureaucratic procedures with which they must comply to get aid, by the conditions of poverty itself, and sometimes by abusive police or other officials. Question: What "compelling reasons" (if any) are there for others to assert control over the lives of the poor in these ways?)

What is at stake in the cases of Bill and Judy? No one has attempted to deny them their religion or culture or their projects. We think that first and foremost what is at stake for Bill is his dignity and self respect. Fred has essentially told Bill that his interests and his needs don't count, denying Bill's dignity.

Judy was asked to engage in significant disclosures, not only about herself but also about her family. No doubt Rachel's mother, who seemed motivated only by a desire to include Judy, would have felt affirmed by Judy's trust if she'd shared these facts. It would have brought them closer together.

However, it is also true that Judy had just met Rachel's mother. In effect, she was being asked to place considerable trust in a stranger. She had no real way of knowing whether Rachel's mother would react positively or negatively to what she said. Moreover, Judy had no way of knowing with whom Rachel's mother might choose to talk about her. Rachel's mother has little sense of privacy. Perhaps she might find it quite normal to discuss Rachel's roommate and her family with everyone and anyone. Judy and her family thus might be subject to appraisal by complete strangers. Does this harm Judy or her family?

Thus far we have sided with Bill and Judy. Fred has not respected Bill's basic dignity. Rachel's mother, while well meaning, has insisted on self-disclosure under conditions that may not warrant it. Trust may be an important prerequisite of self-disclosure, and trust may need to be earned.

However, we still need to say something about how we might go about describing the boundaries of privacy. There may be no principled way to decide this. Consider the question of the use of Bill and Fred's room. At the extremes, we can draw reasonable conclusions. Neither Fred nor Bill may behave as though the space is theirs alone and the other person's needs don't count. But is there some moral principle that will help decide exactly how the space should be used? Here we are doubtful. No doubt if Bill feels that neatness is important, Fred should try not to be too messy and might help with occasional cleaning. But how much? When? We do not know, and we doubt that there is any way to know.

There is an approach that could be taken to deciding such matters. Bill and Fred might discuss the matter and seek a mutually acceptable agreement. Bill has, in fact, proposed this. He has asked Fred to talk about the problem. Perhaps Fred's essential denial of Bill's dignity is his refusal to talk. He has taken the position that because he is able to impose his will on Bill, there's no need for him to consider Bill's views.

We suggest, however, that his refusing to discuss the matter with Bill is inconsistent with Bill's dignity or (and this is the same point in different words) the principle of *respect for persons.* Bill and Fred need to talk about the matter. We want to describe the kind of talk as a "dialogue." In Chapter 1 we said that a dialogue has two purposes: it seeks mutual understanding and a consensus, or agreement. Given these purposes, a dialogue should have three important features to reach its goals:

First, it seeks a *voluntary* agreement. An agreement that is coerced is no agreement at all. Just as the authority of democratic governments is said to rest on the consent of the governed, the moral force of any agreement rests on the fact that the parties in the agreement all knowingly and freely agreed to its terms. Had Fred forced Bill to accept Fred's view of the use of their room, it is hard to see that Bill would have any duty to keep the agreement. One point of having a discussion is that the process of talking until an agreement is reached is conducive to uncoerced agreements, and this gives agreements their moral force.

Second, a dialogue assumes the equality of the participants. No one is allowed to decide the outcome of a dialogue by an act of authority. No one's welfare is more important than the welfare of the other participants. Everyone's view and everyone's interests count equally.

Third, a dialogue seeks an agreement that is as informed as possible with all of the relevant facts and arguments. Dialogue is a way of getting out the relevant facts and of making the relevant arguments. We do not mean that whatever facts and arguments there are must be sufficient to decide the matter. Even after everyone knows all there is to be known and has said all there is to be said, it may be that people will continue to disagree. And it may be that no one will have taken a position inconsistent with any relevant fact or argument. We do not believe that moral argument can settle every issue. However, it does not follow that there is nothing to say. Fred might discover that Bill is having trouble studying and getting enough sleep. Even more important, he might discover how Bill feels about this. They might explore a schedule for using the room. If both Fred and Bill begin with the assumption that they have an equal right to use the room and that they will respect each other's dignity and needs in the matter, a dialogue might very well enable them to achieve a mutually agreeable outcome, even if the facts and arguments they give don't determine the nature of their agreement.

The need for dialogue seems equally important in the case of Judy and Rachel. They do seem to respect one another's dignity and needs. Indeed, they like each other and are friends. But they do not understand one another, even though it seems likely that they could. Rachel does not understand Judy's need for privacy. Judy does not understand the importance of personal disclosure in Rachel's family and why her resistance seems rude. Perhaps these differences are rooted in different cultures, perhaps not. However, there is nothing incomprehensible about either view. Merely taking the time and effort to try to understand each other's outlook, given good intentions and mutual respect on each side, seems quite likely to resolve the matter. The point isn't that when Judy and Rachel understand one another's perspectives, it will become clear just how much self-disclosure and touching is appropriate. That seems unlikely. What is more likely is that if Judy understands how Rachel's family works, her willingness to talk about herself will increase; and if Rachel and her mother understand Judy's feelings, they will be less likely to press the matter.

Perhaps neither Judy nor Rachel will be able to articulate their feelings clearly. They may have to struggle to give a name to concepts such as self-disclosure, trust, or inclusion. But that is another reason for dialogue. It is a means to self-understanding as well as agreement.

What makes agreements achieved as a result of dialogue ethical? We assume here that one thing that makes something the right thing to do is that we have agreed to do it. An agreement is a promise. We should keep our promises. Perhaps Fred and Bill might agree that Fred and his friends can have jam sessions in their room between 8:00 and 10:00 P.M. while Bill studies in the library. There isn't anything inherently right in this agreement, but having agreed to do this, it becomes the right thing to do. Such agreements don't make things that are otherwise wrong right, but they can define what's right in many cases. "Let's talk about it" is morally central in a society whose members respect one another's dignity.

EXAMPLES OF COLLEGE AND UNIVERSITY CODES ON PRIVACY

Students' privacy regarding visitors:

Thirty years ago, most colleges limited the hours and places in which students could entertain guests of the opposite sex. Since the student revolution of the 1960s, few colleges see themselves as acting "in loco parentis" (in the place of parents), and students increasingly are allowed complete freedom regarding visitors in their rooms. Colleges vary widely, however, in the freedom and privacy they allow students in this regard.

A. *Excerpt from the student handbook of Hope College*[2]

Maximum guest hours for members of the opposite sex are:

Sun–Thur. 11:00 a.m. to 12 midnight
Fri and Sat. 11:00 a.m. to 2:00 a.m.

During restricted hours, stairwells are off limits (with the exception of those serving both women and men) during hours when the hallway and rooms are closed for visitation. Residence hall lobbies and basement common areas, and cottage or apartment living areas are the only open areas during restricted hours.

B. *Excerpt from the survival handbook of Antioch College*[3]

Visitors and Guests

[. . .] In the past few years there have been some problems with 'permanent' visitors. If you have someone visiting you who is staying for more than one week you should clear this with the Housing Office first.

---

[2] *1994–95 Student Handbook*, Hope College, p. 24.
[3] *1994–95 Survival Handbook*, Antioch College (Community Government), p. 61.

Students' privacy regarding their records:

A. *Excerpt from the student handbook of Tompkins Cortland Community College*[4]

Public Notice Designating Directory Information

Tompkins Cortland Community College hereby designates the following categories of student information as public or "Directory Information." Such information may be disclosed by the College at its discretion, for any purpose.

Category I. Name, address, telephone number, dates of attendance, classes for which currently registered, enrollment status (full-time, part-time, new, continuing, transfer).

Category II. Previous institution(s) attended, major field of study, awards, honors, degree(s) conferred (including dates).

Category III. Past and present participation in officially recognized sports and activities, physical factors (height, weight of athletes), date and place of birth.

Currently enrolled students may withhold disclosure of any category of information under the Family Educational Rights and Privacy Act of 1974. To withhold disclosure, written notification must be received in the Office of the Registrar within the first two weeks of the semester. . . . The College assumes that failure on the part of the student to specifically request the withholding of categories of "Directory Information" indicates individual approval for disclosure.

B. *Excerpt from the code of student ethics of Indiana University*[5]

'Public information' is limited to name; address; phone; major field of study; dates of attendance; admission or enrollment status; campus; school, college, or division; class standing; degrees and awards; activities; sports; and athletic information. Records of arrests and/or convictions and traffic accident information are public information and may be released to anyone making inquiry. [. . . .]

[. . .] Public information shall be released freely unless the student files the appropriate form requesting that certain public information not be released. [. . . .]

[. . .]. A student's record is open to the student, with the following exceptions:

---

[4] *1994–95 Student Handbook*, Tompkins Cortland Community College (Dryden, NY), p. 33.

[5] "Appendix 4: Indiana University Release of Student Information Policy," *Code of Student Ethics*, Indiana University (University Faculty Council, 29 March 1977), pp. 43–44.

1. Confidential letters of recommendation [. . .] [if they] carry waivers signed by the student relinquishing the right of access to the document.
2. Records of parents' financial status.
3. Employment records.
4. Medical and psychological records; [. . . .]

[. . .] Student records are open to members of the faculty and staff who have a legitimate need to know their contents [. . . .]

[. . .] Normally, records can be released—or access given—to third parties (i.e., anyone not a member of the faculty and staff) only at the written request of the student. Without the consent of the student, releases to third parties may be given only as follows:

i. To parents of students who are dependents as defined by IRS standards.
ii. To federal officers as prescribed by law.
iii. As required by state law.
iv. To research projects on behalf of educational agencies for test norms, improving instruction, etc. (provided that the agencies guarantee no personal identification of students).
v. To accrediting agencies carrying out their functions.
vi. In response to a judicial order or lawfully issued subpoena [. . . .]
vii. By IU Police to other law enforcement agencies in the investigation of a specific criminal case.

ADDITIONAL CASES

Case 4.3: The Assignment

Brian has enjoyed his Women's History class and enjoyed being one of the few male students in the course, but the assignment for the final paper (half of his grade!) angers him. "Interview the women in your family (as many as possible) and write their personal histories, analyzing them in terms of the demographic trends and social categories we have discussed," it read.

After class, Brian tried to explain to the instructor why he couldn't do this. "First, I don't have any female relatives that I'm in touch with except my mother and my sister," he said.

"Fine! Just interview them," the instructor said. "Or maybe you could use this assignment as an excuse to get in touch with some of your other relatives!" she added brightly.

Brian tried to imagine how his intensely private and bitter mother, estranged from her parents for thirty years, would react to this idea (his father's parents were dead, and he had no aunts). He changed his tack. "Besides, I don't think it's appropriate for me to try to get my mother and sister to tell me their problems and innermost thoughts; we don't do that in my family."

The professor was not dissuaded. "This assignment might be just the way to open your family up, then. You'll probably learn a lot about them that will give you a new respect and empathy for them, and they will be touched that you care."

That was ridiculous, Brian thought. Rather than feeling "touched," they would be outraged that he presumed to violate their privacy just to get a grade, sharing their secrets with a complete stranger to mark up with a red pen. Brian gave one last try: "I don't feel comfortable putting them in little niches like the "trends and categories" we've talked about—they're too complex for that, they're individuals."

The instructor clearly was starting to lose patience with him. "Just do the best you can," she said as she turned to talk to the next student waiting for her.

Questions

1. Brian sees the assignment as an invasion of his privacy, whereas his instructor seems to see it as a means to self-understanding and perhaps family therapy, in addition to measuring how well students have absorbed the concepts taught in the course. It is probably true that we can learn much from making connections between the subjects we study in school and our personal lives. But can such connections be mandated? Do teachers have a right to make students dissect their personal feelings or family backgrounds in class, or for a grade?

2. Do such assignments show a lack of respect for students' differing cultural backgrounds, or is it merely a matter of different personalities liking different assignments?

3. How should a student respond when faced with an assignment he or she regards as overly intrusive?

4. More generally, can, or should, a college force students to analyze their opinions and become more self-reflective? Where does the professor's duty to stimulate reflection and critical thinking (and the right to grade students on their abilities in this regard) end, and the student's right to privacy begin?

Case 4.4: Raided!

At 9:45 P.M. on Thursday, an unidentified number of students (wearing stockings over their heads to disguise their features) burst into Hamilton House, a small co-ed residence hall on the edge of campus. Screaming like maniacs, they sprayed shaving cream wildly, threw rolls of toilet paper into every open door, and then ran out again before their stunned victims could respond.

Maggie was hard at work studying in her room when the raid occurred. She knows that raids like this are supposed to be good clean fun and part of college life. But she, like Queen Victoria, Is Not Amused. In fact, she thinks raiding is pretty stupid and immature, and she's angry about having her studying disturbed. Not only did she completely lose her train of thought when the raid started, she couldn't get back to work at all that night because her housemates were so noisy and excited as they exclaimed over the mess and planned for a return raid on the suspected perpetrators, the inhabitants of Jackson Hall. Worst of all, the shaving cream left permanent streaks on the photographs Maggie hung on her wall. They are the only large prints she has of her best pictures, taken over several years, and many of them are irreplaceable. She's furious!

Questions

1. Maggie's housemates seem to feel that the best response to a raid is "Don't get mad, get even." Is this an appropriate response if they aren't even sure who raided them?
2. Even if some residents of Jackson Hall are responsible for the raid, is a retaliatory raid likely to prevent, or encourage, future raids? Is it fair to Jackson Hall students who may not have known anything about the original raid?
3. Because Maggie thinks raiding is "stupid and immature," presumably she won't want to participate in a retaliatory raid no matter how mad she is. What other options might she have for punishing the raiders and/or ensuring that no more raids take place?
4. The raiders would probably claim that they hadn't meant any harm and hadn't realized that the shaving cream would ruin some of Maggie's prized possessions. Does Maggie really have a right to get so bent out of shape about a very temporary invasion of her space (the raid took all of three minutes) and accidental damage of her property?
5. Because everyone at Maggie's college knows about the possibility of raids, is it Maggie's responsibility to protect her belongings from damage during a raid, perhaps by keeping her special photos in a drawer rather than on the wall?

Case 4.5: Searching

Sam had a rather lonely first semester at college. Actually, it wasn't much worse than high school, but all though high school he'd kept thinking that things at college would be different. He imagined college as the place where he'd have long talks about the meaning of life with people who thought about the deeper things. He'd read The Important Books and learn from fascinating professors. Perhaps he'd even meet a girl who cared more about ideas and spirituality than looks and popularity. However, it hadn't worked out that way. He was still searching.

Toward the end of Spring semester, his luck seemed to change when he met Melanie and Ben. They were very friendly and outgoing, and somehow they got Sam talking about the missing spiritual dimension in his life, even though he hardly knew them. "You know," Melanie said, "there just happens to be a spiritual retreat this weekend that we're going on. We went to one before, and I loved it—lots of good talk, good people, and good food. I bet you'd like it too." "Why don't you come with us?" Ben smiled engagingly. "It's a great way to meet people you can really talk to. And it will be fun—we'll camp out together, play volleyball, do the whole campfire thing."

And so it was that Sam found himself that weekend at an isolated campsite with about fifteen people he didn't know. At first, it did seem rather fun and adventurous. Friday night they played volleyball and had a campfire as advertised. But Sam soon began to feel that he had been misled. It rapidly became clear that the "retreat" was not just vaguely spiritual, but an intense indoctrination into a religious sect. The group sat in a large circle, where the campers took turns describing their spiritual failings and pressuring Sam to come up with similar confessions. This emotional discussion continued until late at night, when the talk turned to ways to be "saved." Sam was very tired, but they mocked him for wanting to sleep when his soul was at stake and badgered him to confess and be saved.

This intense pressure continued all weekend. Sam stayed up all night Friday and barely got any sleep at all on Saturday. By Sunday, he was so tired and had had so many heated exchanges about various points of belief and exhausting emotional ups and downs (he had been both hugged by everyone in the group and shouted at for over an hour) that he didn't know what to think anymore about anything. The group had convinced him that his life was lonely and alienated, and that perhaps the way to happiness lay in bonding with them and accepting their doctrines. So before he left on Sunday, he agreed to start coming to their prayer meetings on Tuesdays and Thursdays. "I'm so happy you've seen the light!" Melanie sobbed with tears streaming down her face. "I'll come pick you up at your room at 7:00 P.M. on Tuesday. Welcome, brother!"

Unfortunately, by Tuesday morning, when Sam had caught up on his sleep and had a chance to think things over, he was no longer at all sure that he wanted to be part of their group. But Melanie and Ben seemed to read his mind. They found him in his room after lunch, and in their friendly way managed to stick near him until seven o'clock, when Sam found himself heading off with them to the prayer meeting.

But the more they pressured him in the days ahead, the more resistant Sam felt. Finally he told them outright that he'd decided he wasn't interested in their group, and that they should leave him alone. But this did not seem to deter them. "You promised to try it out, Sam. Open your heart, and you'll never be sorry you did," said Ben. "We care about you!" Melanie added. "A battle is going on in your soul, and we can't let you fight it alone. We're your friends, Sam!"

Sam thought with a shock, "Some friends. How am I going to get rid of them so I can figure things out for myself?"

Questions

1. Is intense religious proselytizing of this nature an invasion of privacy? How?
2. Did Melanie and Ben deceive Sam, and if so, can such deceit be justified?
3. Sam volunteered to them that he was searching for something spiritual in his life, and he chose to go to both their retreat and some prayer meetings. Does this mean that he owes it to Melanie and Ben to give their faith (more) serious consideration?
4. Are Melanie and Ben really friends to Sam? Why or why not?
5. Which moral principles might be relevant to this case, and how would you apply them in giving Sam advice about what to do?

Case 4.6: Smooching in the Lounge

Rita and Anna were in love, and radiantly happy. But at their small, conservative school, there were few opportunities for lesbian couples to hold hands, much less have sex. Like all first-year students there, Rita and Anna had each been assigned to live in triples, rooms they shared with two other roommates. They thus found themselves limited to long talks, hugs, and furtive kisses. And then late one night they were "caught" kissing in the residence hall lounge. Three students suddenly came upon them cuddling in a dark corner and immediately started hassling them. Anna knew one of them, Paul, who lived down the hall from her and her roommates, and she and Rita had seen the other two around the school. But the fact that they all vaguely knew each other didn't stop Paul and his friends from swearing and shouting at Rita and Anna. "This is disgusting! You dykes are polluting the lounge—get out of here! You make us sick!" and more in the same vein.

Anna and Rita were so embarrassed and taken aback that at first they didn't respond. But then Rita started arguing that what they did was none of his business and that they had every bit as much right to use the lounge as anyone else.

At this Paul grabbed Rita's arm and roughly yanked her off the couch. "You have NO right to be here, you dirty little creep!" he shouted menacingly. "God hates perverts, and you belong in hell!"

"C'mon Rita," said Anna, getting up too. "Let's get out of here before Mr. Religious does something really stupid."

Questions

1. Have Anna's and Rita's rights to privacy been violated?
2. Since the lounge is public space, can students forbid behavior they find offensive there, such as lesbians' kissing? If not, how should offended students deal with public affronts to their sensibilities and perhaps to their religious beliefs? If so, which students should get to decide what constitutes "offensive behavior"?
3. Would your answers be the same regarding straight couples' making out in the lounge at night? In other words, should public space be off limits for all sexual activity if it bothers some students, or should those students mellow out?
4. Because gay students are often ostracized and persecuted, do they deserve special consideration here?
5. Arguments about acceptable uses of the common lounge might be similar in some ways to debates in some communities over the use of (semi-)public spaces. Neighborhoods' attempts to ensure "standards of decency" in common areas can range from efforts to get rid of "adult" bookstores to the imposition of zoning and yard maintenance requirements on homeowners. In all these cases, the questionable behavior is legal, and probably not offensive to some members of the community. The question is how to balance the competing interests of a community's consensus on public morals and appearances, and individuals' rights to privacy and the pursuit of happiness. What is the fairest way to make decisions about the use of public space? How might the principle of benefit maximization apply here?
6. How could dialogue between people with such radically different positions work?

Case 4.7: *Telephone Harassment*

Laura likes to think of herself as a kind-hearted person who is sympathetic to the underdog and open to new people. But recent events have challenged her self-image. A couple of times last semester, she had listened sympathetically to a lonely guy named Dan who talked to her after class about his problems. Gradually, Laura realized that Dan seemed both to have a crush on her and to be slightly disturbed. So Laura smiled at him but made excuses not to talk any more. She didn't want to encourage him, but she also didn't want to hurt his feelings by rejecting him outright. Then Dan stopped waiting for her after class, and Laura was relieved. The school year was almost over, and she was busy with exams, papers, and goodbyes. She forgot about Dan.

Back at her parents' for the summer, Laura got a call late one evening. Her mother handed her the phone with a sharp reminder to have her friends call before 11:00 P.M., and Laura sleepily said, "Hello?" It was Dan. He'd gotten her parents's phone number and address from the Student Records Office, and said that he had to talk to her. He loved her and needed her; she was the only one who understood him. Laura tried to extricate herself from this embarrassing conversation and finally hung up, saying, "I'm sorry, I have to go to bed!" But Dan was not dissuaded; he called her right back.

This time Laura was firmer. "You can't call me this late!" she said. "I don't want to talk to you!" But as soon as she hung up, the phone rang again. This time, she turned the ringer off and let the answering machine pick up, but her heart was racing as she heard Dan's voice saying, "I know you're there! Talk to me!"

These calls turned out to be the first of literally hundreds. Dan called so often, at all hours of the day and night, that Laura's parents finally had to get an unlisted phone number. Now Laura no longer hears from him, but she is still angry and frightened. He has her address. What if he tries to come to the house? She has no idea how far away he lives or how likely he is to carry his telephone pursuit into a physical pursuit. He seems to be a harmless crank, but she wonders what might happen if his telephone harassment turns into something scarier. Her parents are worried, too, but also irritated with Laura. They seem to think that somehow she must have encouraged Dan's crazy attentions and "led him on." Laura feels sure she hasn't, but can't understand why he is picking on her. What will happen when she returns to school in the fall?

Questions

1. Is Laura somehow at fault for Dan's harassment, as her parents think? If you said yes, what could she have done differently?
2. Are her only future options either fearfully keeping to herself or being open to new people who may hurt or bother her? How might she protect herself from further harassment?
3. Does she have any duty to help Dan, perhaps by trying to get him into counseling or by finding out more about his life and why he thinks she, a

virtual stranger, is the only one who understands him? Is dialogue with Dan a reasonable way for Laura to deal with him, or has he proven himself unsuitable for such an approach?

4. Colleges often allow all kinds of information about students to be divulged without the students' express permission (see Examples of College and University Codes on Privacy, pages 69–71). Students are usually told (in fine print) that they can forbid the release of personal information, but they must sign a special form in advance. And because the Records or Registrar's Office is often the only way to locate a long-lost college friend, many students hesitate to tell the college not to give out their home address or phone number. Other students never worry about this; in fact Laura never signed the waiver forbidding the Records Office from giving out this information. Alumni groups and other organizations also may have legitimate reasons for wanting to get in touch with the members of the class of 1999. How can colleges help prevent situations like Dan's telephone harassment of Laura? If you were a college administrator, how would you try to balance students' right to privacy with others' legitimate desires for information about them?

Case 4.8: Apartment 3-G

Robin, Tracy, and Juanita share an apartment with a common kitchen and living area, and each student has her own bedroom. The three women like each other personally, but their different sexual styles are driving them apart. Robin is practically married to her boyfriend, Glenn, and he sleeps at the apartment regularly. Tracy occasionally has short affairs with men she brings home, rarely seeing the same one for more than a few nights. Juanita is a virgin and doesn't approve of having men in the apartment at all. At first Juanita was shocked that her roommates were having sex, but now she just resents having men around because their presence intrudes so much on her privacy.

When Glenn or one of Tracy's guys stay overnight, Juanita feels that she can't walk around in her underwear or eat breakfast in the morning before she's got her "face" on. They also seem so inconsiderate: men always seem to leave the toilet seat up; a guy once walked in on her in the bathroom without knocking; and she finds it distracting, to say the least, to hear sex through her wall when she's trying to sleep or study. She also hates the surprise of waking up to find some strange man (Tracy's onenight stand) sitting at the kitchen table. Glenn is bad in a different way. Although he's friendly, he never does chores around the apartment, and he leaves his clothes and books in the living room, or forgets the remains of a late-night carton of ice cream on the kitchen counter. Robin has tried to pick up after him ever since Juanita mentioned the problem, but

Juanita thinks Glenn should pick up after himself. And she says that if he's going to be there so often, he should pay rent, too, and share household cleaning jobs and the phone bill.

In fact, Robin, Glenn, and Tracy have agreed to share the apartment and split the rent if Juanita wants to move. Juanita does want to leave, but housing is tight and she can't move before next semester or perhaps even next year. Besides, she feels that she is being forced out by their inconsiderateness. They shouldn't just get their way and make her go through the hassle of finding somewhere else to live and moving all of her stuff. It's not fair.

Questions

1. Robin feels that she's trying to accommodate Juanita by picking up after her boyfriend. Is this enough to make up for the inconvenience his presence causes Juanita? What else could, or should, Robin, Glenn, and Tracy do?
2. Someone else might not be bothered at all by the men's presence and Robin and Tracy's behavior. Does this mean that Juanita has no right to be upset?
3. Does Juanita have a right to insist that no men be allowed in the apartment, or is this too great an imposition on her roommates?
4. There is a difference between Glenn and Tracy's one-night stands in the inconvenience they cause Juanita. Should there be a difference in how she responds or what she asks of them?
5. Should Juanita try to talk with the bothersome men directly, or with her roommates, who are responsible for inviting the men there?
6. At least for now, the apartment is home to all three women. How can they decide whose rights to privacy should be paramount?

Case 4.9: Noise Pollution

It's a beautiful spring day toward the end of the final exam period. Out in front of West Hall dorm, students are celebrating the end of exams by playing frisbee and hackysack to the sound of music blasting out of the open windows of their rooms. Like a giant amplifier, the front of the multistoried dorm picks the music up and sends it echoing out across the quad. Windows are open all over to let in the fresh air, glorious sunshine, and sounds of spring. The scene looks idyllic, except for one jarring detail: first one student, and then another, leans out of the dorm windows and shouts something at the celebrators that can't be heard, their faces contorted with annoyance and anger.

A few minutes later, several of the angry students are outside arguing with the music lovers. It seems that they can't study with the music playing, even when they shut their windows. The music players think that requests to turn the music off or way down are unreasonable. They want to be able to hear music on the quad as they celebrate. They point out that most students are finished with their exams and papers, and they suggest that the few people who aren't should go to the library if they need quiet. The angry students respond that they feel pressured enough without all the noise. They don't want to go to the library because they have too many books to lug, and it's not convenient. "We should be able to study in our own rooms!" they shout. The two groups seem at an impasse.

Questions

1. Should one group of students clearly have priority in this situation? If so, which one, and why?
2. How might they negotiate a compromise that respects everyone's interests? Might the principles of benefit maximization, community, and respect for persons suggest different solutions to this conflict?
3. Does the fact that noises and smells are less tangible invasions of one's space than the presence of other people mean that they are less important intrusions on privacy, or that they should be treated more leniently?

Case 4.10: Smokers' Rights?

Hippocrates Community College recently designated all buildings on the entire campus as "smoke free." Student smokers have vocally protested this decision. They see the College's action as an invasion of their privacy and freedom to make the choice to smoke. "It's just nosiness on the part of our obsessively health-conscious and paranoid administration," a sophomore named Phil told the student newspaper. His view is apparently shared by a number of students, faculty, and staff (especially those with European or Third World backgrounds, who find Americans' obsession with secondhand smoke bizarre). Phil went on, "What the administration is really saying is that 'smoking is morally bad,' although they pretend it's a health issue. If it were really just about secondhand smoke bothering some people, they would have places for smokers to go. But they really want to *punish* smokers and make them go outside in freezing weather for a smoke. They like to see smokers suffer for their sins."

Questions

1. Does Phil have a point? Do smokers have privacy rights? That is, should they be able to smoke in private (say in their private rooms, or in a public bathroom when no one else is in it)?
2. The College might argue against allowing smoking anywhere not only because of the dangers of secondhand smoke for nonsmokers, but also

because smokers should be discouraged from hurting their own health, and because of the danger of fire. But is harming your own health anyone else's business? Why or why not?

3. People have been smoking on the Hippocrates campus since it was founded forty years ago, and there have been no reported cases of fires being caused by cigarettes. Does this record mean that the administration has no right to use fire safety as a grounds for forbidding smoking?

4. Which moral principles might apply here, and how?

BACKGROUND READING

David L. Kirp, "Proceduralism and Bureaucracy: Due Process in the School Setting" in *Stanford Law Review*, 1976, vol. 38, p. 841. This article discusses the advantages of "structured conversations" (slightly more formal versions of what we call dialogues) over the legal route of due process hearings and so on, for resolving disagreements, especially in college settings.

The Family Educational Rights and Privacy Act of 1974 (20 U.S.C. 1232g, "The Buckley Amendment," subsequently amended and clarified by U.S. Senate Joint Resolution No. 40) is a piece of federal legislation that guarantees all students access to their personal educational records (with some limitations), allows them to challenge these records as "inaccurate, misleading, or otherwise inappropriate," and protects their privacy when a third party (other than a school official) wants to see their personal records.

Several sources discuss the almost unnoticed loss of privacy that is occurring as society becomes more computerized and personal information becomes available to merchants, the direct marketing industry, social service workers, and various officials without our knowledge or consent. Such information includes material generally considered private, such as educational accomplishments and records, credit ratings, income levels, purchasing habits, health records, job histories, and psychiatric records. See Anne Wells Branscomb, *Who Owns Information? From Privacy to Public Access* (New York: Basic Books, 1994); Jeffrey Rothfeder, *Privacy for Sale: How Computerization Has Made Everyone's Private Life an Open Secret* (New York: Simon and Schuster, 1992); *Privacy Journal: An Independent Monthly on Privacy in a Computer Age* (P.O. Box 28577, Providence, RI 02908, (401) 274-7861); and Peter McGrath with Patrick Rogers, "Info 'Snooper-Highway' Privacy: As Computer Power Grows, So Does the Personal Information Available. Have We Compromised Ourselves?" in *Newsweek*, 27 February 1995, p. 61.

ADDITIONAL MATERIALS

1. "Student Sues College, Saying Party-Animal Roommate Drove Him Into Therapy," in *The New York Times*, 27 May 1994, sec. B, p. 5, col. 1. This ar-

ticle relates the case of an Albright College freshman who requested a docile, studious, and philosophical roommate on the "compatibility" questionnaire the school sent out over the summer. Instead, he was paired with a football player who did not study, played loud music, and partied late. The student then dropped out after two months, claiming that he developed posttraumatic stress disorder because of his assigned roommate and had to go into intensive psychotherapy. He finally decided to sue the college for negligence, and his ex-roommate as well. If you were on a jury for this case, would you believe that someone could develop "posttraumatic stress disorder" as a result of two months with an incompatible roommate? Would you allow the college to be held financially liable for roommate incompatibility? Which moral principles might apply here, and how?

2. Bob Levey, "Holiday Question: Who Sleeps Where?" in *The Washington Post*, 13 December 1994, sec. B, p. 11, col. 1. This is the story of a student who refused to come home for the holidays unless his parents let him and his girlfriend sleep in the same bed at their home. The parents felt that in their house, their son should not sleep with a woman unless he were married to her. He thought this was hypocritical because they knew he slept with his girlfriend at school. Is the son's behavior an example of emotional blackmail, or a principled stand? The student and his parents obviously have different ideas about acceptable social norms regarding premarital sex. How can they respect each other's views and stay in the same house? Who should decide who sleeps where, and why should their views be given priority? How might this argument be framed in terms of competing rights to self-ownership?

3. Geeta Anand, "Waltham Police Appeal to Parents of Noisy Students" in *The Boston Globe*, 27 November 1994, sec. WW, p. 1, col. 1. In the two years since a new letter-writing policy began to deal with noise complaints, Waltham, Massachusettes police mailed twenty letters of complaint to parents of students at both Brandeis University and Bentley College. The letters drew outrage from students, who wanted to be treated equally under the law and not have the police go over their heads to their parents. Are such letters an invasion of students' privacy? Should students (or anyone else) lose their rights to privacy if they break laws or regulations like the Waltham noise ordinance? Do you think writing to parents would be an effective way to deal with noisy students? Is it fair? Why or why not?

4. Peter McGrath with Patrick Rogers, "Info 'Snooper-Highway' Privacy," in *Newsweek*, 27 February 1995, p. 61. "Last month, 28 Harvard students were mortified to learn that the campus newspaper, *The Crimson*, had identified them as consumers of pornography simply by tracking their Internet activities through the university's network." Did *The Crimson*'s actions violate the students' privacy? Could there be any ethical reason(s) for publishing the names of students (or others) who "consume pornography"? Which moral principles might you use in analyzing this incident, and how? Is there anything wrong with the monitoring of Internet users' hobbies and interests by others for various purposes? What can on-line computer users do to protect their privacy? For more information, see the third set of items under Background Readings in this chapter.

5

LOYALTY, FRIENDSHIP, AND COMMUNITY

Two Cases: United We Stand?

Case 5.1: Loyalty Test

Barbara Stalking Bear is president of the Native American Student Association. Her friend Roger Turner is treasurer. They have been friends for the three years that they've been at Amigos Community College and have worked together on a number of projects for NASA—an acronym whose irony they both enjoy.

They became friends despite some significant differences in their backgrounds. Barbara comes from a middle-income family in a suburb of a large eastern city. Barbara's father teaches biology in the local high school. Her mother is a lawyer. Although her parents encouraged her to explore her heritage, they have not been active in any community of Native Americans, so Barbara's exploration of Native American cultures and history has been academic. Friends occasionally comment on her last name, but Barbara's father is two generations removed from being a functional part of a Native American community, and Barbara's mother has a French and Irish background with only a small amount of Native American blood. Until she went to college, being Native American was not part of who Barbara was. Roger helped change that.

Roger was born and raised on a Cheyenne reservation in Oklahoma. He grew up poor and angry. Barbara has learned something about Native American culture from her parents, but she has learned about the oppression and reality of Native American life from Roger. There are other differences. Barbara's Iroquois father's ancestors were from somewhere in central New York. Barbara supposes that the Iroquois and the

Cheyenne shared about as much common culture as the French and the Germans did—perhaps less, but she also thinks that solidarity among Native Americans is important and that discovering or even inventing a shared culture is worthwhile. Here, too, Roger has been her guide. He has many insights into Native American traditions and helps Barbara see themes and commonalties. Roger is a traditionalist, but he is quite willing to incorporate the wisdom of various Native American cultures into his beliefs.

Thus their friendship has developed despite the differences in their backgrounds. Roger has been the mentor, Barbara the devoted apprentice. Nor has their friendship been strained by one durable difference in their views of what is involved in being Native American. As Barbara learns about contemporary Indian life, she has come to see herself as a modernizer. She now thinks of herself primarily as a Native American, and she respects Native American traditions. She also believes that Native peoples need to become more integrated into mainstream society to escape their poverty and stigmatization. She wants to see them become doctors, lawyers, and business people. She wants them to avail themselves of opportunities off the reservations. Indeed, she quietly hopes for a form of life for her people in which reservations will disappear.

Roger, however, is not only a traditionalist, but a hard-core traditionalist. He is intensely committed to restoring the traditional values and lifestyles of Native Americans. This commitment has often led him into conflict with other Native Americans and with whites. He has actively resisted the emergence of casino gambling as a way for reservations to generate income and develop capital. He often criticizes other Native Americans on campus because they see their education more as a means to advance their careers than to improve the welfare of their people. In contrast, he views his college education as a way to "learn the white man's ways in order to resist white oppression."

The sharpest point of contention between Roger and Barbara has to do with spirituality. Curiously, both Roger and Barbara have been raised as Presbyterians. Barbara isn't sure how seriously she takes her Christianity. She rarely attends church anymore and doesn't miss it much. However, her lack of faith extends to religion generally. She isn't very interested in converting to one of the Native faiths, which seem puzzling to her and unsuited to the life she is likely to live after graduation. Roger, however, is deeply committed to the recovery of Native American spirituality. He has worked to discover what traditional Indian religions teach and to distill an understanding of spirituality that is authentically Cheyenne. He and a group of friends have begun to meet to discuss and practice what they are learning. Often they invite Native American leaders renowned for their high level of spirituality to campus to instruct them. Roger and his friends believe that spirituality is the foundation of everything Native American, and increasingly they make commitment to that spirituality the litmus test for who is a real Native American.

Barbara's friendship with Roger has survived even this difference. She has attended a few meetings and made polite and noncommittal excuses to avoid others. She respects Roger's commitment. As president of NASA, she has agreed to use some of the organization's funds to bring in those whom Roger identifies as spiritual leaders.

Now Roger has gone too far for her. He signed two large checks that, as far as she can see, were not approved by her or anyone else. After a little investigation, she found that the checks were apparently used to conduct a peyote ceremony. One went to the man who led the ceremony. The other paid for the peyote. Both checks were for nontrivial amounts, considering the modest budget of a student organization.

Barbara is stunned. A little checking reveals that the sale, purchase, or use of peyote is illegal in their state. Peyote is a controlled substance. Roger has very likely committed a felony and involved others in it. He has also used NASA funds without submitting the expenditures for approval. In short, he has stolen them, and because some of NASA's money comes from the college's student organization fund, he has very likely spent college money on an illegal activity. She earnestly hopes that she won't have to justify these expenses to anyone from the student activities office.

Her meeting with Roger is a disaster. He is utterly unrepentant. He claims to have "liberated" some of the white man's money and considers it reparations, but what bothers her most is his attitude toward her. He makes her support of his actions a test not only of their friendship, but also of whether she is a true Native American. "It's time you decide," he says. "Are you one of us, or an apple? You need to get a red soul to go with your red skin."

Case 5.2: Group Guilt

Dean Travers decided that the problem might be solved by an approach that involved a little open discussion instead of a judicial hearing. The brothers of Tau Rho Epsilon were not known to be troublemakers. They didn't violate the university's liquor regulations. The TREs were normally good students. They were what a fraternity should be—harmless.

Except for their Christmas initiation rite. Pledges were expected to provide the fraternity's Christmas tree. There were only two rules: they had to cut it themselves, and they could not pay for it. No doubt there were a few legally cutable trees in the nearby state forest, but they were not the right size or well shaped. Competition for sunlight did not a good

Christmas tree make. Thus the TRE tradition effectively required pledges to steal a tree.

After a few years of this, campus security knew where to look if anyone reported that their trees had been molested, but it was difficult to do much. It was hard to prove anything, given that one Christmas tree was much like another. One year the pledges had gone so far as to purchase a second tree merely to be able to produce a receipt for the one they stole.

This year they went too far, and they were stupid. They didn't raid a rural resident's recent plantings or a "You Cut" Christmas tree farm. They cut a tree from the university arboretum. Not only that, they cut a rare tree. It had been given by a delegation from Nepal, and it was estimated to be worth several thousand dollars. The head of the arboretum was beside herself. She wanted something done to the perpetrators, apparently along the lines of *The Texas Chainsaw Massacre*.

The pledges didn't even get rid of the evidence. Custom required that the tree team cut off a few extra inches from the bottom of the tree when they brought it back so that there was no danger of the bottom of their tree matching the top of the victim's stump. This year's pledges had tossed the cutting into the dumpster behind their frat house, where it was discovered by the inquiring officer. They were dead meat.

The problem in prosecuting them was that the police had to charge someone, and they had no way of knowing who actually cut the tree. Nor was anyone talking. The TREs were good at solidarity. Thus there seemed no way to prove anyone in particular guilty. This was when Dean Travers opted for sweet reason. He had the following conversation with TRE's governing council:

Dean Travers: I'm not going to charge anyone, but I want to end this. I want you to see that it's wrong and stop cutting trees.

TRE Council: No doubt it is wrong. We hope you can persuade whoever's doing this to see it your way.

Dean T: Isn't there any way I can get you to be responsible about this?

TRE: Isn't it really the fault of the arboretum or Security? Everybody knows that someone cuts an occasional tree before Christmas. If they haven't got the brains to guard a valuable tree, it's their fault. Not ours.

Dean T: You really think it's all right to destroy other people's property?

TRE: No, we really don't. We aren't destructive people. But this is your rule, your tree, and your problem. We have our relationships with our brothers to worry about. We aren't going to rat on them, and we aren't going to do your job for you. Sorry, Dean.

Questions

1. Both Barbara and Roger are Native Americans. Do they have different relationships to the Native American community? In what ways?
2. Do the members of Tau Rho Epsilon have a still different kind of relationship to the fraternity? In what way?
3. How would you characterize the ways in which these communities are important to their members?
4. Loyalty and friendship are usually counted as virtues. What is the basis of loyalty? What kinds of obligations follow from it?
5. Should Barbara turn Roger in?
6. Should one of the TREs turn in whoever cut down the tree?
7. Should citizens support the law by informing on lawbreakers? If so, does this obligation change when the lawbreakers are members of one's group or are one's friends?
8. Suppose that the incidents described above were more serious. Suppose, for example, that there had been a murder. Would you feel differently about informing?
9. If everybody is equal, why should we be more loyal to those who are members of our group than to outsiders?
10. Do the demands of loyalty or friendship change depending on the group? Should we be more loyal to members of our race, religion, or culture, than to members of our age group, sorority, or softball team? Why should we be loyal at all?
11. It is usually viewed as prejudice if white people try to promote the hiring of other white people at the expense of members of other races. Is it similarly wrong for minorities to look out for the welfare of other members of their groups? Why or why not?
12. How does loyalty to or solidarity with members of our race, culture, or religion differ from prejudice?
13. What role does solidarity with a community play in our lives?

ISSUES

Human beings are communal beings. That is why our opening chapter included *"community"* among the ethical principles we consider important to think about. Not only do we form communities to accomplish various purposes, but we are also formed by our communities. At least some of our affiliations are important to our sense of who we are. Moreover, some values seem significantly attached to the idea of community—loyalty and solidarity, perhaps. At the same time, the idea that we are communal beings and that community is important can generate some questions and problems. Suppose that we belong to a group but reject some of its values or actions. Should we support it when we think it is wrong? Are there occasions when it is wrong to be loyal to our friends or our group? Is loyalty to particular people inconsistent with equal respect for everyone? The principle of community generates some hard questions.

Important differences exist between various communities and how they fit into our lives. We affiliate with some kinds of groups or communities because of who we are or what we think we need. Some of these associations have little influence on who we are. Credit unions, community choirs, or chat groups on the Internet are likely to have this character. We join them because they provide us with a service or allow us to express some interest. Our relationship to them is instrumental. They are not likely to define or shape us.

However, some communities do shape us. This is likely to be true of a religious or ethnic community, especially if we are born into it. Our membership in these communities helps to make us who we are. Such communities may provide us with values and moral commitments that guide our choices or orient our lives. That we belong to them may itself be part of who we are. We will call communities that significantly define and shape us "constitutive communities."

These differences between communities depend in part on the nature of the community, but also on us. It is unlikely that a credit union will function as a constitutive community for very many people, even its employees. We join such associations because they provide a service for us. Although businesses may try to cultivate the loyalty of their customers, they tend not to be perceived as proper objects of loyalty. We usually choose a bank because it provides the service we want, conveniently and at a favorable cost. We change banks when it is convenient. We are unlikely to accept poor performance out of a sense of loyalty. We are not inclined to say, "Well, even if they have messed up my account three weeks running, they are, after all, my credit union." However, this is the kind of thing we often do want to say about our family or our church or our ethnic group. These groups seem more plausible as constitutive communities and as objects of loyalty.

Other communities are in the middle. Colleges and universities may be such communities. Students and faculty may treat them instrumentally, as places to learn a valuable skill or as the source of a pay check. People may also bond to their institution, and often this is encouraged. For better or worse, the promotion of such school spirit is one function of school athletic teams. For some people, an intellectual community can be transforming and life-defining. In colleges people not only learn chemistry or philosophy, but they also sometimes become chemists and philosophers. They come to identify themselves with their intellectual craft and with those who practice it at their own institutions.

Often the degree or character of the affiliation, whether it is constitutive or instrumental, depends on us as well as on the character of the community.

Barbara and Roger have different relationships to the Native American community. It seems clear that for Roger, the Native American community is a constitutive community. He is not just a member of a group interested in exploring Native American culture. He *is* a Native American. It defines him. He does not seem to view his membership as a choice. It is a fact—perhaps *the* fact—about who he is. Barbara's relationship to the community, on the other hand, is less clear. She has an identity independent of her membership in the Native American community. If the Native American community is to be a constitutive community for her, that will have something of the character of a choice. It may be a choice informed by her ancestry, but it is still a choice.

Roger, too, might make a choice about his relationship to the Native American community, but it would be a very different choice. His identity is already strongly formed by his being Native American. Could he choose to disaffiliate? What would that mean? Some choices are possible. Roger could stop attending meetings with or about Native Americans. He could decide to become an accountant or an engineer, take a job with an appropriate corporation, move to a suburb, and attempt to take up a conventional middle-class life—one much like the life of Barbara's parents—unrelated to his Native American heritage. However, such a transition is not as simple as this description suggests.

Consider two difficulties. One has to do with how others see and respond to Roger. To the extent that people treat or continue to treat Roger as a Native American, it will be difficult for him to be anything else. For better or worse, we are much influenced and constrained by our interaction with others and their expectations of and response to us. If Roger is a Native American in the eyes of others, he may have difficulty choosing to be something else.

The other difficulty is that to the degree that being Native American defines Roger and structures his understanding and orientation to the world, an attempt to disaffiliate requires the reconstruction of his identity. He must change his orientation to the world, his fundamental ways of thinking about it. How would one do this critically or intelligently? On what basis would one decide to change something that structures one's reasons for making decisions? (Question: In what ways is a disaffiliation from a constitutive community like a religious conversion, or like the rejection of one's childhood religion?)

The members of TRE have a very different relationship to the fraternity. On one hand, their affiliation with the fraternity probably means more to most members than belonging to a credit union. It may have something of the flavor of a constitutive community. Members may be strongly bonded to the fraternity and may have internalized some of its culture. However, it seems unlikely that TRE would be life-defining for members in the way that being Native American is for Roger. For Roger the claim, "I do this because I am a Native American and this is what Native Americans do" will be true in many cases. In some cases, this can also be true for fraternity members. There may be traditions to be followed or a mindset that orients members to their college life. However, members also have outlooks on life that are far more central in their orientation than their fraternity membership. As Roger discovered what it meant to be a Native American, he found he could not also be a Presbyterian. It is doubtful that this is the case for the TREs.

At the same time, the TRE brothers' bonds of affiliation are likely to be strong enough to sustain loyalty to the fraternity and its members. There will be times when it will be important to be loyal to the fraternity and its members. To take an obvious case, the members may find their membership a sufficient reason to play for or support the fraternity baseball team. However, there may also be cases in which commitments external to membership will trump loyalty. Most students will not miss an important exam to play for the fraternity team, nor (if the group is reasonable) will they be expected to do so.

We need to say some things about the values associated with community and about the concept of loyalty. One set of values consists of those that are central to the community's character. For example, religious communities are, to a degree, defined by their theological commitments. The values that underlie a community are often described as its culture.

We should note two things about these kinds of values. First, to say that they are central to the community does not mean that they are clear, universally agreed upon, or may not be contested. Roger actively tries to debate and formulate a picture of Native American culture. He doesn't see the values that characterize Native culture as a package that he must accept to be a member of that community. Community affiliation, even within constitutive communities, is often a matter of having a vague sense of commonality with others with whom one can then join in a shared argument about how these values should be understood.

Second, the values that characterize a constitutive community are often discovered by their new members, rather than understood and agreed to beforehand. Roger discovered that being a Native American required a view of spirituality that was inconsistent with being a Presbyterian. This was something he discovered about himself, rooted in his affiliation. He did not become a Native American because he found that their sense of spirituality seemed correct. (Questions: Might he have? Or can white, New Age religious seekers legitimately adopt Native American spirituality without having any such heritage?) Barbara is also in the process of discovering what it is to be a Native American. She differs from Roger in that she is also open to defining herself in other ways, and must balance her affiliations.

To be a member of a community is to be loyal to its values and commitments. This loyalty need not be expressed as mindless subservience. It is more a matter of being committed to a process of reflection and discovery that focuses on the values of this community rather than some other.

Being a member of a constitutive community also involves loyalty to its members. Most constitutive communities tend to prefer their members or extend privileges to them in ways that are not available to outsiders. Members of religious groups, even those that teach universal love, may feel a higher level of duty to care for their own members than for outsiders. Usually only members of the community are permitted to participate in deliberations about how it will conduct its business. Thus, it seems appropriate for Roger to be committed to helping his people, and it would be strange if those who were not TREs were allowed to vote in the fraternity's elections.

Friendships are often established within communities. We are more likely to befriend those who are like us, enjoy what we enjoy, understand us, or share our basic values than we are to befriend outsiders.

Thus communities play an important part in our ethical lives. Our community memberships are connected to our sense of identity, our basic commitments, our loyalties, and our friendships.

Community affiliations can also be the source of some of our most perplexing moral dilemmas. Few of us are members of a single, all-encompassing, community. Instead, we are members of a variety of groups. Even Roger, who identifies with one primary community, is still a member of a college community and a civic community. Barbara, too, is a member of the Native American community as well as the college community. However, because her attachment to the Native American community is not as deep or unconditional as Roger's, other communities may be significant to her. She isn't clear how to feel about her earlier religious commitments. Her family thinks of themselves as ordinary middle-class professionals who happen to have some Native American ancestors. This still seems to be an option for Barbara.

Similarly, the TREs are members of a fraternity, but they are also members of a university community and a civic community. No doubt they also belong, with a variety of degrees of commitment, to a wide range of religious groups, ethnic groups, and other associations, sharing important values and a sense of group identification.

These differing affiliations can generate several different kinds of ethical conflict. We will discuss three.

1. Some conflicts stem from the fact that we may belong to multiple groups with different histories, purposes, values, or commitments. Our membership in these varied communities can generate conflicts of several types.

One type is identity conflicts. People who have strong attachments to more than one constitutive community may not know who they are. Barbara is not sure that she is either a Native American or a middle-class suburbanite.

Another type is loyalty conflicts. Should the TREs be loyal to each other or to the university community? Should Barbara be loyal to Roger, to the University, or to the civil society whose laws Roger has broken? And what action would count as being loyal to the Native American community?

Finally, there may be a conflict of principles or of values. Is there any sense in which Native American spirituality is superior or inferior to Barbara's Presbyterian heritage? Is one of these her "real" heritage? Is there a question to be asked about which religion (if any) is true? Do the TREs have a moral obligation to support the civil society's antitheft values?

2. Another way to look at such conflicts is to emphasize the difference made by an insider's perspective versus an outsider's. Roger, for example, seems not to be bothered by the fact that he has violated the law and the college's regulations. He is inclined to judge his conduct only in terms of how it affects or serves the aspirations of the Native American community. He does not see himself as a member of either the college community or the civil society. He may even view them as oppressors or enemies. Because he is not a member, their law is not his law, and he does not feel an obligation to abide by their laws. He sometimes seems to view the rules of the college or society's laws as we might view the laws of Mongolia. They may or may not be good laws, and because they are not our laws, we need not obey them.

The TREs (with less justification) seem to have taken a similar view toward the university. That is how they are able to take the view that "this is your rule, your tree, and your problem." Here the TREs have not disavowed the basic idea that it is wrong to steal or to destroy others' property. But they have clearly disavowed any responsibility for accommodating or enforcing these standards in the current case. We might say that they recognize the validity of the rule, but they do not recognize any ownership of the rule. Thus they regard themselves as entitled to violate it when it conflicts with their fraternity's traditions, and they have no sense of any duty to assist in its enforcement.

Here we might also notice Roger's ambivalence about the legitimacy of the civic or college regulations that he has violated. Perhaps he holds that the state's laws banning peyote should not apply to Native Americans. "What right do they have to regulate our religious ceremonies?" is a useful question for Roger (as well as the authorities) to ask. Peyote may be a narcotic, but its use in Native American ceremonies does not make the users junkies. Arguably the context makes a great deal of difference.

However, Roger's us-versus-them analysis might be more difficult to support regarding stealing the money. Roger is not in favor of theft generally. Moreover, it is unclear whose money he has used. Although it may have come from the college, it was currently NASA's. Has Roger used his alienation from the college and the civil society to rationalize his misappropriation of NASA's funds? Roger's remarks about liberating the money don't seem to ring true, and his attack on Barbara might be motivated by a need to cloak his guilt.

We should also ask about the basis Roger and the TREs have for viewing themselves as outsiders in the university. Plausible reasons are not hard to find for Roger. As a Native American, he is rooted in a different culture than the one that dominates the college. This culture functions as a constitutive community for him. Moreover, he may quite reasonably view his status in American society as the consequence of a history of oppression of his people. It may be that he is often defined as an Indian by others. It is easy to see why Roger might view himself and all Native Americans as "other."

It is hard to see similar grounds for the TREs. Culturally and religiously they are indistinguishable from the other members of the university and the larger society. The fraternity is not merely an instrumental community for most of them, but neither is it a constitutive community.

The TREs, nevertheless, may feel themselves to be outsiders. Many sociologists claim that that is a common feeling of youth in our society and claim that it is, in part, a consequence of the high level of age segregation fostered by our educational system. Youth, they argue, come to adulthood in institutions in which they are more influenced by their age peers than by adults. The adult world is largely invisible to them. As a consequence, they view themselves as outsiders in the adult world.

This may explain why the TREs, although they accept the norms of private property and honesty held by the larger society, nevertheless do not feel any ownership of these norms or responsibility to uphold them. They may consider themselves outsiders in their own society, and they may thus experience its rules and laws as something imposed on them by adults.

Do you think this is a plausible explanation for why the TREs might take the attitude they have shown toward honesty and private property? If so, does it justify their attitude?

3. A final perspective on the moral conflicts that flow from community membership is that some moral ideals seem to apply broadly and generally. Others seem to apply within the context of a community. For example, the principle of *equal respect for persons* seems to apply to everyone who is a person; thus it applies to all human beings. Let us say that it applies universally. That someone is black or white, Christian or Jew, male or female, is not a reason that they should be given unequal treatment (although what "equal" means may sometimes be unclear). Many moral concepts seem to function this way. It seems just as wrong to steal from someone, to murder someone, or to lie to someone who is not a member of our group as it does to do these things to someone who is. Dishonesty and murder seem wrong, regardless of the communities of the victim and perpetrator.

However, not all moral ideals can be like this. Loyalty means nothing if we must be equally loyal to everyone. Is it wrong to give gifts to our children or loved ones without giving them to everyone? Don't we have stronger bonds of obligation or care to our families or to members of our communities than to strangers?

Sometimes universal moral precepts such as honesty seem to conflict with the special bonds we feel toward our loved ones, friends, and the members of our communities. Citizens should be honest, and citizens should help their communities sustain honesty generally. If we see a stranger rob another stranger, it seems reasonable that we should help the victim and turn in the offender. But what if the offender is a friend, a loved one, or a member of our constitutive community? Do we have the same obligation?

One response might be to say that we do have such an obligation. We have an obligation to treat people equally. Thus we should turn in an offender regardless of whether or how we are attached to the offender. Fairness and justice demand no less.

Can this be true? Suppose that the offender was our child or our partner, a brother or sister, or a close friend. Do love and loyalty count for nothing?

You have probably noticed that we are not answering our own questions. We do have views on some of these matters. For example, we have little sympathy for the TREs. We have more sympathy for Roger. He is motivated by some positive ideals, whereas the TREs are not, but we do not think that he was right to steal from NASA (which is what he did). Should the TREs turn in those who stole the tree? We think the leaders should begin by acknowledging their own responsibility. Should Barbara turn in Roger? We don't know.

We think that it is rare that affiliation or community membership justifies the harming of one group by members of another. We also believe that community and loyalty count. Turning in one's friends or community members when they have done something wrong may not be wrong; nevertheless, the reluctance we all feel expresses something commendable: loyalty. Such reluctance is not just bias or selfishness.

Faced with such conflicts, we believe that there are few clear rules. The character of the bond with others is a consideration. For example, our society has made it a rule of law that one spouse cannot be forced to testify against another, no matter what the spouse did. The bond between wife and husband is viewed as important enough to override society's interests in prosecuting criminals. The seriousness of the harm also counts. If Roger or the TREs had committed murder, we do think they should be turned in by other members of their communities.

What can we learn from this? One thing is that living an ethical life often requires that we balance conflicting principles. Here we have tried to juxtapose conflicts between loyalty to a particular community and friendship on one hand, and universally applicable concepts such as honesty on the other. There are no rules that produce clear decisions in such hard cases. What we need are virtues such as judgment and wisdom. We get these through experience and through discussion with others who can help us to see what is at stake in a choice.

This tells us some important things about making ethical decisions. Often ethical situations are not clear-cut. Often our judgment will depend on knowing the context. Sometimes general rules don't seem to help much. What does help is wisdom—a virtue that comes with experience, practice, and discussion. None of us is so wise that we can afford to overlook the moral wisdom of others.

ADDITIONAL CASES

Case 5.3: Hazing

Although hazing is forbidden at the University of Eastern West Texas, several fraternities there practice it secretly. For example, Chi Chi Chi's initiation rites require that inductees prove their mettle by downing enormous quantities of hard alcohol during a special drinking game; and Sigma Epsilon Chi requires that pledges describe in vivid detail a lovemaking session with a girlfriend or date whom they must then bring to a large frat party.

In past years, XXX pledges have occasionally had to go to the hospital to have their stomachs pumped, and many have passed out for periods of time. Fortunately, no one has ever died, although death by acute alcohol poisoning is a very real threat from such a drinking "game." While SEX pledges run no such health risks in proving their devotion to their house, they do have to prove their loyalty at the expense of unsuspecting non-initiates, at least some of whom they may be supposed to care about. Other fraternities merely require members to wear strange uniforms, or to be accompanied by a frat brother everywhere they go (even to the bathroom), or always walk around campus in a single file with other pledges throughout the rush period.

Questions

1. Hazing activities take place in the name of bonding and forming group loyalty. Of course, some fraternities substitute community service requirements or other more socially acceptable means for pledges to prove their commitment. Yet hazing persists on many campuses, despite being outlawed. Why is hazing so persistent, even when colleges attach severe penalties to any fraternities that they discover hazing their pledges? What benefits might pledges and previous members of the frat get out of hazing that would motivate them to continue such traditions at all costs?

2. Do the hazing practices of the XXX and SEX frats violate different ethical principles? Is one type of hazing morally worse than the other?
3. If you were an XXX or SEX pledge, how would you respond to being told to do something potentially harmful to yourself or someone else because "it's a frat tradition"? Where would you personally draw the line, and why?

Case 5.4: Sharing Secrets

Scott and Val have been dating for two years, and they are very close; they will probably get married after they graduate. Scott is also very close to three other guys, and he regularly spends time hanging out with them when Val isn't welcome. Val accepts the exclusive friendship of "the Four Musketeers" because she knows that Scott needs time alone with his friends. Secretly, she is proud of never seeming possessive of Scott or of grilling him about what he and his friends do together. "I'm too mature for that," she thinks to herself. All of Scott's and Val's friends admire their relationship, which seems so strong that it precludes the petty jealousies and fights that trouble weaker matches.

However, now Val is shocked to learn that Scott has told his buddies a painful secret from her past. Scott doesn't see a dilemma, saying "I never promised that I wouldn't discuss something about you, because if I need to talk about you, they're the only ones I can talk to. And we were all talking about our relationships." Val thinks he has no right to share her private life with people she hardly knows (or with people she knows well, either), especially without her permission. For the first time, she sees his male friendships as a threat to their relationship as a couple. And she feels that she can never trust Scott again.

Questions

1. Should Scott's loyalty to Val override his loyalty to his male friends, or vice versa? Why?
2. Is telling someone else's secret always a breach of loyalty? Might it be justifiable in some circumstances? (See Chapter 4.)
3. Is discussing the details of an intimate relationship with someone outside that relationship disloyal, or can it be a healthy way to learn from others' advice?
4. Is it "mature" to have close friends outside a couple bond? What if some of those friends are of the opposite sex?
5. In addition to sexual faithfulness, what might "loyalty" mean for a couple?

Case 5.5: Ratting: A Roommate's Dilemma

Ruth was caught buying a term paper from Ever-Ready Student Services, an organization that writes papers and take-home exams for college students in exchange for cash. Honoria College has been trying to locate Ever-Ready and get enough evidence to close it down, and unfortunately for Honoria junior Ruth, they finally conducted a raid just when she was in the Ever-Ready office, paying for "The Role of Market Factors in the Development of the Health Insurance Industry." Caught red-handed, Ruth had no choice but to confess. In her confession, she mentioned that many other students knew about Ever-Ready too; for example, her roommate Smita knew about her activities. Ruth quickly added in Smita's defense that Smita had urged her not to resort to Ever-Ready, but she'd ignored this advice.

Smita, Ruth's roommate, was president of the student body, a hardworking and ambitious student. She and Ruth were both well aware that Honoria College has a strict honor code requiring that faculty and students turn in any students they suspect of cheating. However, Ruth refused to reveal whether she knew anyone who used Ever-Ready's services.

When the Honor Board confronted Smita, she said that she had tried to get Ruth to write her paper herself, warning her that everyone knew the college wanted to bust Ever-Ready and catch its customers, but to no avail. She then had hoped that if Ruth got away with her cheating this time, the college would shut down Ever-Ready before she could be tempted again.

Ever-Ready Student Services was the most blatant example of a persistent cheating problem on campus, and Honoria College wanted to make an example of any of its customers they could identify. Therefore, they expelled Ruth for the remainder of the school year, telling her she could reapply for admission after that. The college administration also wanted to send the student body a message that they must take seriously the honor code's requirement to turn in students who cheat. Because the administration felt that Smita had not fulfilled her obligations as a leader of the college community in this regard, they asked for her immediate resignation as president. Her permanent college record showed that the resignation occurred as the result of disciplinary action. Smita's stellar record thus contained a black mark that could haunt her future career.

Questions

1. Are there situations in which one student ought to report another to the authorities? How would you decide which situations merit such "ratting," and which do not?

2. How might a student leader resolve the conflict between loyalty to a friend and responsibility to the office she holds? Which moral principles might she use, and how, in deciding what to do?

3. Was Ruth really a friend to Smita? What ethical principles did she violate?

4. Should higher standards of behavior be expected of people in positions of authority and power, like Smita?

5. Do you think the college administration should give Smita (or Ruth) another chance?

6. Is the honor code requirement that students turn in other students unrealistic? (See Chapter 2.) Is it unfair to force students to choose between loyalty to their peers and friends, and loyalty to the college community as a whole?

Case 5.6: Secret Abuse

Late one evening, several members of Pi Alpha Lambda sorority are discussing a shocking scene that two of them, Maureen and Joan, have just witnessed. Maureen and Joan were walking through the sorority parking lot after a late night at the library when they noticed two people fighting inside a car. The street light was fairly bright there, and they thought they saw a man punching a woman. Joan recognized the car; it belonged to Matt, a junior who is dating Leah, one of the sorority sisters. Joan and Maureen had argued about what to do, and then continued walking. The car windows had been pretty fogged up, so they couldn't be sure about what they'd seen, and they didn't want to butt in inappropriately.

Now that they're back in the House, Joan is feelingly increasingly bad about not interfering. "I'm sure I saw him hit her!" she exclaims. "And I think he's beaten her up before. Remember that time Leah had a black eye that she said she got from slipping on an icy sidewalk? Well, that was just after she and Matt were out together." The others soon add their observations and suspicions.

It turns out that a majority suspect that Leah is being beaten regularly by Matt, who otherwise seems likes a dream date: good-looking, charming, athletic, funny, polite. "We should do something!" says Joan, and they resolve to talk to Leah when she comes in.

A moment later, Leah does come in; but she runs up to her room before anyone has a chance to speak to her. When Joan and Maureen knock on her door, a muffled voice says, "I don't feel like talking right now. I want to be alone." It sounds as if Leah is crying.

Over the next few days, several PAL sisters try to talk to Leah, but she denies that anything is wrong. When they suggest that she try counseling anyway, because she often seems to cry after phone calls or dates with Matt, she gets angry. "Look, I appreciate the concern, but everything is fine! My relationship with Matt is really no one else's business. And I don't need some busybody counselor making trouble between us. Matt would never go to therapy, and if I even suggested it to him, or went by myself, he'd be really ticked off."

Questions

1. What should the women of PAL do if Leah doesn't want help?
2. Is it a breach of loyalty to her as their friend and sorority sister to go to a counselor or other knowledgeable person against her expressed wishes? Does loyalty to her require getting her help even if she doesn't want it?
3. What if the sorority sisters do convince Leah to go to therapy, and Matt beats her up as a result?
4. If, after weighing the good and the bad in her relationship with Matt, Leah has privately decided that an occasional beating is worth it to keep him as her boyfriend, can this be a legitimate decision?
5. Should Maureen and Joan have interfered when they thought they saw Matt hitting Leah? Is interfering in a case of suspected physical abuse a violation of the participants' privacy, integrity, and freedom to run their own lives?
6. Can you make an argument for why Leah's situation should be the legitimate concern of her PAL sisters? What ethical principles might you use?

Case 5.7: *School Spirit*

Mountain College prides itself on being a small school in which students have a big sense of community and college spirit. Mountain spirit peaks during homecoming week, when the gold and blue school colors are everywhere, and all minds are on The Big Game with perennial rival and neighbor Plains College. Students express their loyalty to Mountain by spending weeks preparing floats for the big pregame parade, planning elaborate halftime programs, and of course arranging for the best-ever homecoming dance. Some of them also traditionally express their loyalty by getting into postgame fights with Plains students.

This year, the Plains Tigers beat the Mountain Bulldogs 14–13, and feelings were high when the game ended. Mountain sophomores Randy, Jonathan, and Will were heading out of the stands, talking angrily among themselves about the unfairness of the referee's last call, when they saw several Plains students (obvious in their grey-and-red sweatshirts emblazoned with huge Ps) celebrating their victory. One of the Plains students banteringly shouted out to them, "Those Bulldogs suck!" This insult was too much for the Mountain sophomores. Not about to let such a challenge pass unanswered, they exchanged a number of blows with the Plains students before Security broke up the fight.

Questions

1. The flip side of loyalty to a school or group is often hostility toward outsiders. Are fights like the one involving Randy, Jonathan, and Will a natural outgrowth of (excessive) competition between schools?
2. Are such fights and other extreme shows of loyalty to a school somehow the fault of the institution, or only of the individuals involved?
3. Can a college promote school spirit without also promoting intense rivalry with other colleges? Why might sports be the primary means schools use to develop school spirit? Are there other possible ways to build a feeling of loyalty to a school?
4. Promoting a strong sense of loyalty is obviously beneficial to the college: school spirit often translates into alumni loyalty and financial donations to the school. Having school spirit also seems positive for students because expressing loyalty to their alma mater might make them feel a sense of belonging otherwise missing in their lives and give them the satisfaction of working with others for common goals. Are there negative aspects of school spirit (expressed, for example, at sporting events) for colleges or students?
5. Is school spirit a distraction from "the real point" of school (academics), or *is* it "the real point," as many older alumni seem to recall fondly?
6. What do you think of the school spirit at your college?

Case 5.8: Stand By Your Man?

Thorndike Community College is in an uproar over allegations by juniors Mindy Engelhardt and Lisa Fernandez that Associate Prof. Joe Washington has sexually harassed them. (The students' names were supposed to be kept anonymous, but someone leaked them to the local newspaper.) Mindy and Lisa were talking to Professor Washington after one of his "Africa: The Continent and Its Peoples" lectures when, they claim, he made an obscene joke about the sexual abilities of women in a certain African tribe compared to American women. He then followed this embarrassing comment with a joking question, apparently addressed to them both, about their abilities in the same regard. Mindy and Lisa said that they were not the only ones to be embarrassed and humiliated by this exchange—their fellow students Latifa Lee, Charlene Johnson, and Janice Howard were standing nearby. However Latifa, Charlene, and Janice have refused to support Mindy's and Lisa's story.

What actually happened between Professor Washington and the students has largely become lost in an ugly, campuswide debate. The hullabaloo seems to center around the fact that Mindy and Lisa are not African Americans, and Professor Washington (and Latifa, Charlene, and Janice) are. Charges of racism mingle with countercharges of sexism, as defenders of each party accuse the other of the lowest motives.

Latifa, Charlene, and Janice have had many soul-searching discussions with their friends about their mutual decision to deny Mindy and Lisa's report. The talks have been soul-searching because all three women did hear Professor Washington's obscene comments. Furthermore, they know other female African American students who have heard worse from Professor Washington, and even been propositioned outright by him. However, the three women have decided that they should support him because they feel that whites are always trying to keep African American men down by means of trumped-up sexual charges.

"Our men have a hard enough time without having us women attack them too, especially in front of whites," Latifa said. "Look how white people are always trying to pull down any black man who gets some authority."

Charlene agreed. "There are hardly any other African American professors on this campus, and we have to stand behind him, no matter how much of a jerk he can be."

"I don't think he really means any harm," added Janice. "He thinks he's being friendly, or funny, or something. You just have to ignore it."

Thus the three students resolve to lie to the college administration in order to defend Professor Washington. However, they do privately feel bitter about his harassment and about his stupidity in showing his crass character to white students and thus putting them in the difficult position of having to decide whether to be loyal to their race or their sex (not to mention to the truth).

Questions

1. Did Latifa, Charlene, and Janice make the right decision?
2. Might their argument that black women need to stand behind black men in a hostile white world have merit?
3. Are they as much (or more) victims of sexism as Mindy and Lisa are?
4. Are there times when lying may be justified by a feeling of loyalty to a fellow member of one's group? If you disagree that Latifa, Charlene, and Janice are justified in lying to the administration, would they would be more justified if Professor Washington were their father or other close kin?
5. If the three women are not willing to accuse Professor Washington of harassment publicly, is there anything they can or should do privately about his behavior? Is there anything they can or should do (privately, if not officially) to support Mindy and Lisa?
6. Can you say whether your sex, your race, or your social class more fundamentally defines you, and thus ultimately demands your loyalty when push comes to shove?

7. Why might "the women's movement" consist primarily of white females, and "the gay movement" consist primarily of white males, rather
than either "liberation" movement including a proportional number of
people of color?
8. What factors determine our strongest group loyalties?

BACKGROUND READING

James Coleman (United States President's Science Advisory Committee Panel on
Youth), *Youth Transition To Adulthood* (Chicago: University of Chicago Press,
1974).
This is one of the first and best-known sociological accounts of youth alienation, which Coleman blames on the high level of age segregation in our educational system.

The ethics of the use of peyote in Native American religious rites are explored in a
documentary film, *The Peyote Road*, directed by Gary Rhine, Fidel Moreno, and
Phil Cousineau. Other sources of information about the subject include Linda
Kanamine, "'Good Medicine' vs. the Law," in *USA Today*, 11 August 1994, sec. A,
p. 2, col. 4 (describes a Senate bill to lift the last barriers to Native American use
of peyote in religious ceremonies, thirty years after the cactus was listed as a controlled drug); "For Indian Church, A Critical Shortage," in *The New York Times*, 20
March 1995, sec. A, p. 10, col. 4 (discusses the law regarding peyote use and cul-
tivation and provides some background about the Native American Church of
North America); and "The Mescal Religion" in Natalie Curtis, recorder and editor, *The Indians' Book: Authentic Native American Legends, Lore and Music* (New
York: Bonanza Books/Crown Publishers, 1987), pp. 162–65 (a reference work that
describes peyote ceremonies and provides historical background.)

Michael Lind, "To Have and Have Not: Notes on the Progress of the American Class
War" in *Harper's Magazine*, June 1995, vol. 290, no. 1741, pp. 35–39, 41–47.
The author explores the idea that beyond race, sex, or religion, social class
(especially for the "hidden" upper class) determines Americans' ultimate loyalties. He argues that the contentious divisions between various disaffected minorities in American society are really diversions encouraged by the upper class
to keep potential rebellion down.

"To Tell or Not to Tell: Conflicts About Confidentiality" in *Report From The Center for
Philosophy and Public Policy*, Spring 1984, vol. 4, no. 2, pp. 1–5.
This article explores the ethics behind issues of confidentiality and loyalty in
various situations. *The Report* is available from The Institute for Philosophy and
Public Policy, School of Public Affairs, University of Maryland, College Park, MD
20742, (301) 405-4759.

Kenneth Taylor, "Hill, Thomas, and the Politics of Race" in *Report From The Center
for Philosophy and Public Policy*, Spring/Summer 1992, vol. 12, no. 1, pp. 16–19.
The Report is available from The Institute for Philosophy and Public Policy,

School of Public Affairs, University of Maryland, College Park, MD 20742, (301) 405-4759.

The author analyzes the turmoil in the black community over Anita Hill's testimony during the Senate Judiciary Commitee's confirmation hearings for Supreme Court Justice nominee Clarence Thomas. Taylor explores the ethics behind the issues of loyalty to race versus sex, African American group identification and affirmative action brought up by the case, as well as the broader political and social implications of each.

ADDITIONAL MATERIALS

1. The O.J. Simpson murder trial brought up questions concerning racial solidarity for many in the general public. African Americans in particular were often questioned by pollsters and media pundits about their reactions to the case: for example, did they view Simpson's inter-racial marriage and opulent lifestyle as examples of race treachery, or as proof that blacks could make it in a white world? (See Donna Britt, "For O.J., They Can't Cross That Color Line," in *The Washington Post*, 24 June 1994, sec. D, p. 1, col. 1; and Meri Nana-Ama Danquah, "Why We Really Root For O.J.," in *The Washington Post*, 3 July 1994, sec. C, p. 9, col. 4.)

Why might the O.J. Simpson trial have become a sort of loyalty test for many black Americans? When people suggested that African Americans ought to support Simpson because he was black, how did they use the principle of community to make this argument? When they argued against black support for Simpson, what ethical principles did they seem to use? (See Karen Grigsby Bates, "What Color is Conscience?" in *The Los Angeles Times*, 13 April 1995, sec. B, p. 7, col. 2; Kenneth B. Noble, "The Simpson Defense: Source of Black Pride" in *The New York Times*, 6 March 1995, sec. A, p. 10, col. 5; Sam Fulwood III, "Separating Black and White," in *The Los Angeles Times*, 22 July 1994, sec. A, p. 1, col. 1; and Earl Ofari Hutchinson, "Race and Sex—The Last Taboo Lives," in *The Los Angeles Times*, 30 June 1994, sec. B, p. 7, col. 2.) Is such loyalty justifiable? Do the vast majority of African Americans really have much in common with Simpson? Why or why not? (See Seth Mydans, "In Simpson Case, an Issue for Everyone," in *The New York Times*, 22 July 1994, sec. A, p. 16, col. 4; and Mary Schmich, "Seeing Simpson in Different Ways," in *The Chicago Tribune*, 3 July 1994, sec. 2C, p. 1, col. 1.)

2. When people allow the principle of community to become their sole ethical standard, they become racists or nationalists. The Bosnian civil war offers a striking warning of the dangers of community run amok. What light do the moral principles we have discussed shed on the Bosnian conflict? Some possible sources of information about the moral and human side of the war in Bosnia include Tom Gjelten, *Sarajevo Daily: A City and Its Newspaper Under Siege* (New York: HarperCollins, 1995); Misha Glenny, *The Fall of Yugoslavia: The Third Balkan War* (New York: Penguin, 1993); Brian Hall, *The Impossible Country: A Journey Through the Last Days of Yugoslavia* (Boston: David R. Godine Publisher, 1994); and David Rieff, *Slaughterhouse: Bosnia and the Failure of the West* (New York: Simon and Schuster, 1995).

Can you think of illustrations of the destructive potential of the other principles (benefit maximization, respect for persons, relationships, and character growth) if taken to extremes? What does this suggest about ethical argument in general?

6

SEX, RELATIONSHIPS,
AND POWER

Case 6.1: Seduction or Rape?

Carlotta Gomez was stunned by Peter Andretti's blunt response to her question. "I don't rape," he had said, "I seduce." He was clearly proud of his "moral" outlook on the topic. After her interview with Peter, Carlotta summarized his view to herself as involving essentially two ideas. The first was, "If it feels good, do it"; the second was, "Let the woman beware."

Carlotta was a counselor in the Office of Student Services at Columbia County Community College. Her job at Four Cs was to provide both academic counseling and emotional support to Four C students. While the emphasis in her job was academic, she was a warm and open person who often achieved the kind of trust and rapport with students that led them to discuss more personal problems with her.

Susan Black was one of her students. She had been in several times to discuss her schedule and her academic problems. Susan was usually an adequate student. However, her family was not a model of stability. Her parents were divorced, and her father's support payments were irregular. Often Susan was unable to pay even Four C's modest tuition. Even when her father came through, Susan often felt that she had to turn over some of the money to her mother to keep the rest of the family going. The need to work and the stress didn't do much for Susan's grades.

The last few months had been a disaster. Susan was failing all of her courses. Carlotta called her in to see what was going on. Susan was clearly troubled by something, and for a while she was unwilling to discuss it. Finally she blurted out, "Ms. Gomez, I was raped."

The story, as Susan told it, was this: She was at a party with a few friends and ten or so other people whom she didn't know. They listened to some music and had a few beers. She met Peter Andretti there. She enjoyed his company and spent much of the evening talking and dancing with him. At about one in the morning, when the party was breaking up, Peter asked Susan if he could give her a ride home. Susan agreed. When they were in the car, Peter suggested that they go over to his place to talk and listen to a new CD that he thought she would like. Susan wasn't very interested. It was late, she was tired and a little tipsy, and she didn't really trust Peter. However, Peter drove to his apartment over her objections, saying that he would be glad to drive her home after they had listened to the CD.

After they got to the apartment, Peter put on the CD and opened a bottle of wine. About halfway through the CD and the bottle of wine, Peter became sexually aggressive. For a while Susan made light of it, joking with Peter while pushing him away and suggesting that she should go home. Peter, however, was persistent. Moreover, he belittled her resistance. He wanted to know why she was so frigid and hung up, asking whether she was religious, or a lesbian. He made both things sound like some disease. He made her feel as though she had to prove to him that she was a normal human being, and that the only way that she could do that was to have sex with him.

Susan was fuzzy about most of what followed. There was more wine. The tension of the situation had seemed to her to be a reason to drink more. The next thing she could remember clearly was waking up in Peter's bed, plainly after having had sex with him. She dressed as quickly as she could and fled into the street. She remembered his laughing at her distress.

Although Susan wasn't very clear about some of what had happened, she was clear that she had repeatedly told Peter that she wasn't interested in having sex with him. At one point she recalled having said, "Maybe I'm not a virgin, but I'm not a whore either. I don't sleep with people two hours after I've met them." Thus, she concluded, "he raped me."

Carlotta wasn't so sure. She wasn't a lawyer, and Susan wasn't clear about the facts. In any case, Susan was unwilling to take the matter to the police. She had thought about it for a while, and she had even read an article on rape prosecutions. It was clear to her that any lawyer who defended Peter would pay a lot of attention to the question of why she had gone to his apartment, and that there would be other questions about other romantic involvements. She was afraid she would end up looking like a slut, and she couldn't prove anything. She didn't want to deal with it.

Because Susan was unwilling to pursue the matter, Carlotta thought that she herself should drop it. It wasn't part of her job to inform Peter of the error of his ways. However, her anger and her need to find out what kind of person Peter was led her to call him in.

Much to her surprise, Peter willingly confirmed almost all of the details of Susan's story. He was obviously proud of his "conquest." He bragged that there were others much like Susan. And he added a few details of his own. He admitted that Susan had resisted coming to his apartment and having sex with him, but he also noted that at no point had he forced her to do anything. "I just kept at her until she said yes," he said. "She was a little reluctant; girls like to say 'no' for a while. It makes them feel more valuable and less guilty. But she was certainly willing in bed. In fact you might tell her when you see her that she's a damn good lay. I'll be happy to accommodate her again. Besides, I'm sure she really wanted it, no matter what she says now. Why else would she come to my apartment? She just needed a little help to relax!" That was when Carlotta accused Peter of rape, and Peter smugly replied, "I don't rape, I seduce."

Questions

1. What's the difference between rape and seduction? Does rape necessarily involve force?
2. What makes rape wrong? Is seduction wrong? If both are wrong, should both be criminal offenses?
3. Suppose that Susan had been willing and eager to go over to Peter's apartment and have sex. Suppose also that both understood that their sex was a casual matter for the pleasure of the moment, and that no long-term relationship was envisioned. Is there anything the matter with that?
4. Often these days, talk about responsible sex emphasizes either the prevention of pregnancy or the prevention of AIDS. Are avoiding consequences such as unwanted pregnancy or AIDS the only reasons for resisting casual sex?
5. What do you think about "If it feels good do it?" Susan seems to feel that casual sex is wrong. Is it?
6. Is casual sex inconsistent with some benefits or desirable ends that can be achieved through sex? Does this question ask about what is right or wrong?
7. Many traditional religions frown on premarital sex and are strongly opposed to adultery. Aside from the question of whether these prohibitions might reflect the will of God, are there other reasons for opposing premarital sex or adultery?
8. Most marriages involve vows of faithfulness that are broken by adultery. Why should there be such vows? What value is added to sexual relations when they are expressed within a long-term commitment?
9. Suppose Peter had seduced a male student rather than Susan. Would anything about your answers to these questions change? Does anything

prevent same-sex relationships from realizing the benefits possible in heterosexual relationships?

ISSUES

Probably nothing we discuss in this book is likely to be as controversial as sex, nor is there a topic about which human beings have had more, and a wider variety of things, to say. Here we can suggest only a few approaches and questions about the ethics of sex. First, we want to discuss minimal standards for sexual conduct. Second, we want to make a few suggestions about how one might think of sex as part of durable and meaningful human relationships, and compare this position to another view of the significance of sex.

In most Western societies, the minimal standard for sexual conduct between adults is that it should be consensual. Coerced sex (rape) is commonly criminalized. Why should this be the case?

One response is that forced sex is a form of exploitation. One person uses another person for his own ends. Thus forced sex violates the principle of *respect for persons*. This seems true enough, but perhaps it understates the case. Rape seems a particularly serious and violent form of exploitation. The act itself can be experienced as highly degrading, painful, and intrusive, and often it has quite emotionally destructive long-term consequences for the victim. What is the basis of such feelings? Why is rape usually considered even more heinous than other crimes of violence?

Note that it seems clear that Peter has exploited Susan. Susan did not want to have sex with Peter. Nevertheless Peter put a great deal of effort into getting her to have sex with him. Why shouldn't Peter's behavior be considered rape? One response might be that Peter didn't use force. That seems to be the point of his comment that "I seduce, I don't rape." But why should the use of force define rape? Isn't the point that sex should be consensual? The very meaning of seduction, however, is that that the victim is persuaded to do something against her will or better judgment, even though physical force isn't used. Peter got Susan drunk. He brought her to his apartment when she wanted to go somewhere else. He lied to her. He applied psychological pressure in manipulating her until she gave in. There seems little doubt that Peter had every intent of exploiting Susan. Then why not view his action as rape? Indeed, why distinguish between rape and seduction?

Perhaps we should not treat rape and seduction as different acts. What should define rape is not force, but more simply the lack of consent. This thinking lies behind the idea of criminalizing adult sex with minors (statutory rape). Statutory rape is considered a violation of a minor even when no violence or threat of violence is used, because minors are presumed to be unable to give meaningful consent to sex.

Another view, however, is that the idea of consent in this case is ambiguous. Susan did, it seems, give in eventually. When we say that she didn't "consent," perhaps we mean something like this. Giving in to Peter is something that Susan would not have done under reasonable circumstances, in which she had not been drinking and was not being pressured. Giving in seems a different thing than freely consenting from the outset. Yet she did give in. Is this "ambiguity about consent" a reason for distinguishing between rape and seduction? Does the fact (if it is a fact) that Susan became fully involved in the sex act change anything?

One might argue that rape and seduction are different for legal purposes, but not moral ones. They are different legally because the ambiguity about consent makes it difficult to know the extent to which sex was consensual. Consider, for example, that it has been common for women to marry men whom they would not otherwise wed for the economic security that such a marriage can provide. Is sex in such a marriage consensual? Some feminists have argued that all sex under conditions of gender inequality is a kind of rape, that in a patriarchal society, marriage differs little from prostitution in being an exchange of sex for needed economic benefits. If the idea of "consent" is ambiguous, perhaps the point of treating force as a defining characteristic of rape is that the use of force seems to make it clear that the sex was not consensual.

However, in this case it seems clear that Peter's intent was to exploit Susan. Should we then conclude that his behavior is every bit as immoral as rape, even if it is not every bit as illegal?

The questions and responses we have discussed above are part of what might be viewed as a minimalist view of sexual morality. We have raised questions about how people ought to be treated and what kinds of conduct are wrong. A number of other perspectives might be used in questions of sexual ethics. For example, we have hinted at, but not developed, equality as a feature of an ethics of sex. Not only should sex be consensual, but it also should occur under conditions of equality and reciprocity. This could mean a number of things. It might mean that sex cannot be fully consensual in a society in which women are likely to be economically dependent on men or in which they have less power than men. It might mean that standards of sexual conduct should not differ for men and women. The common assumption that men should take what they can get sexually and women should resist is an example of inequality in standards of conduct. It might mean that the benefits of sex should be equal. It might mean that men and women should share familial responsibilities equally. What else might it mean? Can you think of other examples of gender inequality?

Another perspective that we will not pursue here has to do with lying and promise keeping. Sex is often connected with love and expressed within a context of promises. We may feel that sex is more appropriate with someone whom we love or for whom we have at least some affection. Susan seems to feel this way. We may express our love not only through sex, but also verbally. We may also express fidelity and faithfulness in connection with sex. Some of the ethical issues here are simple and straightforward: It is wrong to lie. It is wrong to make promises you do not intend to keep, and to fail to keep promises you have made. Thus it is wrong to do these things in the context of sex. However, there are complexities: Is it all right to lie if my purpose is benevolent rather than selfish? May I break a promise if circumstances change radically or unexpectedly? Might such promises sometimes be coerced? You might wish to consider how these questions can apply to sex. But also note that these issues are primarily about lying and promise keeping; they are not, except by implication, about sexual relations.

"Responsible sex" offers another perspective on sexual ethics. When people talk about "responsible sex," they often seem to assume an ethical outlook something like this: Sex is valued largely because it is pleasurable. However, like some other pleasurable activities, sex can have undesirable consequences. Among these are unwanted pregnancy and sexually-transmitted diseases, the most chilling of which currently is AIDS. "Responsible sex" is consensual sex under conditions that avoid these unwanted consequences.

In one sense, this picture seems entirely reasonable. Sex that is not consensual, or that unreasonably risks unwanted pregnancy or disease, certainly is not responsible. However, we also think that the framework for thinking about sex needs to be broader than this. Discussions about responsible sex appeal to a moral principle—perhaps a variation of the principle of *benefit maximization*—that says we should not seek pleasure in ways that significantly harm ourselves or others. But this principle does not take a position about the significance of sex.

Another approach we might take is to examine some traditional social mores about sex. Is premarital sex wrong? Why have many human societies wished to confine sex to marriage, and to insist on faithfulness in marriage? Are there clues here to the benefits or meaning of sex beyond immediate sensual pleasure?

In what follows, we are not going to say much about sexual mores. But we do wish to make a few points, both so that you can understand our reluctance to discuss this important matter further, and so that you can have some idea how such questions might be approached.

At least two kinds of important considerations influence the way we think about sexual mores. One set of concerns is religious. Many of the religions in our society have historically taken a dim view of sex outside marriage. Do such views carry moral force? We think that this is a matter for you to decide, given your own religious convictions or lack of them. However, we do want to make some observations on the matter.

First, because our society emphasizes freedom of conscience, we must be cautious about assuming that anyone's religious convictions can be made the basis of obligatory sexual standards for others. We are not suggesting here that religious views cannot be true or false or that one religion is as good as another. Rather, we are suggesting that even if religious convictions are true, that is not a sufficient reason for believers to seek to use governmental power to give them the force of law. We believe that this applies to religiously in-spired views about sex. Thus, while you may feel that those who violate your religiously based sexual mores do wrong (and you are entitled to those views), you do not as yet have any reason for coercing them to do right.

Second, we want you to question one view of the connection between re-ligious beliefs and ethics because we think that this understanding does not do enough justice to religion. (We discuss this in more detail in Chapter 9.) Many religious people seem to hold what we will label a "command theory" of ethics. Such a theory says that what makes actions right is that God has commanded them or at least permitted them, and what makes actions wrong is that God has forbidden them.

God may or may not have made various commandments. That is not the issue. A command theory of ethics tends to trivialize religiously inspired views of sexuality because most religions have an understanding about the point of sexuality. They interpret it within their particular frameworks, and the mores they promote or the commandments they follow have larger meanings. Viewing them simply as commands cuts them off from their broader significance about the point of sexuality. To put this point differently, many religions interpret the meaning of sex in terms of spiritual understand-ings of what we call the principles of *relationship* and *community.* If we view sexual ethics solely in terms of God's commands, we miss some of what reli-gions have to say about relationships and community.

For example, some religions view marriage as sacramental. It is not sim-ply a relationship between two people, but also a picture of the relationship between God and the individual or between God and the religious congre-gation. This relationship is sacred and holy and should not be capriciously undertaken or broken. Sex is pictured as a form of union with significance far beyond the production of pleasure or children.

Various religions have interpreted the point of sex in a wide range of ways, some of which do not support monogamy. For instance, some groups have considered nonmonogamous sex a way to establish meaningful connec-tions among fellow believers. The very openness of sex in such circumstances was intended to allow practitioners to connect to the divine within each other; by not choosing partners based on erotic attachment or other "superficial" qualities, practitioners hoped to embrace them in their spiritual essence.

Instances of such religiously (or semi-religiously) motivated polygamous sex include sacred prostitution in the ancient world (male believers wor-shipped at temples by having sex with women representing the gods); Chris-tians who took Christ's command to love one another literally, such as the

American nineteenth-century Oneida community in which all male members were "married" to all female members; "free love" advocates such as anarchist Emma Goldman; and poets such as Walt Whitman, who wrote, "Divine am I inside and out, and I make holy whatever I touch or am touched from."[1] In this view, open sex can express the divine love that binds us all, in contrast to more "selfish" monogamous sex.

Our point in noting these cases is to emphasize that religious views of sex are rooted in understandings of human relations, what a good life is, and the proper relationship between God and human beings. In considering the implications of religion for sexual conduct, our basic suggestion is that you approach the question not so much by worrying about what God may have commanded you to do or not to do, but by trying to understand and appraise the picture of sex and of human relations that such commands express. Perhaps the important question to ask isn't whether you should do what God has commanded (although if you believe God has commanded something, no doubt you should do it). It is whether you understand and accept the picture of life your religion teaches and wish to realize the benefits associated with sex in its teachings.

One more way to consider sexual mores is to view them in the context of the kinds of human relationships required in order to provide healthy and stable conditions for nurturing children. As you will recognize, this is a hotly debated and most controversial topic. Although we think it is crucially important, we do not plan to discuss it further because we cannot discuss it without taking a long detour into sociology. Nevertheless, we think that no full picture of appropriate social mores about sex can be developed apart from such considerations.

The rest of this chapter explores this question of the larger meaning of sex and how it can fit into various views of a good life. To help us in this discussion, we want to describe two characters representing opposing views about the meaning of sex, whom we will call the *bonder* and the *aesthete*.

The Bonder

The bonder views sex as a means for developing a special kind of relationship between a pair of human beings. The bonder thus brings the principle of *relationship* to bear on the question of the good of sex. A sexually involved couple can form a bond so intense and so valued by the partners that it becomes life-changing. Why might this be? What conditions are necessary to experience this kind of bond?

---

[1] Walt Whitman, "Song of Myself," line 524, from *The Norton Anthology of Poetry*, Revised Edition, ed. Alexander Allison et al. (New York: W.W. Norton and Co., 1970), p. 819. Originally published in *Leaves of Grass* (1855).

Considering the concepts of vulnerability and privacy might help us answer these questions and understand the bonder's view of sex. Suppose we think of privacy as involving the right to control, or not to have to disclose, information about ourselves. (For more on privacy, see Chapter 4.) Think of "information" broadly here. It involves more than data about our incomes or our grade point averages. It may include the privilege of disclosing or not disclosing our bodies. Perhaps one reason that few of us would be comfortable in going nude or dressing provocatively most of the time is that this would subject us to constant sexual appraisal. The right to privacy protects us from having to reveal information about ourselves that would subject us to harm or unwanted evaluation.

Privacy also allows us to reveal information about ourselves under special conditions. Most of us have told an embarrassing story about ourselves to friends. We are likely to do this only if we believe that it will result in some form of sharing—perhaps humor, perhaps the recognition of mutual weakness. Sometimes such revelations are a form of exploration. They ask, "Can I trust you enough to tell you this about myself and to know that you will not misuse the information?"

Note that such revelations both require and build trust. We are unlikely to engage in any self-revelation if we think it likely that the other person will belittle us or tell other people in a degrading way. The willingness to engage in such self-revelation says, "I trust you. If you prove trustworthy about this, perhaps I will trust you in more important matters." Trust is developed. A stronger bond is forged.

Privacy is a condition of such self-revelation. We could not selectively disclose things about ourselves to special people if everyone knew all there was to know about us.

Having sex might be thought of as a form of such self-disclosure. Perhaps mutually satisfying sex requires the form of privacy that used to be referred to as modesty. To the degree that our sexuality is there for all to see, we might be left with nothing to reveal to a special person or under special circumstances. Thus there may be a connection between such concepts as privacy, modesty, vulnerability, self-revelation, and bonding that explains why we often feel that something is missing in sex with an unfamiliar person, engaged in only for the pleasure of the moment. Because we are especially vulnerable to embarrassment or humiliation in sexual encounters, they may be especially valuable occasions for building trust and cementing strong bonds.

Another approach to understanding the bonder's view of sex lies in the observation that bonds between human beings are often strengthened by activities that are shared with that special person and with no one else. A feeling that "you are the one I share this with" builds relationships. The special activity may be anything from childhood memories to fishing. But sex is an activity that seems especially likely to help build a strong bond with a special person when it is shared exclusively with that person. Restricting the activity to the relationship enhances its value to the relationship. If sex is to build trust and cement bonds, one of the virtues required is fidelity or faithfulness. A promise to be true and the conviction that it will be honored are necessary.

If this argument for the bonder's view of sex carries some force, it is, nevertheless, important to see what does and does not follow from it. Nothing about it supports the claim that premarital sex, casual sex, or even significant promiscuity are morally wrong. (We are not here suggesting that they are right, either. The point is that social or personal mores about such matters depend on other kinds of arguments, such as the conditions for nurturing children or religious considerations.) The bonder's view of the meaning of sex doesn't address the question of which sexual mores are right or wrong. Instead it expresses beliefs about the conditions necessary for bonding and about the role sex might play. Bonders believe it is difficult to treat their sexual partners simultaneously both as "that special someone" and as one among many sexual partners.

If bonders are correct, at most this suggests that monogamy is a precondition of a certain kind of human good. This view is silent about what kind of sexual mores I should have before meeting my special someone, and about how long I should expect the relationship to last. Indeed, it is not an argument for marriage. The fidelity it requires may find a variety of social expressions. Additionally, the bonder's view of sex does not necessarily define concepts such as modesty or casual sex. Perhaps these concepts are culturally relative. For example, in societies in which topless or nude beaches are common, they are not experienced as sexually provocative, whereas certain forms of dress may be. (Question: what do you think "modesty" and "casual sex" mean in your social circle?) The bonder's view of sex is distinctive in that it considers bonding the main way to add meaning to sex beyond its immediate sensual pleasure.

The Aesthete

In contrast to the bonder, the aesthete views sex principally either as a potential "art form" or as a means of self-expression. The aesthete additionally rejects the idea of limiting sex to socially predetermined roles or mores as unreasonably constraining.

What might speaking of sex as an art form mean? Art forms often take an experience that is usually considered pleasurable or beautiful and seek to enhance it by making it more complex, sophisticated, or varied. They try to enhance our enjoyment in participating by increasing the skill required, and our enjoyment in perceiving by increasing the discrimination required for the experience. Analogies occur in sports, in which increased skill enhances our enjoyment in participating, and art, in which the ability to "see" a complex work of art is important for enjoyment. (See our discussion of drinking in Chapter 7.)

Applied to sex, the aesthete's view emphasizes that enjoyment of sex is enhanced by skill and by learning to be discriminating and nuanced in experiencing sex.

Aesthetes also view sex as a form of self-expression or self-realization. We are, they would claim, sexual beings. Perhaps sexuality is central to our natures. Self-expression, or the expression of something that is central to our natures, is good. Denial or repression of this self-expression is bad or even harmful. Some have argued that sexual repression is the source of much neurosis. Thus the expression of self involved in sex is a part of its significance, and whatever prevents us from such expressions is harmful.

So far there is no clear reason why the view of the aesthete is inconsistent with that of the bonder. Why not seek both bonding and enhanced enjoyment? Certainly we have not said anything inconsistent with the idea that one can both bond with some special person and treat sex within the relationship aesthetically.

We can begin to consider what makes these views alternatives by noting that the aesthete may have a particular view of social mores or of moral constraints about sex. Aesthetes often view these as placing arbitrary boundaries on enjoyment or self-expression. Sometimes they see them as sources of sexual inhibition or repression and thus as deeply inconsistent with their aesthetic values. The aesthete is perhaps someone who is, first and foremost, dedicated to enjoying and enhancing experience. For the aesthete, novelty and experimentation may be highly valued. Moral obligations or strong ties to other persons, the kinds of ties important to the bonder, may be viewed as overly restraining and, thus, inconsistent with the psychic freedom necessary to be an aesthete.

Perhaps, however, the aesthete's values are not sharply opposed to those of a "liberated" bonder. Indeed, some people may move from one view of the meaning of sex to the other over time, as in the case of a twenty-year-old sexual aesthete who "settles down" into a marriage with children in his or her thirties. Bonders, as we have described them, need not be committed to a traditional or religiously based morality (although they may be). Their position is not based on any arbitrary social constraints or on the supposed commands of a prudish God. Rather they are focused on the development of relationships, in a way that does not obviously exclude the enjoyment of sex.

We suspect, however, that there is a real tension between even the "liberated" bonder and the aesthete. Perhaps the center of the tension is a different view about what is crucial to a good life. Bonders find the good life principally in relationships. It is being with others, sharing with others, caring for others, enjoying with others, that constitutes the good life. The bonder's ethic is an ethic of relationships. Bonders need not oppose pleasure, including the pleasure of sex, but bonders are likely to subordinate pleasure to the goods of relationships and thus to argue that sex within bonded relationships ultimately provides for a richer life. The aesthete's picture of a good life is one in which the enjoyment of experience is central. The aesthete need not reject the benefits of relationships, but these will be subordinated to the intrinsic quality of the experience. Thus the aesthete is likely to find any picture of sex in which the experience of sex is subordinated to some deeper good as restraining and undesirable.

To illustrate this tension, suppose that A and B are bonded. And suppose A finds C, a willing sexual partner who has mastered some technique with the potential to significantly enhance A's sexual experience and pleasure. Should A take C as a sexual partner? The aesthete seems likely to answer yes, the bonder no. For the bonder, the relationship has now become essential to the value of sex. Either faithfulness to the partner is more important than any enjoyment that might be gotten from a new partner, or, where bonding is advanced, faithfulness is inconsistent with even enjoying sex with a new partner. In contrast, the aesthete may view a sense of commitment or an incapacity to enjoy sex with a new partner as undesirable inhibitions.

Another reason that the bonder and the aesthete may differ at a basic level is that they may value novelty differently. For the aesthete, novelty may significantly enhance the experience of sex, and novelty may require new partners. Although bonders may agree that novelty enhances the experience, they may find that they value their relationship more, or they may find that apart from their relationship, they cannot fully enjoy sex.

Finally, the aesthete may want to reject the kind of question the bonder is asking. The bonder seems to be seeking the "deeper meaning" of sex, and finds it in relationships. "But," the aesthete might ask, "why must sex have a deeper meaning? Why must there be anything beyond the experience? Does sex have to be part of something larger or deeper? Indeed, perhaps looking for something more just distracts from the experience. Perhaps all the meaning there is can be found in appreciating the pleasure and joy of the act." Thus the aesthete may consider the very attempt to find the deeper meaning of sex in relationships, in religion, or in anything beyond the experience a mistake, one that lessens the experience.

(Question: the aesthete may not value such traditional virtues as faithfulness or bonding, but does the aesthete value casual sex? The aesthete's view of sex may require that it be studied and mastered. Perhaps sex is a practiced art. Is this casual?)

Unfortunately, we think, the bonder's various views of the deeper meaning of sex (or life) do not get much press in our society, nor does the contrasting picture of the aesthete. Instead the mass media generate strong pressure for casual sex (both outside meaningful bonds and unstudied), although they do not seem to make any logical arguments. Advertising, television, and movies seem to promote the idea that casual sex is good because (a) it feels good; (b) it avoids commitments (and the ensuing "hassle" of working out a long-term relationship); and (c) it reassures participants about their sexual desirability, general attractiveness, and even basic self-worth. Religious people who oppose these contemporary trends often seem to do so in ways that exude confidence about what God has commanded about sex, while being uninformed about the meaning of sex even within their own traditions.

For young men especially, the mass media suggests that if you're not "getting it," preferably from a number of women, you are not really a man. For women there is a double standard: if men, preferably several, aren't sexually pursuing you (the woman is not supposed to be active in initiating sexual encounters), you are not really a woman. However, at the same time that male interest is reassuring, it is also threatening: should the woman "give in" to sex, or to sex with multiple partners, she loses her status and becomes a "slut." In other words, everyone's doing it (rather mindlessly), and so should you—up to a point.

Is the view of sex promoted by the media and advertising a third view? Can you describe and argue for its values? To what extent does the media portrayal of sex seek to manipulate both men and women for commercial gain? In what ways is its view of sex inconsistent with the views of both the bonder and the aesthete?

Up to this point we have tried to avoid any judgments about sexual mores. We have emphasized a minimal sexual ethic that emphasizes consent, and several ways of constructing a deeper understanding of the role of sex in a good life. Do any of these views provide a perspective from which to judge the kind of popular culture we have described above?

Although we have not developed the idea, we have also suggested that sexual relationships should be egalitarian. What might this mean? Does it lead to a critique of popular culture?

Throughout this book, we have been developing and applying the five ethical principles discussed at the beginning of the book (as well as a few others). Do the principles we haven't mentioned in this chapter also suggest additional perspectives from which one might think about the ethics of sex, the meaning of sex, or the picture of sex generated by popular culture? What kinds of virtues or behavior ideals (such as self-restraint, openness, honesty, unselfishness, faithfulness, and so on) do different views of the significance of sex require of sexually active people? Do all of the views we have described imply necessary virtues? If some do not, what might this suggest about them? Which view seems most compelling to you, and why?

We particularly suggest that you try to apply the principle of *character growth* to questions of sex. Peter, for example, has adopted an exploitive stance toward women. Has Peter damaged his capacity to form a meaningful and equal relationship with a valued partner? Has he harmed himself in the process? How might unequal, exploitive, or casual attitudes toward sex form character? Does popular culture damage people?

EXAMPLES OF COLLEGE AND UNIVERSITY CODES GOVERNING SEXUAL BEHAVIOR

1. Excerpt from the Antioch College policy on sexual offenses.[2]

Under the sexual offense policy:

All sexual contact and conduct between any two people must be consensual;

Consent must be obtained verbally before there is any sexual contact or conduct;

If the level of sexual intimacy increases during an interaction (i.e. if two people move from kissing while fully clothed—which is one level—to undressing for direct sexual contact, which is another level), the people involved need to express their clear verbal consent before moving to that new level;

If one person wants to *initiate* moving to a higher level of sexual intimacy in an interaction, *that person is responsible for getting the verbal consent of the other person(s) involved before moving to that level;*

If you have had a particular level of sexual intimacy before with someone, you must still ask each and every time;

If you have a sexually transmitted disease, you must disclose it to a potential sexual partner.

Don't ever make assumptions about consent; assumptions can hurt someone and get you in trouble. Also, do not take silence as consent; it isn't. Consent must be clear and verbal (i.e. saying: yes, I want to kiss you, too).

Special precautions are necessary if you, or the person with whom you would like to be sexual, are under the influence of alcohol, drugs, or prescribed medication. Extreme caution should always be used. Consent, even verbal consent, may not be meaningful. Taking advantage of someone who is "under the influence" is never acceptable behavior. If, for instance, you provide someone with alcohol and get her/him drunk so that person will consent to have sex with you (figuring you wouldn't get "as far" if that person were sober), then their consent may be meaningless and you may be charged under the sexual offense policy. If you are so drunk that you act inappropriately with someone (in a way maybe you wouldn't if you were sober), or if you are so drunk you don't hear "no," you may still be charged under the sexual offense policy.

---

[2] Selection from *"Sexual Violence and Safety"* in the *"Antioch College '94–'95 Survival Handbook"* (Karen Hall, The Sexual Offense Prevention and Survivors' Advocacy Program Director, Antioch College, Yellow Springs, Ohio, June 1992), pp. 17–18. [This policy is currently under revision.]

2. Excerpt from the policy on sexual harassment of the University of New Hampshire.[3]

Policy on Sexual Harassment of Students

[. . .] It is the policy of the University System of New Hampshire that no member of the University System community may sexually harass another. The intent of this policy is not to create a climate of fear but to foster responsible behavior in a working environment free of discrimination.

Unwelcomed sexual advances, requests for sexual favors, and other verbal or physical conduct of a sexual nature constitute sexual harassment when such conduct has the purpose or effect of unreasonably interfering with an individual's work performance or creating a hostile or offensive working or academic environment; when submission to or rejection of such conduct by an individual is used as the basis for employment or academic decisions affecting that individual; when submission to such conduct is made either explicitly or implicitly a term or condition of an individual's employment or academic work. (Section 1604.11 of the EEOC's Guidelines on Sex Discrimination)

Examples of conduct that may, if continued or repeated, constitute sexual harassment are unwelcomed sexual propositions; graphic comments about a person's body; sexually suggestive objects or pictures in the work place; sexually degrading words to describe a person; derogatory or sexually explicit statements about an actual or supposed sexual relationship; unwelcomed touching, patting, pinching, or leering; derogatory gender-based humor.

Such conduct, whether intended or not, constitutes sexual harassment and is illegal under both state and federal law. Violations of this policy will not be permitted. Any faculty member, staff, or student who violates this policy will be subject to discipline up to, and including, dismissal.

3. Excerpt from the student handbook of Hope College[4]

The College is committed to fostering an environment in which all persons have an equal opportunity to work and pursue learning freely, whether in group settings or in close relationships between individual students, faculty, and staff. This entails an obligation to protect the dignity, safety, and self-respect of all students, faculty, and staff. As an academic community valuing the moral teaching of Jesus Christ, Hope

---

[3] "Administrative Policies and Regulations" in *University of New Hampshire 1994–1995 Student Rights, Rules and Responsibilities* (University of New Hampshire, July 1994), p. 35.
[4] "Sexual Harassment Policy" in *The 1994–95 Student Handbook*, Hope College, Holland, Michigan, pp. 19–21.

College is committed to the belief that each individual is of unqualified worth. God values each person, male and female, as a unique work of divine creation. Therefore, the College condemns covert and overt acts which interfere with this commitment and will not tolerate any form of intimidation, abuse, or harassment.

Description and Explanation

Sexual harassment is a form of discrimination. It includes any inappropriate or unwanted conduct of a sexual nature which has a negative effect on the educational process, employee benefits, campus climate, or opportunities of any student or employee. [. . . .]

An abuse of privilege or power, sexual harassment can threaten a person's academic status, economic livelihood, sense of safety, well being, and personal dignity. The effects of sexual harassment may include feelings of anger, resentment, embarrassment, humiliation, fear, and lowered self-esteem. [. . . .] Nothing in this policy should be construed to limit the scholarly, educational, or artistic content of written, oral, or other presentations or discussions. Academic freedom should be extended to all members of the academic community. Sexual harassment includes the following categories:

A. Actions Which Create a Hostile Environment

    1. Generalized Sexist Remarks or Sexist Behavior
    This involves demeaning remarks or actions serving no scholarly, artistic, or educational purpose that are directed at individuals or groups because of their gender.

    2. Sexually Offensive Remarks or Behavior
    This includes lewd, obscene, or sexually suggestive remarks or actions serving no scholarly, artistic, or educational purpose, which would be found offensive by a reasonable person in that situation. This category also includes the public display of sexually offensive audio and visual materials serving no scholarly, artistic, or educational purpose.

B. Sexual Advances

    1. Sexual Advances Without Intimidation
    This includes repeated unwanted requests for a social or sexual encounter. It also includes unwanted or inappropriate touching or kissing.

    2. Sexual Advances With Intimidation
    This refers to sexual advances that are accompanied by the threat of punishment or the promise of reward.

C. Sexual Assaults

This includes sexual advances that are accompanied by actual or threatened physical violence. [. . . .] [It] also applies to any of the following, if lacking explicit verbal consent: physical contact with groin, genital area, inner thigh, buttocks, and/or breasts; penetration that involves sexual or anal intercourse; cunnilingus; fellatio; or placing any other object in the genital or anal opening.

Romantic Relationships Between Employee/Student

A. Implicit in the concept of professionalism is the recognition by those in positions of authority that their relationships with students include an element of power. It is incumbent on those with authority not to abuse, or seem to abuse, the power with which they are entrusted. Therefore, the initiation of or consent to a romantic or sexual relationship between an employee of Hope College and any current Hope College student for whom the employee has a direct professional responsibility is unacceptable. [. . . .]

C. The initiation of a romantic or sexual relationship is strongly discouraged even where there is not a direct professional responsibility. In these situations, there may still be an element of power or authority which could diminish the individual's freedom of choice. Additionally, a change in the situation may establish a direct professional responsibility between the individuals. [. . . .] Furthermore, for individuals who enter into a relationship where a power differential exists, it will be difficult to prove immunity on grounds of mutual consent if a complaint alleging sexual harassment is lodged.

D. Such romantic or sexual relationships frequently can have a detrimental effect on other students or employees who share a work or classroom environment with the involved parties. [. . . .]

4. *Excerpt from the policies and procedures handbook of the University of Pennsylvania*[5]

[. . .] For the purposes of this policy, acquaintance rape/sexual violence is defined as any act in which a member of the university community forces another with whom he or she is acquainted to engage in sexual activity against his or her will or without his or her consent. Assent shall not constitute consent if given by a person who because of youth, mental disability or intoxication is unable to make a reasonable judgement concerning the nature or harmfulness of the activity. This policy applies to groups as well as individuals."

[5] "Acquaintance Rape and Sexual Violence Policy" in *The PennBook 1994–95: Policies and Procedures Handbook of the University of Pennsylvania* (Office of the Vice Provost, 1991), p. 38.

ADDITIONAL CASES

Case 6.2: Pregnant!

Lorraine and Tim are sophomores who have been dating for several months when Lorraine finds out that she's pregnant, despite the fact they've been using some contraception. Both are very upset by the news. After thinking long and hard, Tim promises to help support the child and to marry Lorraine. Lorraine, however, has settled on having an abortion. She knows that she isn't ready to be a mother, she wants to finish school, and she doesn't want to marry anyone yet, including Tim. Even though he no longer goes to church, Tim's Catholic childhood rises up to remind him that abortion is a mortal sin. He pleads with Lorraine, but she remains firm through both of their tears.

Questions

1. Please note that this case does not ask you to discuss the morality of abortion. Instead we want to focus on the issues of power involved in this dilemma. Which member of the couple should have the deciding vote about whether or not to terminate the pregnancy, and why? Would your response differ if Lorraine wanted to have the baby and Tim wanted her to get an abortion?

2. Do Lorraine and Tim have an obligation to tell their parents about their predicament? Why or why not? If you believe that they don't, would you change your mind if they were fourteen instead of eighteen years old? Why?

3. If you were counseling Tim and Lorraine, what would you tell them (separately and together) to do?

Case 6.3: Best Buddies

Mark and Demetri have been close friends since the beginning of the semester. Leaving a party late one night, as they stumble drunkenly home together with their arms around each other, Demetri confesses to Mark that he loves him. At first Mark takes Demetri's declaration as an excess of drunken male bonding, but when Demetri stops and looks deeply into his eyes and says, "I really mean it, man, anytime you want . . . ," Mark's stomach turns over. He keeps his voice under control as he asks, "Are you gay or something?" After Demetri's quiet "I think so," Mark wants to run away and throw up. How could he not have realized?! Everyone else probably knows and is talking about them behind his back!

The next day Mark starts shunning Demetri and spreading vicious rumors about his ex-friend. Demetri is crushed by Mark's cruelty and feels lonelier than he ever has in his life. He's also angry with himself for having seen cues in Mark's behavior and body language that apparently weren't there—or did Mark "lead him on" and not have the courage to admit it, even to himself?

Questions

1. What do you think of Mark's reaction? What concerns seem to be motivating him? How would you analyze his behavior in terms of the principles of respect for persons, relationships, and personal growth?

2. If you were Demetri's friend, therapist, or minister, how would you counsel him? Would your advice change, depending on which role you assumed?

3. Can a person "lead someone on" without being really aware of it? If so, should people be held ethically responsible for things they do without being fully conscious of them? (Other examples might be unwittingly hurting a friend's feelings or making a racist or sexist comment without intending any insult.) Another way of asking this is, are we morally responsible for our feelings (whether of love, hate, jealousy, lust, snobbery, and so on) and any "unconscious" behaviors they inspire, or only for acts we have consciously planned?

Case 6.4: Cheating

Nick and Katie have been a couple for two years, and despite some minor fights, they feel firmly committed to each other. They often talk about getting married eventually and have even planned many details of their future life together. One night when Katie went out with her girlfriends, Nick met Olivia at a party. Olivia was very sexy, exotic, temperamental, and rather wild—everything that Katie was not. They began an affair almost at once. Nick knew, even while he was "in lust" with Olivia, that he had no intention of dropping Katie for her. Katie was the person he wanted to marry someday, and Olivia was merely the person with whom he wanted to do unprintable things right now. Therefore he took great care to avoid making Katie suspicious, and he saw Olivia only on the sly, when Katie thought he was studying or out with his friends.

In fact, no one knows Nick's dirty little secret except for Linda and Omar, mutual friends of Nick's and Katie's who saw Nick and Olivia embracing passionately under a tree. Linda and Omar argue about whether or not to tell Katie what's going on. (They don't know Olivia, and they feel no loyalty to her). Omar thinks it's none of their business; perhaps Katie already knows about it and has decided to ignore the affair until it blows over. "We'll just embarrass them both if we tell her what we saw," he says. "And maybe this is something Nick just needs to get out of his system."

Linda disagrees. "He has no right to treat Katie like this! When I see Katie with Nick, I'm sure she doesn't know. And she would never forgive us if she found out that we knew and didn't tell her."

Questions

1. What sort of duty does Nick have to Katie, and to Olivia? If the affair with Olivia doesn't mean much to him compared to his commitment to Katie, is it then less, or more, important for him to be honest with Katie about it?

2. If it turns out that Nick's affair with Olivia is brief and Katie never finds out, is any harm done?

3. How might Nick's character and his relationship with Katie change depending on whether or not he admits his duplicity?

4. Do friends have an obligation to tell friends painful truths, or should their role be only supportive? In other words, is it kinder to tell Katie something she will find painful, or to let her remain in ignorance and support her if and when she finds out? Should Omar and Linda tell Katie what they know?

5. Should they go to Nick, tell him what they saw, and ask him to tell Katie himself if he doesn't want them to? Is it fairer to Nick to approach him directly, or is this a kind of blackmail?

6. Consider the fact that the risk of AIDS (and other sexually transmitted diseases) increases exponentially with every new sexual partner a person has. Does this affect your answers?

7. Would your responses to any of these questions be different if Katie were the one having an affair behind Nick's back? If so, why?

Case 6.5: Dating in the Age of AIDS

After several dates, Cheryl and Ray find themselves in bed together. Ray has a condom in his wallet, but he's embarrassed to bring it out because then, he thinks, Cheryl will know he's been planning on having sex with her, which might insult her. Besides, a condom would really ruin the spontaneity of the moment. For her part, Cheryl has had little sexual experience. She feels shy and uncomfortable about sleeping with Ray, even though she's powerfully attracted to him. Like Ray, she is too embarrassed to mention contraception or safe sex until it's too late. It's almost as if she can tell herself that she isn't having sex (being a slut, as her mother would say) if she doesn't make any preparations for it.

After the deed is done, the two of them lie quietly side by side. Finally Ray works up the courage to say that he really cares about Cheryl and hopes they'll "get together" again, and next time, maybe they should use some contraception. Cheryl agrees, relieved. After a pause (during which she is thinking about pregnancy and AIDS and whether this might be the start of a long-term relationship), Cheryl asks Ray if he's had a lot of girlfriends. Ray knows that Cheryl has had only one boyfriend before him. He doesn't want her to think that he's slept around as much as he has, so he claims to have slept with only two women before her.

He wonders if Cheryl is worried about AIDS. He rationalizes lying to her with the thought that his ten or twelve previous partners "weren't the kinds of girls who get AIDS," although he knows that the risk of AIDS increases with the number of partners one has. "I really should get HIV testing," he thinks to himself. But he says none of this out loud, because he doesn't want to scare Cheryl away.

Questions

1. Ray has begun his relationship with Cheryl with a lie. What repercussions might this act have?
2. Do sexual partners have a moral duty to report honestly on their pasts, no matter how unsavory, or are their past relationships their own business?
3. Do we incur ethical obligations by having sex with someone, even if only once? If so, what kinds of obligations?
4. How might practicing safer sex, getting tested for HIV, and talking together about the results affect Ray and Cheryl's personal growth and the health of their relationship?

Case 6.6: Sexual Harassment I

"Dick Reynolds gives me the creeps!" Helen Wong told her friends. "I try to avoid him, but it's hard, because he's in two of my classes. I think he's been trailing me, and I've caught him spying on me! No matter where I go, he keeps walking up behind me and muttering stuff like 'you turn me on, baby' and making lip-smacking noises, then running away. I'm going to report him. He's such a disgusting, immature jerk!" Helen's friends were sympathetic, but they reminded her that Dick hadn't done anything Helen could officially complain about. Besides, everyone knew he had a "thing" about Asian women, and the other girls he pestered just ignored him.

Then one night Dick exposed himself to Helen while they were both on a deserted floor of the library. After he dropped his pants, he immediately pulled them up again and ran away, but Helen was still scared, embarrassed, and upset for many minutes after the incident. Finally she went downstairs to the pay phones and called one of her roommates to come and walk her home. The next morning she reported Dick's actions to the dean of students, expecting that he would be quickly punished.

Instead it seemed that Helen was the one who was punished. She had to spend many weeks and considerable emotional effort in following up the matter. She had to give humiliating testimony, twice, before a faculty review board. One member even said, "Some women would consider Mr. Reynolds' actions flattering. He never actually touched you or threatened you, so what's the problem?"

Finally the board told her that Dick would be leaving the college. Helen was relieved until she found out that the school hadn't expelled him. Instead the administration had told Dick that if he left voluntarily, nothing would appear on his record and he'd have no trouble applying to another school. Helen also found out where Dick was transferring to, and she decided to write them a warning letter about him . . . It seemed that everyone, from the board to her friends, thought that Helen should drop the matter. "He's been punished enough by having to change schools," they said. "Leave him alone and get on with your life."

Questions

1. Has Dick been punished enough for what he did to Helen (and, perhaps, to other women) by having to transfer?
2. Does the fact that Dick was known to "have a 'thing' about Asian women" make his harassment of Helen less, or more, offensive and actionable? Why?
3. If he never touched or threatened anyone, but did bother women and make some of them feel uncomfortable or scared, is he still guilty of harassment?
4. Can he be accused of sexual harassment if he is a peer of those he bothers, rather than their professor or boss?
5. Does Helen (or her school) have a duty to the unknown members of another college community who might be bothered by Dick, or should she (or the school) let him start over there?

Case 6.7: Sexual Harassment II

Professor Kulbrick is the only professor at Karen's large, impersonal college with whom she has ever had a private conversation, and he gave her her only A last semester. Now that Karen wants to transfer to a smaller school, he seems the logical person to ask for an academic recommendation. However, he sometimes makes her uncomfortable. Once when she'd gone to his office to talk about a paper, he extravagantly flattered her, intellectually and physically, and made a double entendre comment about her "endowment." Karen was embarrassed and didn't talk to him alone again, although she continued to participate actively in his class discussions.

Now, because she wants his recommendation, Karen again finds herself alone with Professor Kulbrick in his office. He says that he would be happy to write a recommendation, but again he embarrasses her. He sits very close to her, touches her arm and leg several times while they talk, and makes a suggestive joke about "uncovering her secret abilities." Finally Karen gets out the door with his promise to write the recommendation.

Six weeks go by, and Professor Kulbrick hasn't written Karen's recommendation. Feeling uncomfortable about seeing him again, Karen calls him to see whether he's forgotten his promise. He assures her that he plans to write the recommendation and suggests that she meet him again so that he can "get more background information." Karen makes excuses for not being able to meet him, but she's feeling anxious—she's counting on his reference, and time has almost run out. She leaves him notes several times to remind him, but nothing seems to happen. Finally Karen mentions the situation to her parents. They are outraged by what they regard as Professor Kulbrick's sexual harassment of their daughter, and Karen's father writes a letter to that effect to the dean.

Two days before the final submission date for all the application materials, Karen calls the professor one last time. He is furious and claims that he never harassed her. "You crazy, sex-starved bitch!" he shouts. "Do you know how much trouble you've gotten me in? You made up all this crap just to entrap me! Your recommendation," he adds nastily, "will be waiting for you with the department secretary, but I doubt it will be much help."

Questions

1. Do you believe that Professor Kulbrick's behavior (prior to the final telephone call) counts as an example of sexual harassment, or was this all a big misunderstanding? If he were genuinely unaware that he was embarrassing Karen, would this matter?
2. Could Karen have handled the situation differently? If so, what should she have done?
3. The professor retaliated by writing a bad recommendation. Is this action sexual harassment, unprofessional in some other way, or an understandable reaction to what he saw as Karen's harassment of him? How might he have better handled the situation?
4. Do you think that if she wanted to pursue the matter, Karen would have enough evidence to be able to win a sexual harassment complaint against Professor Kulbrick? What might the evidence be?
5. Suppose that Karen had offered herself sexually to Professor Kulbrick as a bribe for a good recommendation. What, if anything, is wrong with an exchange of sex for an improved grade or recommendation?
6. Can a student who sexually pursues a professor despite the professor's objections be considered guilty of sexual harassment, or does "harassment" necessarily imply that the harasser has some sort of power over her or his victim?

Case 6.8: *The Affair*

"I can't believe you're having an affair with Professor Woolf!" Suzanne exclaimed to her friend Patsy. But actually, now that the cat was out of the bag, she *could* believe it; with hindsight she could see that there had been signs all semester. She remembered now that Patsy had confessed to having a crush on Professor Woolf when they'd both been in the archaeological field work seminar for only a couple of weeks. Then there were all those times Patsy and the professor seemed to catch each other's eyes during class discussions and talk after class, and Patsy did seem to know a lot of obscure details about cultural anthropology for a junior.

"I've wanted to tell someone for weeks; this whole thing's been like an incredible dream come true!" Patsy gushed. "It's been so hard keeping such a big secret and sneaking around all the time. It started that day Grant and I—"

"'Grant?'"

"You know, Professor Woolf. It started the day he took me out to look at the site by myself. We had this amazing long talk about Mound Builder culture, Indian history, mythology, the supernatural, everything in the universe—and then he told me about how lousy his marriage is, and how he wished he could talk to his wife the way he can talk to me. Then, well, one thing just led to another, as they say," she giggled. "Actually, I'm really flattered that he confides in me; and I'm learning so much from him. He's so sophisticated! And he makes me feel really attractive."

Suzanne thought to herself that of course Professor Woolf found Patsy attractive; stunningly beautiful was more like it. Suzanne was surprised to feel herself growing angry. "Am I jealous?" she wondered. "Shouldn't I be happy for Patsy?" Out loud she asked, "But you said he's married—what about his wife?"

"Oh, he's been very honest with me. He told me he wouldn't leave his wife, and she doesn't suspect anything. But I know how unhappy he is. She doesn't understand him or support him, and he really needs me. We're in love!"

Suzanne didn't know what to say. She couldn't pretend that she shared Patsy's enthusiasm. In fact, she felt betrayed by both Patsy and Professor Woolf, although she couldn't say exactly why. This whole secret relationship just didn't seem fair to her and the rest of the class, or, of course, to Professor Woolf's wife.

Questions

1. If Professor Woolf weren't married, would there be any harm in Patsy's having an affair with him?

2. Patsy seems to be learning a lot from Professor Woolf. What might be the long-term effects of the affair on her intellectual development, emotional life, and character growth?
3. Is there anything wrong with students' and professors' sleeping together? Is a student's having an affair with a teacher ethically different from an employee's sleeping with a boss, or with a May-December romance between any consenting adults? Would it make a difference if Patsy were a graduate student the same age as the professor?
4. What are the effects on the class and the college community of an affair between a student and a professor? Are the other students in the class being harmed?
5. Would it make a difference if Patsy were doing an independent study with Professor Woolf, so that he wasn't grading other students with her?
6. In addition to being a grader, Professor Woolf is also a learning resource for his students. How might his secret affair with one of his students affect the learning of the others? If everyone knew that Patsy and the professor were romantically involved, would there still be a problem?
7. Is a private relationship between Patsy and Professor Woolf Suzanne's business? If so, does her duty lie with her friend, who has confided an important secret to her, to the other students in the class, who don't know about the affair, or to Mrs. Woolf, whom she has never met?
8. What should Suzanne do?

Case 6.9: *First Comes Love, Then Comes Marriage . . .*

Seniors Jerome and Wendy are deeply in love, but they may have to break up with each other. Although they share the same conservative religion, Jerome takes their religion's prohibition against premarital sex much more seriously than Wendy does. He decided years ago that he would remain a virgin until he married, and he's not ready to get married yet (although he may want to marry Wendy eventually).

Wendy thinks it's important for potential life partners to have sex before they commit themselves to each other. She feels that they can't know how compatible they will be in the long term until they have an intimate relationship. She believes that sex is a powerful way to both show their love and increase their intimacy. But Wendy also respects Jerome's feelings about sex; she even finds his devotion to religious duty admirable, if frustrating. However, she cannot promise to wait indefinitely until he feels ready. At this point in her life, she wants to get serious about someone, and for her, "getting serious" means having sex as well as considering marriage. Jerome loves Wendy, understands her reasoning, and doesn't want to lose her, but it's important to him to save sex for his wedding night. As Wendy tearfully asked Jerome, "It seems bizarre to say, 'I love you so much, but I have to look for someone else!' Isn't there some way to save our relationship?"

Questions

1. Do Jerome's views about virginity and sex have merit? That is, should a believer remain faithful to his religious convictions and traditional ideas about sex in a situation like this? Why or why not?
2. If Jerome's desire to remain a virgin until marriage were based on non-religious beliefs or feelings, would it be less defensible?
3. What other arguments might Jerome and Wendy use with each other for and against the idea of sexual abstinence?
4. Using the ethical principles we've discussed throughout this book, what would you advise Wendy and Jerome each to do?

BACKGROUND READING

Joan Blythe, John Boswell, Leon Botstein, William Kerrigan, and Jack Hitt, "Forum: New Rules About Sex on Campus: Should Professors Be Denied Admittance to Students' Beds?" in *Harper's*, September 1993, vol. 287, no. 1720, pp. 33–42.

This is a lively discussion of sexual harassment versus sexual freedom and privacy, carried out by several professors and administrators over dinner. Attitudes range from "students and professors are both adults, and some students only want to lose their virginity to a professor like me," to "a fair amount of data shows a long tradition of abuse of students by professors."

Catherine MacKinnon, *Only Words* (Cambridge, Mass.: Harvard University Press, 1993). This work offers a deliberately shocking and graphic description of the harm done to women by pornography. It argues against giving pornography free speech protection because "social inequality is substantially created and enforced—that is, *done*—through words and images." Similarly, the author defines sexual harassment broadly ("unwelcome sex talk is an unwelcome sex act") and makes legal arguments for punishing verbal as well as physical sexual harassment. She finds that colleges (and workplaces) are sites of confrontation between women's rights and free speech arguments protecting harassment and pornography, because college and the workplace both "crucially enforce inequality and crucially guarantee equality."

Gertrude Himmelfarb, "New Victorians Don't Earn That Label" in *The Wall Street Journal*, 12 January 1994, sec. A, p. 10, col. 3.

The author discusses the use of the word "Victorian" to describe the school of feminism led by Catherine MacKinnon. She critiques feminists who would prohibit pornography, censor "hate speech," punish sexual innuendos on the grounds of sexual harassment, prescribe detailed codes of sexual conduct, make "date rape" as odious an offense as violent rape, and subject offenders to "sensitivity" and "consciousness-raising" sessions.

Karen Lehrman, "Has Sexual Correctness Gone Too Far?" in *USA Today*, 4 April 1994, sec. A, p. 15, col. 2.

> The author explores the deleterious impact that bloating the definitions of "sexual harassment" and "date rape" has on the notions of romance and courtship, particularly in the workplace and on college campuses, as a result of the debate's focus on the extreme rhetoric and policies of "some radical feminists."

Katha Pollitt, "Not Just Bad Sex: a Review of *The Morning After: Sex, Fear, and Feminism on Campus* by Katie Roiphe (Boston: Little, Brown, 1993)," in *The New Yorker*, vol. LXIX, no. 32, pp. 220–224.

> This author also castigates what she sees as the excesses of the movement on campus to control sexual behavior through conduct codes and harassment policies. However, as an avowed feminist, Pollitt has different reasons for opposing this "climate of fear" than does Lehrman.

The ethics of faithfulness and infidelity within a pair-bond are explored in Bonnie Steinbock, "Adultery" in *Report From The Center For Philosophy and Public Policy*, Winter 1986, vol. 6, no. 1, pp. 12–14. *The Report* is available from The Institute for Philosophy and Public Policy, School of Public Affairs, University of Maryland, College Park, MD 20742, (301) 405-4759.

ADDITIONAL MATERIALS

1. Richard Bernstein, "Guilty If Charged," in *The New York Times Review of Books*, 13 January 1994, vol. xli, nos. 1 and 2, pp. 11–14; Jeremy Rabkin, "Rule of Law: New Checks on Campus Sexual-Harassment Cops," in *The Wall Street Journal*, 19 October 1994, sec. A, p. 21, col. 3; Anthony Lewis, "Time To Grow Up," in *The New York Times*, 14 October 1994, sec. A, p. 35, col. 1; and Joanne Jacobs, "College Professors Are Compelled to Tiptoe Around Student Sensitivities," in *The Atlanta Journal*, 5 October 1994, sec. A, p. 8, col. 1.

J. Donald Silva, a tenured English professor at the University of New Hampshire, was found guilty of sexual harassment in 1993 and severely punished. He was suspended from his job without pay for "at least one year," ordered to undergo a year of "weekly counseling sessions" with a "professional psychotherapist approved by the university," to "reimburse the university $2000 to cover the cost of setting up an alternative section of his course," and to "apologize, in writing, for creating a hostile and offensive academic environment." What had he done? (a) In class, he said that "belly dancing is like jello on a plate with a vibrator under the plate" as an example of a simile. (b) He explained the concept of "focus" by comparing it to sex ("you zero in on the subject . . . you move from side to side . . . you bracket the subject and center on it . . . you and the subject become one"). (c) When a female student said, "I guess I'll jump on a computer before someone else does," he replied "I'd like to see that!" (d) When he saw a student at the library, pulling out a card index on her hands and knees, he joked that "you look like you've had a lot of experience on your knees."

Do you think these are examples of sexual harassment? Do you agree with the University of New Hampshire's definition of sexual harassment (above under "Examples of College and University Codes Governing Sexual Behavior")? What role might generational differences (Silva was late middle-aged; his students were young) play in perceptions of sexual harassment? Is mandatory psychotherapy an appropriate punishment for convicted harassers?

2. Laura Miller, "May I Touch You There?" in *The San Francisco Examiner,* 19 December 1993, pp. D1–D4; Comment: "Different Strokes" in *The New Yorker,* 29 November 1993, vol. LXIX, no. 40, pp. 8–10; and Edward Felsenthal, "Campus Dilemma: The Risk of Lawsuits Disheartens Colleges Fighting Date Rape" in *The Wall Street Journal,* 12 April 1994, sec. A, p. 1, col. 1.

Antioch College's Sexual Offense Policy (see above under "Examples of College and University Codes Governing Sexual Behavior") has become notorious recently. Is the policy an unwarranted intrusion into private life or a legitimate and helpful way to prevent the crime of date rape? Does the view of sex implicit in the policy make women into automatic victims? If so, could this attitude be harmful to women, or to men? How? What other implications might such a policy have?

3. How big a problem is (date) rape on campus? Different sources disagree. Some claim that one-fifth of all college women are victims of date and acquaintance rape and one-quarter experience either attempted or completed forced sex: Carol Bohmer and Andrea Parrot, *Sexual Assault on Campus: The Problem and the Solution* (NY: Lexington Books, 1993), p. 26. These sources describe the "typical" victim of a college sexual assault as a female freshman who has been drinking alcohol, especially during a frat party drinking game; she is unlikely to report the rape to the police or even to the college administration (ibid., p. 19). Fraternity pledges are the students "most likely to rape in college." Fraternity members in general and basketball and football players at NCAA colleges are significantly more likely to assault women sexually in college than are male members of student government or students not affiliated with other organizations (ibid., p. 21). Other sources say the estimate that 20–25 percent of women are victims of sexual assaults in college is inflated; few rapes are reported at least partly because women don't consider what happened to them "rape," and if they don't know they've been raped, it isn't rape (Neil Gilbert, quoted in M. Collison, "A Berkeley Scholar Clashes With Feminists Over the Validity of Their Research on Date Rape," in *The Chronicle of Higher Education,* 26 February 1992, vol. 38, no. 25, pp. A35, A37).

Looking at these figures in the context of the debate about date rape (see "Background Reading" above), what might be some of the problems involved in collecting accurate rape statistics? Should the actual number of campus rapes affect rape-deterrence policies? Aside from sexual conduct codes and anti-harassment policies, what can colleges and students do to help prevent (date) rape? Which methods seem the fairest to all involved, and why? What aspects of fraternity life might support a climate in which rape is tolerated or even encouraged? What can women do to protect themselves from rape? For more information, see Bill Hendrick, "Rape a Big Problem for Freshman Women" in *The Atlanta Constitution*, 18 May 1994, sec. A, p. 9, col. 1.; Bill Brubaker, "NCAA Intensifying Effort to Educate Athletes on Issues of Sexual Responsibility" in *The Washington Post*, 13 November 1994, sec. A, p. 24, col. 1; and Bohmer and Parrot, *Sexual Assault on Campus*.

4. Tamar Lewis, "If Flames Singe, Who is to Blame?" in *The New York Times*, 25 September 1994, sec. 4, p. 3, col. 4; and Tamar Lewis, "Dispute Over Computer Messages: Free Speech or Sex Harassment?" in *The New York Times*, 22 September 1994, sec. A, p. 1, col. 1.

Several students at Santa Rosa Junior College in California recently complained about a computer network "flame" (an insulting message) that they considered sexually harassing. Can someone be sexually harassed via computer, rather than in person? How should computer users respond to sexually harassing (or racially intolerant, or otherwise offensive) messages on line? How much responsibility should computer networks take for potentially offensive words posted on their bulletin boards? How might colleges try to balance computer users' freedom of speech with their right not to be intimidated or harassed?

5. "Date Rape and a List at Brown" in *The New York Times*, 18 November 1990, p. 26; and Bohmer and Parrot, *Sexual Assault on Campus*, p. 13.

A number of female students at Brown University believed that the University didn't take complaints of rape seriously, so they made a list of male students whom they claimed had raped them and wrote it on the bathroom walls to warn other women on campus. What consequences might such a list have for the rape victims and their assailants? Would you expect such a measure to be effective in preventing further rapes? What if a man's name was put on the list by mistake, or because of rumor, or because a woman wanted to "get him" for a reason unrelated to sexual assault? What are the ethics of taking matters into your own hands, bypassing official channels for punishing suspected rapists or other criminals?

6. Acquaintance rape has been the subject of a powerful motion picture (*The Accused* (1988), starring Jodie Foster, who won an Academy Award for her performance), and a made-for-TV documentary that focused on date rape on college campuses ("Against Her Will" (1989) narrated by Kelly McGillis on Lifetime cable network). Compare these or other depictions of date rape;

analyze how the moviemakers assign blame for the rape and its aftermath and the solutions they suggest. To what ethical principles do they seem to appeal? How is the victim "supposed" to act? You might contrast these recent portrayals with older images of acquaintance rape, such as a 1979 portrayal on the soap opera *General Hospital.* Luke raped Laura, and Laura left her husband to marry him (cited in Bohmer and Parrot, *Sexual Assault on Campus*). How has public opinion about date rape, at least as reflected in television and the movies, changed?

7. Andre Dubus, "Townies," *Finding a Girl in America* (Boston: David Godine Publisher, 1980), p. 37. In this short story, Dubus paints a disturbing portrait of college acquaintance rape (and in this case, murder) from the assailant's point of view. He seems to suggest that class differences help explain such violence. Do you accept this explanation? Might class or gender differences contribute to a communication gap that results in date rape, or does this type of reasoning remove individual responsibility?

7

DRINKING AND LIVING
THE GOOD LIFE

Case 7.1: The Drinking Survey

George Parker, a senior at Bacchus University, always had a perverse interest in drinking. After all, it was a major factor in his life. His father's alcoholism had broken up his family, impoverished him and his mother, and made his teenage years unstable and unhappy. Maybe he'd overreacted to his dad's drinking, but George hadn't had so much as a beer since he was fifteen. He was a compulsive nondrinker.

Perhaps his experience and attitudes also explained the direction George's job had taken. George was an undergraduate dorm counselor for a freshman and sophomore dorm. He quickly learned that his charges' drinking behavior heavily influenced his job. Alcohol seemed to be behind a significant number of the fights he had to deal with, as well as his occasional trips to the college clinic with an injured or ill person. Just last week he had to call security to provide a ride for a student who had broken his leg in a drunken fall.

These experiences led George to investigate undergraduate drinking for a term paper on the topic of why people drink. The dean of students encouraged his study and agreed to consider it part of George's paid work. George first tried to gather some data on alcohol-related incidents on campus. He interviewed a number of other undergraduate counselors, combed the campus and local newspapers, and interviewed people at the clinic as well as at campus security. Following are some of his findings:

- Campus security estimated that they received ten to fifteen alcohol-related calls a week, involving automobile accidents, fights or disturbances of the peace, or illnesses or injuries. One officer described these calls as "probably the tip of the iceberg." Most incidents, she assumed, either were not reported or were handled by someone else.

- The health clinic similarly saw a steady flow of alcohol-related illness and injury. Most of these were not serious: sprains, abrasions, and contusions. However, the clinic had dealt with several potentially life-threatening incidents, in which students needed to be revived after a binge with the bottle.
- Most of the incidents occurred on weekends. Bacchus University was a fairly demanding place; most students worked hard at their studies during the week. Those who partied continuously or who had serious alcoholism problems usually didn't last to become sophomores.
- The local papers provided a sample of alcohol-related incidents from the past few years:

  — One student died while trying to walk on top of a five-foot brick wall. He fractured his skull when he fell.
  — A second student died after being induced to drink nearly a liter of vodka at a fraternity initiation.
  — A third student nearly died of asphyxiation after being painted green from head to toe by a group of partiers who, after consuming more than a case of beer, decided that this would be a cool way to celebrate St. Patrick's Day.
  — One student appeared to have eased her path to suicide by washing down a bottle of sleeping pills with a large quantity of wine.

These findings suggested that many students abused alcohol. However, Bacchus University had more than twenty thousand students. George supposed that a majority of them drank, but few had these kinds of problems. George himself often went out for a beer with friends (even though he had a soft drink), and there were never any incidents. He decided to conduct a survey of undergraduates. He rounded up a group of students to serve as his sample and asked them three questions. (1) Do you drink? (2) When, where, and how much do you drink? (3) What are your reasons for drinking or not drinking?

In answer to the first question, George found that a majority of students drank. Underage students were only slightly less likely to drink than were older students.

Students tended to drink largely on weekends. Although a few might have a beer before going to bed, most drank while partying with their friends. Some students drank with their friends at bars, but most partied with friends at fraternity or sorority houses or in their dorms or apartments. When students drank, they drank a lot, averaging five or six drinks. A great number seemed to go on drinking binges.

Following are some of the reasons they gave for drinking:

- It's cool.
- To get drunk. I like being trashed.
- There's nothing else to do on weekends.
- It helps me escape the tension of this place.
- Everybody drinks. If you don't, you're a tool.
- It helps me have fun with my friends. It helps us let go.
- It helps me get into the music.
- It helps free me up.

George was a bit surprised at the absence of a few reasons. No students said that they enjoyed the taste of what they drank, or that drinking enhanced the taste of food. Although some students said that drinking helped them have fun with their friends, they seemed to mean either that they enjoyed having someone with whom to get drunk or that it helped them to be more uninhibited. They were willing to do some things when they were drinking that they wouldn't do when they were not. But no one said that it made conversation better or improved his or her sociability.

George had expected mostly answers like these, but the more he thought about them, the more puzzled he became. None of these reasons for and against drinking seemed very convincing to him. For example, what does "cool" really mean? Why should the fact that lots of other people do something be much of a reason to do it yourself? Some of the reasons were escapist: people wanted to escape boredom, stress, or their inhibitions. But why would you want to lose your inhibitions? Is losing them a good thing? Having fun or enjoying music seemed more like good reasons to George, but he noticed that the students didn't seem able to define what was fun about their actions when they drank. And how does drinking help you enjoy music?

The few nondrinking students said that they avoided alcohol because:

- Drinking makes people act like jerks.
- I resent the peer pressure to drink.
- I can entertain myself just fine without drinking.
- I like to be in control, and drinking makes me lose control.
- Someone could take advantage of me sexually if I drank.
- I hate the taste.

George was surprised at the nondrinkers' resentment about the topic. The loosening of inhibitions, which motivated some people to drink, was viewed by nondrinkers as a very important reason for not drinking. Was it all really about self-control?

In search of more satisfying reasons for drinking (or not drinking), George went to talk to Dr. Bates, the instructor of a wine-tasting course. This class was one of the most popular at Bacchus, and every semester the university had to have a lottery to see who would be able to take it. He asked the instructor what she was trying to accomplish. She responded that she tried to enhance the appreciation of experience. "Drinking wine is like any other experience. You have to learn to appreciate what's good. You learn to appreciate good music or good art by learning to see and to hear more discriminatingly. This is true for food and drink, too. Good food and good wine are characterized by complex and subtle tastes. You need to learn to experience them."

For George this was a new thought: you have to learn to enjoy good things. He had always assumed that you liked what you liked and that was all there was to it. But Dr. Bates clearly had a different view. "Taste," she said paradoxically, "is not a matter of taste."

Regardless of whether Dr. Bates was right, George thought that this was the kind of insight about drinking he had been looking for when he'd conducted his survey and interviews. Dr. Bates had a view of how wine fit into the picture of a good life. That's what George had missed in his list of reasons for or against drinking. Only a few of those he'd talked with seemed to have an idea of how drinking could enhance experience. Was that the right question? George wrote in his notes, "So is there a difference between a hedonist and an epicurean?" and congratulated himself on having remembered something from his philosophy class.

Questions

1. Many conversations about drinking seem to emphasize the "bads" of drinking. Certainly there are some, often associated with injury or disease. As the label on any beer bottle will tell you, drinking can harm a fetus and impair one's ability to drive or operate machinery. Addiction is also a "bad." We haven't said much about these negative aspects because we suspect you've heard them all before. Are there other, less often discussed, "bads" to drinking? What might these be?
2. Do these same concerns apply to the use of other drugs?
3. Underage students often find ways to drink. They are frequently helped by older students. Should students be concerned about obeying the law simply because it is the law, or more because they might get caught? Why?

4. In his dialogue "Socrates' Defense (Crito)," Plato describes Socrates as willing to die rather than violate the law of Athens, even though Socrates could escape and believed that he had been unjustly condemned to death. Socrates says that the laws have nurtured and protected him, so he will obey them to the bitter end. Is there anything to be said for Socrates' view?

5. Discussions of drinking, at least the kinds that schools promote, often emphasize the bads rather than the goods of drinking. What are the goods?

6. Have we covered the kinds of reasons you or your friends might have for drinking? What have we left out?

7. Dr. Bates expressed a particular view of what makes drinking wine a good. Would Dr. Bates criticize the kinds of reasons the students gave in George's survey? If so, how might she criticize their reasons or their way of drinking?

8. Estimates of the harm done as a consequence of drinking are always enormous. They include thousands of deaths every year, and the loss of billions of dollars from employee accidents, absenteeism, and poor on-the-job performance. Thousands of families are destroyed through addiction. Are there goods that outweigh these bads?

9. Why not have prohibition? Why was Prohibition (the Eighteenth Amendment to the Constitution, which lasted from 1920–1933) repealed? Are there issues of personal freedom involved? What are they?

10. If you use alcohol, how would you describe your drinking pattern? Is it what you want? If not, what could you do about it?

11. One point of disagreement in the case involves the issue of self-control or loss of inhibition. Is loss of inhibition a good thing or not?

12. When something is described as "cool," what kind of reason for doing it is implied?

ISSUES

As you might guess, we could discuss a large number of issues in connection with drinking. We might talk about how drinking affects *relationships*. We might talk about how drinking affects one's health or sense of well-being. Such a discussion might look at drinking from the perspective of *benefit maximization*. These are worthy and important topics, but we suspect that you have heard much about them. Instead we want to address some different questions, which might seem less familiar. The first one has to do with the issue of self-control. Curiously, there seem to be two quite different perspectives here. Some people think that alcohol liberates them from their inhibitions, and they describe this as being "freed up." Others view the relaxation of inhibitions as a loss of self-control and, perhaps, a loss of freedom. They tend to believe that the removal of inhibition puts them under the control of dangerous forces within themselves that should stay suppressed.

A second issue concerns the way alcohol fits into the quality of life, specifically, how it can enhance or detract from our enjoyment of experience.

A third issue, and one that seems intertwined with the first two, has to do with the idea of moderation. Some philosophers (for instance Aristotle, from whom many of the ideas in this chapter derive) have argued that good living depends largely on our ability to discover a middle ground between extremes. For example, we might think of the virtue of courage as a middle position between foolhardiness and cowardliness. Moderation, or finding a middle way between self-denial and overindulgence, might be a helpful way to think about the use of alcohol.

We hope you have noticed that these issues have to do with much more than drinking. In fact, we think that considerations about self-control, quality of life, and moderation apply broadly to a wide range of activities, from child rearing to sports. They are among the issues that you will need to consider when you reflect on what constitutes a good life for you. (Some additional questions are posed in Chapter 8.) Also, each topic has something to say about what we have called the principle of *character growth*. We want to encourage you to take a long view of your life. We don't mean by this that you need to plan your life in detail right now. Rather, we want to remind you that your choices and actions today help form your future character and personality. Many people delude themselves into believing that they can always change if they want to, can always be more honest, kind, brave, selfless tomorrow, when it's important. However, as we noted in Chapter 1, dishonest (or cruel, or cowardly, or selfish) choices harm not only others, but also the chooser, by building an unethical character.

You might think of this as an issue of freedom. Certain choices can make us into the kinds of people who are less free to choose in different ways. The use of potentially addictive substances such as hard drugs, alcohol, or tobacco can provide graphic illustrations of this point. Someone who chooses to smoke often and regularly becomes less free to choose not to smoke. But these habits are also misleading examples because of the physiological mechanisms behind addiction. Dishonesty is not an addiction in the same way. Nevertheless, it may be harder for the habitually dishonest person to choose honesty.

One way to think about our discussion in this chapter is that it broadens the range of ways to apply the principle of *character growth*. The idea that in acting you choose the person you are to become turns out to apply not only to whether you will become honest or kind, but also to whether you will become someone with good taste and developed sensibilities, someone who can enjoy or appreciate what's worthwhile. The basic idea is the same. When you choose, you should always keep in mind that you are also choosing to be a certain kind of person.

Autonomy and Self Control

Among the reasons students gave for drinking was that drinking was "cool" and that nondrinkers were "tools" or "dorks." These are curious reasons. What does it really mean to be "cool" or "dorky"? We suspect that these terms mean virtually nothing beyond vague approval or disapproval. How can they be reasons?

Other words, such as "good," may be similarly vague. If I say "That's a good movie," my comment won't tell you much more than that I liked it, unless we also agree about what makes a movie good. Perhaps, then, when we hear a reason that suggests little beyond approval or disapproval, we should ask, "Do I know what that person means by 'cool,' 'dorky,' and so on, and do I agree?"

Why care? We can suggest two related reasons. First, it is difficult to evaluate words that merely indicate approval or disapproval unless you understand *the reasons for* the approval or disapproval of the behavior or person. Second, we suspect that such words are often used to manipulate people. Perhaps they convey a pleasant or desirable feeling while also preventing you from questioning that feeling. Perhaps they convey an image. Perhaps they are a vehicle of social pressure or peer pressure. (Note how often vague, approving words like "cool," "excellent," "improved," and "new" are used in advertising.)

Following are some questions you might ask when someone gives you a reason containing such a word:

1. Do I understand exactly what the word means? How can I tell when it is used accurately?
2. If I can tell exactly what the word implies, does it seem like a good reason for the behavior or the purchase of the product it describes? Do I agree with it? Why?
3. If I can't tell whether or not the word is being used accurately, how does the word influence me? Does it make me want to buy or do something I would not otherwise have wanted? Such words might suggest that:

> I will be part of a group to which I want to belong.
> I will be popular or attractive.
> People who don't go along will be undesirable.

Not only can others use language of this sort to manipulate us, but we can also use it on ourselves. All of us sometimes have to confront arguments or evidence that we don't want to consider. We can dismiss such arguments with vague vocabulary that allows us to reject a claim without considering it. For example, saying a person (or position) is "really out of it" dismisses them as unworthy of consideration. Does such dismissive language have a role in our moral reflection? After all, we can't consider every claim and every claimant. Do we sometimes use such language because we are afraid to examine ourselves or our conduct?

Notice that these questions imply that you should have reasons for what you do, and be able to discuss your reasons. These questions also assume that it is bad to be manipulated, and good to be independent or autonomous in your decision making. Do you agree? Might these commitments to rationality and autonomy interfere with spontaneity, doing the will of God, or being deeply committed to a community? Is autonomy linked to some of the moral principles we have discussed, for example respect for persons, but inconsistent with others, such as community? Are there times when we should relinquish our autonomy in order to belong? (Question: How might you reconsider some of the issues in Chapter 5 in light of these questions?)

Another set of reasons for drinking involves self-control. Some of the students George surveyed said that they drank to lower their inhibitions or free themselves up. Others viewed drinking as a kind of social lubricant—something that eases conversation or makes social situations more comfortable. On the other hand, some associated drinking with a worrisome loss of self-control. We want to develop these ideas a little by sketching two positions that we call "Plato's story" and "Freud's story" (although Plato or Freud might not have agreed with everything we put into their mouths).

Plato's Story

Plato (427–347 B.C.) described three parts of the soul: a rational part, a spiritual part, and the appetites. For him, a life was well ordered when reason ruled over the other aspects of human nature. Plato wasn't arguing that either our spiritual sides or our appetites should be suppressed. He did not want a life devoid of enthusiasm or full of self-denial. There is no evidence that he objected to drinking, and much to suggest that he enjoyed it. His point is rather that reason should be in charge. Students who worry about losing control when they drink seem to be expressing a similar idea. They may be suggesting that when they drink, reason no longer rules their conduct.

Freud's Story

Freud (1856–1939) believed that we often repress many of our wants and desires, meaning that although we have them, we are not consciously aware of them. Not only that, but in some sense we are also responsible for the fact that we are unaware of them. We have hidden them from ourselves, or we refuse to admit to them. Freud thought that one reason we repress some of our desires is that we strongly disapprove of them. We cannot simultaneously think of ourselves as good people, or be the kinds of people our parents want us to be, and admit to ourselves that we have evil desires. Thus we repress them and make them unconscious.

For Freud repression is an ambiguous thing. Perhaps we should repress some things, such as a death wish or the desire to have sex with our parents. On the other hand, our repressed desires often find subtle ways to express themselves; too much repression can lead to neurotic or even psychotic behavior. Some of Freud's followers and popularizers saw repression as an unmitigated evil, perhaps because they had more optimistic views of human nature than Freud did. They thought that people needed to be freed from the constraints of social convention to express their true natures and desires. (The aesthete we described in Chapter 6 seemed to think this way about sex.)

Thus Freud's and Plato's stories seem to offer different advice about ridding ourselves of inhibitions. Does losing inhibitions mean silencing the voice of reason and giving reign to dangerous uncontrolled passions, as Plato would say? Or might it mean ridding ourselves of burdensome social conventions and becoming able to express our true selves, as some Freudians suggest? Students who drink to become freer seem to be telling themselves a version of Freud's story. They may feel that sometimes they can't act the way they want to because they are "too hung up." Perhaps using alcohol to get rid of "hang-ups" such as shyness, insecurity, or an oppressive sense of social conventions frees us to be who we really are, or to do what we genuinely want to do. People who claim that drinking helps to improve conversation or to have more fun at a party may be saying something like this.

Are these stories compatible? Might one be true in some cases and the other in other cases? How can we tell?

Recall again the two previous cases from Chapters 3 and 6 that involved excessive drinking. In both cases, people did something when drunk that they would not have done sober. In "Hate Speech" in Chapter 3, Percy yelled racial insults when he was drunk; in "Seduction or Rape?" in Chapter 6, Susan had sex with Peter when she'd drunk too much. What story would Freud tell about these activities? He might suggest that Percy and Susan did what they really wanted to do, or that their behavior reflected their true (unconscious) natures.

If we agree, we probably also have to accept the following: First, our true nature comes out only when we lose our inhibitions; our unconscious desires are what we really want to do. Second, it is good to do what we really want to do and to express our true, or unconscious, natures. Finally, inhibitions are bad because they prevent us from doing what we really want to do or from expressing our natures. Do you agree?

We suspect that Percy would not agree, at least in the case of hate speech. He may have gotten drunk and behaved in a racist way, but he probably wants to deny that his "true nature" is racist. He might ask, "Why assume that what I do when I'm drunk is a better indication of what I'm really like than what I do when I am sober and can make decisions reflectively, in full control of myself? Maybe there is a part of me that is racist, but that is a part of me that I want to keep in check."

Remember that Peter's excuse in his seduction of Susan was that she really (unconsciously) wanted sex with him. Peter might claim that he helped Susan kick her sexually repressed hang-ups. Getting her drunk helped her to express her sexuality without those hang-ups; thus he did Susan a favor by liberating her from her inhibitions.

We don't think that Freud's story is very plausible in these cases. If we drink and then do something we wouldn't otherwise do, it may be true that some part of us wanted to do it. It does not, however, follow that this is what we "really" wanted to do or that it expresses our true natures. Why should we treat these unreflective urges or desires as more real or more truly "us" than what we choose to do or to be when we reflect about our conduct? Aren't our reflective judgments also a real part of who we are? Even if our unreflective urges are somehow more basic to us, it is unclear that it is always a good thing to act on them.

When we call something a "hang-up" we seem to mean that it is an undesirable or unreasonable restraint on what we wish to do. A clear example might be a phobia. One of us has a fear of heights that makes walking near steep drop-offs difficult. Because he is also an enthusiastic hiker who frequently finds himself in such positions, he finds this "hang-up" both irrational and frustrating. That's the nature of hang-ups; they are unreasonable and we don't choose them. People often label most restraints "hang-ups," especially when others' inhibitions are inconvenient for them, as Peter did in "Seduction or Rape?" But are inhibitions against promiscuous sex or racist speech "hang-ups"? Perhaps instead they are reasonable restraints on our conduct, on the way we wish to behave, on reflection.

We are not suggesting that Freud's story is always wrong, even about drinking. Suppose that instead of looking at cases of racist speech or seduction, we consider the claim that drinking helps make socializing freer and easier. Is this implausible? Our conversation with others may very well be restrained by "hang-ups." Maybe we're overly concerned that others will find us foolish or stupid; perhaps we automatically feel embarrassed or tentative in social situations. It may well be that a moderate amount of alcohol can reduce these restraints. Are there other cases in which removing inhibitions may be desirable?

Thus while the "Hate Speech" and "Seduction or Rape?" cases seem to point to Plato's story, there is something to say for Freud's story as well. How to decide which story to tell when? We suggest that you ask these questions:

1. On sober reflection, is the way I act when alcohol has dissolved my inhibitions the way I want to act?
2. If someone else behaved the way I do when my inhibitions are dissolved by alcohol, would I like their behavior, especially if I were its recipient?

The first question suggests that while we think that Freud's story has a point, we think that Plato's story is more important here. You should decide, when your judgment isn't affected by alcohol, how you wish to behave when you drink. The second question is the Golden Rule rephrased for drinking. It reminds us that the way we wish to behave when drinking should take into account the rights and welfare of others.

Another observation we might make about George's discoveries of people's reasons for drinking is the noticeable difference between the students' reasons and the view of drinking held by the instructor of the wine tasting course, Dr. Bates. The principal goal of Dr. Bates's course was the development of a refined taste for wine. George's question to himself about the difference between a hedonist and an epicurean expressed this view as well.

Many philosophers who believe that pleasure or happiness is the ultimate good also hold two additional ideas. One is that what we might call the "higher" pleasures are better, more enjoyable, than "baser" pleasures. The second is that one has to learn to enjoy the higher pleasures. John Stuart Mill says this succinctly on page 410 of *The Utilitarians.*

> *"It is better to be a human being dissatisfied than a pig satisfied; better to be a Socrates dissatisfied than a fool satisfied. And if the fool, or the pig, are of a different opinion, it is because they only know their own side of the question. The other side of the comparison knows both sides."*

Let's consider an example of this philosophy. Suppose we imagine a conversation between Dr. Bates and an undergraduate named Charlie.

Charlie: You know, Dr. Bates, I really like getting ripped. I feel great when I'm blitzed.

Dr. Bates: I can understand that. I've felt high a few times; but you really don't understand what it's all about until you have a chance to enjoy a good Chardonnay with a well-prepared seafood dinner.

Charlie: That doesn't really do it for me, Dr. Bates. I've had wine before, but a glass or two with a meal doesn't give me anything like the good feeling a buzz does.

Dr. Bates: That's because you haven't yet developed the capacity to appreciate fine wine. You need to learn what to look for. That's what I can teach you in my class.

Charlie: No thanks. Why should I want to learn to appreciate something I don't care about now? Why is what you like better than what I like? Aren't you being elitist?

Dr. Bates: Maybe I am, Charlie. But I know that enjoying a good wine is better than a good buzz, because I've had both experiences. You know how to use alcohol only to get high; you haven't learned to appreciate good wine, so you can't judge which feels better.

Charlie: Maybe not; but I still have the right to like what I like.

It isn't easy to say who's right. We'd like to make the case for Mill and Dr. Bates, but first we need to emphasize that we do agree with Charlie that he has the right to like whatever he wants to like. Even when he might be better off if he liked something else, or when this something else, whatever it might be, is genuinely better than what he likes, Charlie should not be coerced. We can only try to persuade him to change his mind.

Mill and Dr. Bates argue for the superiority of "higher pleasures," which result from activities or experiences that require a significant degree of learning to appreciate. Let's consider two examples by comparing chess with tic-tac-toe, and a good wine with a sweet soft drink. Wine and chess have a number of characteristics that soft drinks or tic-tac-toe lack: they are complex and varied, and their potential for novelty is not easily exhausted. Thus they can maintain our interest. Another significant feature is that they both engage and develop our capacities. Playing chess or enjoying a good wine requires that we develop skill, judgment, and discernment. We grow and learn. We become better (more skilled, sophisticated, interesting, and interested) people. And as we do, these activities allow us to express the increased capacities they have helped us acquire.

Often more complex activities are also occasions for forming desirable human relationships. When we have learned a complex activity, we often enjoy discussing it or participating in it with others. Thus such activities often form the basis of friendships and help us to enjoy the company of other people. Consider this point in connection with the principles of *relationship* and *community*, and contrast it with getting drunk, which, even when done with other people, tends to be an isolating and solitary experience.

We have used chess and enjoying wine as examples of higher pleasures, but many other kinds of activities, such as sports, crafts, and making music have similar characteristics. Although there is something cognitive about all of these activities, "higher pleasures" need not be primarily contemplative or intellectual. Someone who can visualize the whole floor in basketball or who can see a beautiful sweater in a pile of yarn has acquired an enhanced capacity for experience much like that of someone who can read the situation in a game of chess or evaluate the nuances of wine. Similarly, making a good pass or a beautiful sweater are as much forms of self-expression as is making a good move in a chess game. When we say that there is something cognitive about these activities, we mean that they involve judgment, discernment, and a sophisticated way of seeing, not that they are passive or merely intellectual.

The fact that these enjoyments depend on judgment, discernment, and a special way of seeing also explains why they depend on learning. As anyone who's watched small children knows, we don't need to learn to enjoy sweet tastes. Similarly, there is little we need to learn to play tic-tac-toe.

This leads to Mill's and Dr. Bates's second point. How do we know that the "higher pleasures" are more enjoyable? It seems the only way to know that something is enjoyable is to note that people enjoy it. We must consult others' experience. However, Mill and Dr. Bates also want to say that not everyone's experience counts equally. They reason that without having acquired the right kinds of capacities, we cannot have or appreciate some kinds of experiences. These kinds of pleasures are learning-dependent. They conclude that when we compare the pleasure of different kinds of activities or experiences, we must consult those who have acquired the capacity to enjoy both. Only they are in a position to make a fair comparison. And Mill and Dr. Bates are confident that, given such a comparison, people prefer the higher pleasures.

Are they right? We suggest that you consult your own experience, but that you do so with their perspective in mind. Are there things you have learned to like? Are there things you like that have been enhanced by learning about them? Are there things you like that are dependent on learning? How do they compare with other things you enjoy?

Are there things you enjoy that do not depend on learning? We enjoy bicycling, hiking, spending time with our families, canoeing, dancing, gardening, drawing, karate, and singing. Do all of these things qualify as "higher pleasures"? Perhaps not. For some of these activities, enjoyment seems to come mainly from the exercise, relaxation, solitude, or excitement involved. Yet people who enjoy bicycling, for instance, often find the activity enhanced by learning about riding techniques or studying bike components. Hiking is more fun when you learn about the plants and animals you might encounter. Singing is more pleasurable when you learn to control your voice and notice musical subtleties. The urge to infuse our activities with cognitive elements and with the opportunity to display skills seems strong.

Moderation

People are often advised to use alcohol in moderation. No doubt this is good advice, but what does it mean? And why should we be moderate?

Moderation is often taken to mean "restraining pleasure." It might seem an old person's virtue, suitable only for someone who lacks the energy or drive to pursue life with gusto—to have it all, now. However, perhaps to enjoy life fully and have real freedom, moderation is important. We will now explore this idea further.

The word "moderation" is sometimes used as an adverb, as in "drink in moderation," and sometimes as a noun. As a noun, "moderation" is one of the character traits that used to be called "virtues": traits such as honesty, charity, fairness, and courage. Virtues are positive behavioral patterns that become habitual, part of one's nature. (Similar, negative, behavior patterns are labelled "vices.") They may also be thought of as excellent characteristics that, when present, make something a praiseworthy example of its kind. Just as strength and flexibility are excellent characteristics in a piece of steel, moderation, courage, charity, and fairness are excellent characteristics (or virtues) in human beings.

Many philosophers have argued that various virtues are essential to leading a life that is fulfilling, enjoyable, or satisfying. One reason is that virtues such as honesty enable people to pursue various worthwhile goals in association with others. They believe that many of the most important goals are social, in the same way that singing in a choir is social, and that they cannot be pursued apart from those virtues that assure mutually satisfying cooperation. It has also been argued that people who fail to acquire virtues, or who acquire vices, harm not only others, but also themselves. They argue that people who are greedy damage themselves in their pursuit of material things even if they succeed. Is this true? How might you argue for this?

One argument is that greedy people, like people with other vices, are ruled by their wants and needs. No matter how much they have, they want more; thus, even when they get what they want, they cannot be happy, because they never have enough. However, people who moderate their desires can be satisfied. Do you agree? Does this reasoning apply to other virtues and vices?

Moderation can also be seen as a capacity for avoiding the extremes of overindulgence or unreasonable self-denial in seeking enjoyment or pleasure. Both extremes interfere with leading a good life. Overindulgence eventually debases pleasure, and we become sated. Either we can no longer enjoy the experience at all, because it has become boring, or we must seek a particular pleasure in increasingly larger amounts or in more extreme forms. Overindulgent people end up going to great extremes to find any pleasure at all, rather as the addict requires ever more of a drug to get even a maintenance high. Ultimately over-indulgers find that they can't enjoy anything at all; they might even find themselves enslaved to something that no longer gives them any pleasure.

Those who practice excessive self-denial, in contrast, seem to reject out of hand the idea that a good life involves the enjoyment of experience. They lose the ability to appreciate even simple pleasures or the beauty around them. They, too, seem to have unreasonably diminished the worth of their lives. (Question: Does this sense of diminishment also apply in the case of religiously-motivated self-denial? For example, stories of the lives of Catholic saints or holy people from other religious traditions are often filled with extreme self-denial, yet practitioners seem to feel closer to God the more they suffer. Why might this be? For some ideas, see William James, *The Varieties of Religious Experience: A Study in Human Nature*, (1902; reprint, with a foreword by Jacques Barzun, New York: Mentor Books/New American Library of World Literature, 1958).

Both overindulgence and self-denial are vices that disrupt communities and relationships. Overindulgent people often end up sacrificing friends to the pursuit of ever less attainable pleasures. They use other people in their search for enjoyment and eventually become incapable of real friendship. Those who practice unreasonable self-denial also tend to be lonely because friendships are usually built around shared enjoyment.

This chapter focuses on drinking, and drinking seems a good example of something that over time best enhances experience when done in moderation. However, the virtue of moderation is a virtue in many areas of life. Unrelenting desires for money, status, popularity, or power become vices when pursued to extremes. When overindulged, they have consequences very similar to those of the over-consumption of alcohol: we crave more and more while enjoying it less and less. The single-minded pursuit of any desire disrupts friendship, marriage, and family.

To say that moderation is a virtue is thus to say two things about it: One is that it is essential to a successful and good life in association with others. The other is that it must be made a part of our character.

We can now summarize the central points we have wanted to make in this chapter. Issues such as drinking are often presented as a matter of making good choices, and a good way to think about making choices is by making lists of reasons for and against them. Of course we are not opposed to making good choices or weighing the pros and cons of a choice. But we think that this approach misses two important things. The first is Mill's point: what you now enjoy, and what you might enjoy if you learned how to appreciate various kinds of experiences, can differ. Moreover, it may be that the experiences and activities that require further learning to be fully appreciated are also among the most enjoyable. Evaluating choices in terms of what you now enjoy doesn't tell you what you might come to enjoy.

Second, making lists of pluses and minuses often overlooks the fact that in making a choice, you are also choosing your self. Little by little, your choices shape your personality and your character. You become a person predisposed to act as you now choose to act. Thus our central point is that you should learn to think of leading a rich and fulfilling life not so much as a series of choices, in which you always try to select the optimal one, but as a project in which you gradually make yourself the kind of person who can enjoy a fulfilling life. You are your most important project.

QUESTIONS

1. Is there such a thing as moderation in the use of heroin or crack cocaine?
2. Are there other areas in which moderation seems difficult, impossible, or undesirable?
3. Suppose that you could be attached to a machine that would sustain your life indefinitely and would also constantly stimulate the pleasure centers of your brain. Would that constitute a good life?

EXAMPLES OF COLLEGE AND UNIVERSITY CODES ON DRINKING AND DRUG USE

1. Excerpt from the student handbook of Hope College[1]

Hope upholds state and local laws regarding the possession and consumption of alcoholic beverages. The concepts listed below are for your consideration:

a) Michigan's drinking age is 21; therefore, most college students cannot drink alcohol legally;
b) alcohol inhibits individuals from functioning at full capacity;
c) alcohol abuse has a negative impact upon the learning environment of the College;
d) peer pressure may intimidate and compel persons to change their behavior to "go along with the crowd";
e) alcohol use has the potential for leading to alcohol abuse;
f) there is a high correlation between alcohol use and sexual assault.

---

[1] College Regulations on Alcoholic Beverages, *The 1994–95 Student Handbook*, Hope College, Holland, Michigan: (1994), pp. 21–22, 37.

While the College affirms that the decision to drink or not to drink is a matter of individual choice, it has established the following regulations regarding the use of alcoholic beverages in order to maintain an atmosphere supportive of its educational purposes:

1) The possession and/or consumption of alcoholic beverages on College property, College housing units, or College vehicles is prohibited. Any alcohol which is found on campus or in campus residence facilities will be confiscated and disposed of by the Residence Life Staff or Public Safety. [. . . .]
2) The use of College or organizational monies to purchase alcoholic beverages is prohibited;
3) The availability of alcoholic beverages may not be used to promote an event;
4) The possession of alcoholic beverage containers is prohibited in campus housing units; this includes "collectable" empty or full alcohol containers. [. . . .]

[. . .] It is important that the student be aware of the potential for legal responsibility when furnishing alcoholic beverages to other persons. If the individual to whom the beverage was furnished subsequently has an accident attributable to the beverage, then the furnisher may be found legally liable.

2. Excerpt from the handbook of the University of Pennsylvania[2]

[. . .] Penn's alcohol policy and programs are intended to encourage its members to make responsible decisions about the use of alcoholic beverages, and to promote safe, legal, and healthy patterns of social interaction.

A. The University of Pennsylvania prohibits:

1. the possession and/or consumption of alcoholic beverages by persons under 21 on property owned or controlled by the University or as part of any University activity.

2. the intentional and knowing selling, or the intentional and knowing furnishing [. . .] of alcoholic beverages to persons under the age of 21 or to persons obviously inebriated on property owned or controlled by the University or as part of any University activity. [. . . .]

3. the consumption of alcoholic beverages by all University employees and students so as to adversely affect job or academic performance

---

[2] "Drug and Alcohol Policy," *The PennBook 1994–95: Policies and Procedures Handbook of the University of Pennsylvania* (Office of the President, 1994), p. 39.

and/or endanger the physical well-being of other persons or oneself, and/or which leads to damage of property.

B. The University of Pennsylvania permits the lawful keeping and consumption, in moderation, of alcoholic beverages on its property or property under its control by persons of legal drinking age (21 years or older).

C. In cases of intoxication and/or alcohol poisoning, the primary concern is the health and safety of the individual(s) who are involved. Individuals are strongly encouraged to call for medical assistance for themselves or for a friend/acquaintance who is dangerously intoxicated. [. . . .]

E. Any advertisement for social events, including but not limited to fliers, posters, and invitations, must also include the statement: "Non-alcoholic beverages will also be provided for those who are under 21 or who choose not to drink." This statement must be as prominent as any reference to alcohol made in the advertisement.

F. Outdoor activities involving alcohol consumption should be limited to areas that are clearly demarcated and in which it is possible to exercise adequate control of access to and consumption of alcohol by anyone on the Penn campus. No drinking in outdoor public areas such as walkways, building steps and porches, unenclosed patios, green spaces and the like is permitted regardless of the age of the drinker. [. . . .]

G. Steps must be taken whenever alcohol is served or possessed to monitor and control access to alcohol to avoid service to underage drinkers. The organizers of any event where alcohol is to be served must have an established plan to ensure that only legal-age individuals have access to alcohol. [. . . .]

ADDITIONAL CASES

Case 7.2: *Alcohol and the Real Me*

Like her friends, Sharon drinks at social events. Unlike them, she recognizes that she needs to drink to relax socially at all. Drinking at a party is not only fun for Sharon; it's necessary. She wishes this weren't the case, but it is. Sharon knows that when she's tipsy, she's much funnier, sexier, and more self-confident than when she's not. In fact, she even wonders whether her friends would like her much if they didn't see her mainly when she's had a few drinks. She's afraid that someday they'll realize the "real," sober Sharon is a shy and boring fool, because she can never think of much to say when she runs into them at the cafeteria or after a class. However, no one seems to have noticed yet, and Sharon is careful to avoid nondrinking situations that might reveal what a dork she is.

Because Sharon only drinks at parties, she doesn't think her dependence on a few beers is a problem—at least she can always count on a buzz to turn her into Ms. Life-of-the-Party. And who knows? Maybe someday she'll learn how to be funny and self-confident without drinking. Right now, however, she's grateful that she's discovered a way to escape her shyness when it matters most.

Questions

1. Is Sharon's "real" personality the tipsy, uninhibited party girl, the shy and insecure nondrinker, or some combination of the two?
2. Is there anything wrong with using alcohol (or other drugs) to let out a side of yourself that you like better than your ordinary personality?
3. Do you think that the way Sharon uses alcohol will inhibit, or help, in her attempt to become a more self-confident person?
4. Is there anything unethical about trying to hide a part of your personality from your friends?

Case 7.3: Sorry, I Was Drunk

The first time Mike hit her, Julie was shocked speechless. They'd just come back from a keg party, where her normally considerate and faithful boyfriend had tried to pick up three different women, practically under Julie's nose. When Julie berated Mike on the walk back, he shoved her hard against a brick wall, told her to leave him the #%@!! alone, and stalked off, leaving her shaken and bruised. They'd both had quite a bit to drink that night, but at the time Julie hadn't connected Mike's outrageous flirting and violent temper to his drinking. His behavior that night was so unlike his usual charming, sober self that it was as if he turned from Dr. Jekyll into Mr. Hyde right in front of her. However, gradually Julie has learned that, as charming and considerate as Mike is when sober (which is almost always), he is violent and sexually predatory when drunk.

Now she is trying to decide whether or not to break up with him. On the plus side, she really enjoys Mike's company when he's sober; he sincerely seems to care about her; and he's very good-looking and popular. On the minus side, he's now gotten drunk four times since she started dating him, and each time it was the same. Frankly, she is scared of him when he's drunk. And when he's sober again, he never remembers anything he's done, although he's always very sorry that she's upset.

"I guess I just lose control if I get trashed," he'd say after each drunken incident. "I'm really sorry, babe. But I can't even remember what happened! It didn't mean anything; you know I'd never hurt you on purpose, because I love you. Next time will be different, I promise. Let me make it up to you." Then he'd kiss her tenderly and buy her roses, or take her out to dinner, or give her that new CD or those earrings she'd been wanting.

"Why don't you stop drinking if it makes you act so crazy?" she once asked him.

"It's not like I get ripped very often," Mike replied, sounding a bit hurt. "And why shouldn't I be able to enjoy myself once in a while like everyone else?"

Julie thought to herself, "Mike can't seem to help what he does when he drinks. Maybe if I just stay out of his way at those times, everything will be cool."

Questions

1. Mike claims that he's not responsible for his behavior when drunk. Do you accept this?
2. Because alcohol overcomes inhibitions, does drinking reveal what Mike is really like beneath his likeable exterior?
3. Either way, should Julie stay in this relationship if she can succeed in staying out of Mike's way when he drinks?
4. By "staying out of his way" and not confronting him, is Julie enabling Mike to continue his anti-social behavior? If so, does she share any responsibility for his actions?
5. Can you think of other cases in which people deny responsibility for their conduct by claiming that they can't help themselves? Are people responsible for being unable to control their behavior if they choose to put themselves in a situation in which they lose control?

Case 7.4: A Friend in Need

Carlos, Steve, and Andy have been friends and housemates for almost a year. At first Carlos bought Steve and Andy beers and Jack Daniels with his fake ID every weekend because he looks the oldest and they are all underage, but Steve has been pressuring him to get booze more and more frequently. It's becoming a strain on their friendship. "I can't be going to the liquor store every other day, man!" he told Steve. "I'm going to get caught, and then where will we be?"

"Don't be such a tool!" Steve replied. "They don't care down at McNally's. They hardly even look at your ID. And it only takes fifteen minutes. I'd do it for you!"

Inevitably Carlos ends up going, although he's tired of being Steve's errand boy. At least they'll all be legal next year, and then Steve can buy his own alcohol.

It's not just the fear of getting caught, and the inconvenience, that makes Carlos hesitate to go McNally's Liquor. He also worries about how much Steve drinks, although he doesn't know how to tell him. Andy thinks it's none of their business if Steve drinks a lot. "It's a free country, and he can do what he likes. You're not his mother. Besides, he seems OK to me." Carlos isn't so sure. Steve seems increasingly depressed and edgy when he drinks. He's stopped going to his 9:00 A.M. biology lab because he's always too hung over. In fact, he seems to have stopped studying for any of his classes. He's also been having a lot of accidents lately. Two weeks ago he fell down while he was drinking and gashed his cheek, another time he smashed his hand through a window when he was drunk, and just three nights ago he fell asleep in the living room with a glass of Jack Daniels in one hand and a cigarette in the other. He woke up with a wet lap and a hole burned in his jeans, and they all laughed—but what if he'd set himself, or the whole house, on fire? "It's a good thing he doesn't have a car," Carlos thought. "He'd probably kill himself!"

Questions
1. Steve's drinking seems to be hurting mainly him. So who is right about their duty toward their friend—Carlos or Andy? Does it show respect for Steve to let him live his own life, no matter how self-destructive, or might his self-destructive acts be cries for help that a friend shouldn't ignore?
2. Because Carlos and Andy both drink regularly, are they in a poor (or good) position to convince Steve to drink less?
3. Who is most responsible for Steve's drinking problem—Steve, who seems addicted to alcohol, or Carlos, who isn't addicted but helps Steve buy alcohol?
4. Assume for the moment that Steve would find some other way to get drunk if Carlos didn't help him. What can, or should, Carlos do about Steve's drinking besides refuse to buy him booze?
5. Does Steve's drinking endanger anyone other than himself? If so, does this fact increase Carlos's duty to help him stop drinking?

Case 7.5: Stoned Sex

Kathy and Rick have been lovers for several weeks, and Rick is starting to feel funny about the fact that Kathy always gets wasted before they have sex. She's explained that it helps her relax and feel freer, and makes the act itself more pleasurable for her. Rick doesn't mind pot smoking in general, and in fact he's often joined her for a toke or two, but he's been wondering more and more why Kathy won't ever make love without first smoking a joint. Maybe she doesn't really like sleeping with him and has to get baked to get into it at all. Maybe she's somehow trying to hide from him at their moment of greatest intimacy and tenderness. He's lightly suggested a few times that they try making love straight, "just to check it out," but Kathy has refused, implying that he's the uptight one. "Why mess with a good thing? It's not hurting anyone."

Yet Rick does feel hurt. Lying in bed together after sex one night, Rick tries out the subject one more time. "Do you always smoke before we go to bed because I gross you out or something?"

"Don't be ridiculous!" Kathy reassures him, but he hears an edge of irritation in her voice. "I think you're very attractive. My smoking has nothing to do with you; I used to get wasted with my old boyfriend too. It's just that weed makes me feel sexy and makes sex so much better. It helps me get totally into it."

"But you always seem sort of far away and dreamy, or silly, when you're high. I want to know what it's like to make love to you when you're all there." Rick hopes he doesn't sound too much like he's whining or begging.

Kathy dismisses the whole subject with a laugh. "I am definitely all here!" she giggles, and gives him a wet, smoky kiss. The conversation ends.

Questions

1. Aside from its illegality, is there anything wrong with using marijuana to enhance sex?
2. Do you think using marijuana (or alcohol or other drugs) before intimacy with a partner indicates a problem in a relationship?
3. Does Kathy somehow "owe" Rick straight sex, or is his desire for this his "hang-up" because Kathy's smoking is her business?
4. Does drug use put up communication barriers between partners (during sex or at other times), or does it remove them?
5. Where Percy in "Hate Speech" (Chapter 3) and Mike in "Sorry, I Was Drunk" (above) use drinking or drugs as an excuse for losing control, Kathy, like Sharon in "Alcohol and the Real Me" (above), seems to use smoking pot as way to access hidden parts of her personality. Marijuana seems to allow Kathy to express her sexuality in a way that she can't or won't do when she's straight. By choosing to use marijuana whenever she has sex, could Kathy make herself unable to enjoy sex without it, and limit her ability to be truly close to Rick?
6. How might habitually choosing to use grass (or alcohol, or other drugs) change one's character and personality? How do the principles of relationships and character growth apply to this case?

Case 7.6: *High Performance*

Dave, like several members of his college track-and-field team, has used drugs to enhance his athletic performance ever since he was in high school. He injured his knee during his sophomore year of high school. Then he began using anabolic steroids to build up his muscles, the stimulant ephedrine to give himself more energy, and dimethyl sulfoxide to deaden his pain so that he could keep running. After he was almost caught in a random drug test during his freshman year of college, he largely stopped using steroids and ephedrine, both of which are banned and readily detectable. Now he uses mainly dimethyl sulfoxide, which he knows doesn't violate NCAA rules and isn't easily detectable anyway because it rapidly passes through the body. Dimethyl sulfoxide, or DMSO, helps reduce the pain and swelling in his knee if it starts acting up and seems to give him a more "pumped up" feeling as it improves his circulation. The only drawback is that it stinks like death and it makes his breath smell like garlic, but this seems a very small price to pay to be able to keep competing when his knee wants to give out.

Dave's teammate Marty never used any drugs, and he was worried when he saw Dave rubbing DMSO on his knee. "If your knee hurts that badly, maybe you should give it a rest," he told Dave.

"Are you crazy?" Dave responded shortly. "Thursday is our big meet, and I can't miss a practice."

Marty didn't retreat. "If Coach knew, he wouldn't let you run. He might even kick you off the team. We're supposed to be 'drug free,' and you could get us all in trouble!"

Dave pondered this last statement. Was Marty going to rat on him? If he did, would Coach really be a hard-ass, or would he make an exception for what was, after all, an over-the-counter drug, used by some of his best runners? "What the other guys and I do as far as using drugs is really no one else's business," he decided, "and if Marty can't see that, well, I can make life unpleasant for him, too." However, out loud he just said, "Chill out, Marty. DMSO helps me run better, and you want us all to perform our best Thursday, don't you?"

Questions

1. In addition to his concern about being punished for his teammates' drug use, Marty might feel annoyed with them for seeking an unfair advantage over those who don't use drugs. Is it unethical to improve athletic performance by using a nonprohibited drug such as DMSO?
2. If you said no, wouldn't it be unethical to use illegal drugs for this purpose? What is the ethical difference between the two drug categories?
3. If yes, to whom is it mainly unfair: opposing teams; other members of the same team who don't use drugs; the drug-using players, themselves; the coach (who expects players to be drug-free); or parents, fans, or others less immediately involved? How?

4. If the drug actually had no physiological effects on performance but made users feel more confident, would using it still be unethical?
5. Concerning Dave's occasional use of other performance-enhancing drugs that have potentially serious side effects (steroids and stimulants), is Dave's drug use really no one's business but his own, or might Marty, the coach, or Dave's friends and relatives have an interest in getting him to stop? Why or why not?
6. In addition to physical effects, what less tangible effects might using drugs to improve his performance have on Dave's character development?

BACKGROUND READING

"Alcohol dependence" and "Drug dependence," *The American Medical Association Encyclopedia of Medicine*, ed. Charles B. Clayman (New York: Random House, 1989), pp. 81–83; 278.

This source provides a medical overview of the physical and behavioral effects of alcohol and other drugs on the body, the signs and stages of addiction, and the effects of increasing blood alcohol levels, in language a layperson can understand.

The use of performance-enhancing drugs among high school, college, and professional athletes is a hot topic at present. The following are a few newspaper articles about the subject: Dick Patrick, "Benefits Are Obvious, But Detractors Find Flaws," in *USA Today*, 12 October 1994, sec. C, p. 1, col. 5. Officials, from the Olympic community to the NFL and NCAA, are proclaiming victory in the drug war, but there is evidence to the contrary, frustrating some coaches and athletes. Larry Meyer, "Powerlifter Flexes Against Steroid Abuse," in *The Chicago Tribune*, 8 November 1992, sec. 18NW, p. 1, col. 4. Disturbed by the rampant and nonchalant use of steroids, Michael Collet of Park Ridge, IL formed Strong Athletes Against Steroids, an organization dedicated to drug-free sport and to educating the public about the dangers of using steroids. Charles Seabrook, "In Haste to Win, Some Athletes Aren't Saying No," in *The Atlanta Constitution*, 23 July 1992, sec. F, p. 8, col. 5. No one knows how many athletes use performance-boosting drugs, but sports medicine experts believe the practice is so widespread that it is wrecking the health and shortening the lives of thousands of athletes.

The Southern Illinois University's Core Institute Student Health Program publishes a semi-annual report called "Alcohol and Drugs in American College Campuses." (The latest available edition at press time was published in January 1993.) This report describes drug, alcohol, and tobacco use patterns and attitudes among various types of higher education students by sex and by region, and is available through Southern Illinois University, Core Institute, Student Health Program, Wellness Center, Carbondale, IL 62901.

ADDITIONAL MATERIALS

1. A number of recent studies suggest that while the general population is drinking less, college students are continuing to abuse alcohol with a recklessness that seems surprising in an increasingly health-conscious society. See Tom Pelton, "Even in Sober '90s, Booze Still Big Thing on Campus," in *The Chicago Tribune*, 30 March 1994, sec. 2C, p. 1, col. 5; and "Editorial: Deadly Drinking," in *USA Today*, 9 June 1994, sec. A, p. 10, col. 1.

A study by the National Commission on Substance Abuse at Colleges and Universities, released on June 7, 1994, by Columbia University, shows that the number of college women who drink to get drunk has more than tripled in the past fifteen years, from 10% in 1977 to 35% in 1994; 55% of all rapes of college women occur when the victim is under the influence of alcohol; and more than one in three college students of both sexes drink excessively, with women now nearly equalling men in the percentage who drink to get drunk. See Brooke A. Masters, "Women Drinking Like Men, College Alcohol Study Finds," in *The Washington Post*, 8 June 1994, sec. A, p. 1, col. 4; "An Alcohol Alert," in *The Christian Science Monitor*, 10 June 1994, p. 18, col. 1; and Marian Sandmaier, "A Tragic Price to Pay for a Drink," in *The Chicago Tribune*, 17 June 1994, sec. 1, p. 21, col. 2.

A University of Michigan survey found that college women in general are drinking more often than previously (as well as more excessively, for some), with academic, social, and health consequences. See William Celis III, "Drinking by College Women Raises New Concern," in *The New York Times*, 16 February 1994, sec. A, p. 18, col. 3. An extensive Harvard study found that nearly half of all students on campuses nationwide are binge drinkers who cause a variety of "secondhand" problems on campus, from vandalism to rape to fatal accidents, that affect nondrinkers too. See Richard A. Knox, "Binge Drinking Linked to Campus Difficulties," in *The Boston Globe*, 7 December 1994, p. 1, col. 1; and Christopher B. Daly, "Nearly Half of U.S. College Students Are Binge Drinkers, Study Finds" in *The Washington Post*, 7 December 1994, sec. A, p. 17, col. 1.

Do you think alcohol abuse is a problem on your campus? What pressures do you think might be causing an increase in college student drinking while alcohol use in the general population goes down? Why might college women in particular be drinking more? Does the push to make college campuses "dry" (see "Examples of College and University Codes on Drinking and Drug Use" above) merely make underage students who want to drink go off campus, so that authorities now have to deal with drinking and driving? What can colleges, and individual students, do to decrease alcohol abuse on campus? See Thomas Gagliardi, "Battling Drinking," in *The Chicago Tribune*, 11 April 1994, sec. 1, p. 16, col. 4 for a summary of some programs being tried.

2. Whereas in the 1980s lighter alcoholic beverages such as wine coolers were the drink of choice among young drinkers, a current drink of choice seems to be Jaegermeister, a 70-proof German brand that has virtually no direct advertising. The hit cordial is peddled in college bars by a squad of 783 scantily clad young women called "Jaegerettes," who shower young men with trinkets when they buy shots of the drink. The Jaegermeister company has also assembled a group of about 100 "Jaegerdudes," who wear tight-fitting bike shorts and cater to the brand's gay following. See Suein L. Hwang, "Partying With the Jaegerettes," in *The Wall Street Journal*, 13 May 1994, sec. B, p. 1, col. 3; Suein L. Hwang, "Marketing: Young Drinkers Do Shots in Potent New Flavors," in *The Wall Street Journal*, 13 May 1994, sec. B, p. 1, col. 3; and Francine I. Katz, "Peer Pressure Key in Shaping Drinking Habits," in *USA Today*, 13 December 1994, sec. A, p. 14, col. 3 (this is a letter to the editor from a representative of the Anheuser-Busch Company).

Is this kind of alcohol promotion unethical? If so, why? Who is ultimately responsible for underage student drinking—the "immature" students themselves, the student peer culture, unscrupulous alcohol advertisers, parents, school authorities, or society at large? Would you answer differently regarding thirteen-year-old drinkers? If so, what is the difference ethically (there is none legally) between a thirteen-year-old drinker and an eighteen-year-old one?

8

ON GETTING A LIFE

Two Cases: What Is College For?

Case 8.1: Finding Herself

Claudia was middle aged—not a bad thing to be. She had married right out of high school, had children who were now out of school and self-supporting, been on the PTA board, gone to church, and done all the things that middle-class women of her age were supposed to do. She still lived with her husband, Ken, and she supposed that she always would. He was all right. He cared for her, and she cared for him. But he had his life, and lately it only slightly intersected with hers. He was one of those men who actually enjoyed his work. He ran a small store where he sold wooden furniture, most of which he made himself. He wasn't a worka-holic. He had time for her, but he was engaged in his work. He thought of himself as someone who made furniture, who incidentally had a fam-ily. That was all right, too. It made him feel engaged and fulfilled. He knew who he was. He was located.

That was the problem. Somewhere in occupying the roles of wife, mother, and community volunteer, Claudia felt as though she had lost herself. She had awakened one day to find that ever since she could re-member, she had been hands and feet, cook and chauffeur, for someone else. This was acceptable but increasingly she wasn't sure just who she was. She was certain that she wasn't only hands and feet. She was a whole person, but she had never had much time to figure out who this person was. She was always defined in what she now thought of as her "servant role." Perhaps that teenager who had married Ken had been on the way to becoming someone, or maybe she even was someone then. It was a long time ago and hard to recall.

Claudia decided to go to college to find herself. She would study literature. She thought that would be a good way to look for herself. Maybe she could even do some writing. So she applied to the local community college. It didn't cost too much, and it was an easy commute.

She soon found out that whoever she was, she was different from the college's view of who students were supposed to be. Although the college had a significant number of older students, it was clearly designed with the assumption that "normal" students were eighteen to twenty-two. Orientation was designed to promote social experiences that only a teenager could love. She wasn't into rap music and didn't especially care to play get-acquainted games with children younger than her own daughter.

Her relations with her advisor were strained. He tried, but he was used to dealing with teenagers and simply had no concept of how to advise a full-fledged adult.

Classes were terrible. She soon discovered that the majority of mature students in college are there to learn something that will translate directly into more cash on the job. The mean age in the college's accounting classes was probably thirty-five. However, she must have raised the mean age of her modern English literature class by five years. She quickly discovered that maturity had something to do with making sense of literature. She found that her experience put her in a position to interact with the story in a productive way. She thoroughly enjoyed the reading. However, the rest of the students were still trying to distill the plot and the theme, and trying to get the best grade for the least work. Their questions and interpretations were, well, juvenile. By the second week of classes, she thought that she had heard the question, "Will this be on the test?" twenty times.

Worst of all was the cafeteria, where she ate between classes. Wherever the other adult students were, they weren't there. She suspected that the classes taken by most adult students were offered in the afternoon or evenings to accommodate their schedules.

"Well," Claudia mused to herself, "I really didn't expect to find myself in the cafeteria. I thought I'd find myself in fiction. Isn't it odd to look for yourself in something made up? Maybe that's not where to look. I don't know. But while I'm looking, it would be nice if I could talk to and be with a few people who understand what I'm about. Maybe I don't need a degree; maybe I need a support group. But that doesn't seem right, either. I came here to change my life. I didn't come to find people to help me endure it."

Case 8.2: Choosing a Career

Allen had wanted to teach first grade for several years, ever since he'd volunteered at a local Head Start program. He loved little kids. He was never happier than when he was reading to them or tying their shoes or even wiping their noses. He especially liked teaching them things because it made such an obvious difference. One day they didn't know their numbers. The next day, through his efforts, a squiggle on a page had magically become the number three. Somehow teaching was what he was meant to do.

Allen particularly liked working on little math activities with kids. He was good at math. In fact, that seemed to be the problem: he was too good at it. He had gotten 780 on the math section of the SATs, and his father was convinced that God had made him to be an engineer. More accurately, his father was convinced that he should be a rich engineer. As always, he had done what his father wanted. He had enrolled in an engineering program, and he was doing well. He had volunteered to tutor kids at a local elementary school. The trouble was that he still liked little kids more than he liked computers, and he still thought he wanted to teach. He looked forward to the time he spent in the school. The time at the keyboard seemed dull in comparison.

At the beginning of his junior year, he had begun to think about transferring into education and seeing whether he could get certified to teach elementary school. He thought that if he switched between semesters, he could get enough credits both to be certified and to graduate. He had written home about it. His mother had said, "Whatever makes you happy, dear," just as he knew she would. His father had provided a detailed economics lecture, beginning with comparative starting salaries for teachers and engineers and ending with some pointed reminders about the stereos and cars Allen was unlikely to have if he became a teacher. However, the letter had ended with, "But it's your life. Do what makes you happy."

Well, that was progress. He wasn't going to be written out of his father's will, but he had hoped for his father's approval. Moreover, in some ways, he knew his father was right. Teachers made a lot less than engineers. He didn't exactly want to spend his life scraping by, but he didn't want to spend it programming, either.

Questions

1. Both Claudia and Allen see college as an opportunity to "get a life," but they seem to understand this differently. Claudia poses the question as one of self-identity. She wants to know who she is. Allen wants to know what job he should pursue. Do these questions have anything to do with each other?

2. Are there other perspectives you might use to view the point of college? Can you connect what you are doing in college with any broad view you have of your own life?

3. If your college education is sucessful, it may change you. You might change your mind about some important ideas, or you might develop new interests, tastes, or skills. You might be a very different person when you leave college than you were when you entered. Is college supposed to do this?
4. If college changes who you are, how can you think about what you'll want from life after college? Do you worry that you'll have to make too many choices about your career before you really know what you want?
5. How do you think about the work you want to do after college? Are you interested mainly in how much you'll earn? Are you interested mainly in whether the work will be fulfilling or enjoyable?
6. Allen seems concerned that he enjoys teaching more than engineering. Is that all there is to it? Perhaps Allen feels "called" to teach—could teaching be what he is meant to do? Do you feel this way about the work you want to do after college?
7. Could Claudia have experienced her work as wife and mother as a calling? Should she have? Could or should men experience their roles as husbands or fathers as a calling?

ISSUES

College is a place for choices. It is supposed to prepare you for life. What does that mean? What is your life? How should you see your education affecting it? Maybe you don't have a clear picture of your life. If not, how can you get one? Do you really need one? Both Claudia and Allen have raised questions about how their attendance at college fits into their concepts of their lives and into their pictures of who they are. However, their questions are not the same. Allen has begun to form a picture of who he is and what he wishes to do. His problems are, first, that his father does not support his aspirations and, second, that he will not make a good living at what he wants to do. Claudia, however, has no currently well-formed picture of herself and her life. She has decided that her old life is somehow deficient, so she is on a quest for self-discovery. She wants to find out who she is and what she is to do with the rest of her life. Although she might or might not take a job after college, she does not seem to define her life in terms of her vocation.

A view of one's life and oneself are important. They are "orienting," which means that they help us make decisions in a certain way. It's not so much that they provide us with information that is relevant to making decisions; it is that having a sense of who we are and a view of our lives helps us to assess the relevance of information.

Consider something as simple as buying a car. If we wish to purchase a car, we'll probably want to know certain things, such as how much it costs and whether we can afford it. We may want to know the car's maintenance record. This information is of little use, however, if we have no sense of who we are and how the car will fit into our lives. Someone who is, for example, the chaplain of a retirement center and whose life is built around service to the elderly may not find a tiny red sports car appropriate. It would not "fit" the person. A film star might find a sedate, low-priced station wagon similarly inappropriate.

College is both a place in which decisions must be made in a way that advances one's view of one's life, and a place where a picture of one's life can be formed, tested, and appraised. Allen, for example, has been in a process of testing a sense of himself as a teacher. He's found that he enjoys teaching and he does not enjoy engineering. But he's unsure whether that is a sufficient reason to change. His family relations are also important to him, and he is unsure whether teaching can sustain an income that will support other things he wishes to do. He needs to balance these concerns. What criteria should he use?

Claudia has no currently functional sense of who she is and what she wishes to do. Not that she is entirely directionless; she has a past. She has a network of relationships that are important to her, including her husband and children. Although her children are grown and her husband is not as central in her life as he once was, she wants to make changes in her life only if they are consistent with maintaining these relationships. At the same time, she needs to discover some things that will allow her to get a firmer sense of direction for herself. How can she do this? Is she right about the potential of literature to help? Perhaps she, like Allen, should test an occupation or an avocation. How are decisions of this sort made?

The Ethics of Getting a Life

Are the ethical principles we sketched at the beginning of this book important to the question of getting a concept of one's life? It seems that some of them are. Allen is asking some questions that could be illuminated by *benefit maximization*. However, we should be careful here. Allen shouldn't uncritically identify making a good income with the benefits he is trying to maximize. Income may count, but he must also consider the satisfaction he gets from teaching and his sense of accomplishment in helping children. These, too, are benefits. Allen must balance them in some reasonable way. How would you do this? How would you advise him? Note also that the principle of benefit maximization is not very helpful right now for Claudia, because she does not know what she wants and is, thus, unclear about what counts as a benefit.

Both Claudia and Allen need to consider how their choices fit into their current set of *relationships*, and how they may form new ones. What duties does Allen owe to his father? What obligations does Claudia have to her husband and her children? How should they think about these concerns? Also, the concept we have of our lives and of who we are will both influence and be influenced by our communities. If Allen chooses to become a teacher, that will locate him in a particular professional community with a certain set of commitments. If he is a member of a religious group, he might see teaching as a form of service to God. Thus his choices might extend his membership in one community while also attaching him to another. (Question: Do the other ethical principles illuminate these decisions? How?)

We want to suggest that the criterion of *character growth* should be considered important in reflections on getting a life. Although we can reflect on who we are and the purpose of our lives, we must also recognize the consequences of and limits on our choices. Our character is not simply chosen. It is built, a little at a time, by what we do and the decisions we make. Moreover, every time we make one decision, we close off others. Some decisions are closed to Claudia by her previous decisions. She can wonder what life might have been like had she not married Ken, but she cannot go back and become that unmarried teenager. She has been formed by her life as a wife and mother. Even though she wishes to change her role, she cannot entirely escape what that life has made her.

The decisions Allen makes may determine not only what he will do for a living, but also what kind of person he becomes. If he chooses to become an engineer, he may have taken a step toward becoming a cynical, bitter, and greedy person who acts largely for monetary gain. Not that engineering makes one this way; it is more the *reasons* Allen would have for becoming an engineer. For him, becoming an engineer might be a matter of allowing his desire for a good salary and what that can provide to take precedence over his love for children. Now he is someone who loves children. In twenty years, he may be someone who loves only money. For someone else, becoming an engineer might mean expressing a love of science or of making things work.

Occupations and the education that trains people for them can form character, but often not in predictable ways. Getting a business degree might make some people greedy. It might give others a sense of accomplishment and public service. Almost every occupation can cultivate some virtues and some vices. If you know or have an idea of your hoped-for occupation, you might ask yourself what virtues and vices it can cultivate. One question you should ask yourself is why you are interested in this occupation. It is quite likely that as you move through your education and into your chosen profession, your current motives will be reinforced. You should ask yourself whether you want to become the kind of person you may become if you are more intensively motivated by these considerations. Also ask yourself what motives you consider worthy in choosing an occupation. Should people be motivated primarily by money? How important should it be for them to enjoy what they do? Should your occupation serve important human interests? Is it acceptable to pursue occupations that are harmful or frivolous? Could you be someone who advertised cigarettes? How might that form your character?

College and Getting a Life

How else might we think about college and the process of getting a life? The stories of Allen and Claudia suggest four components of getting a life.

1. Authenticity. Claudia often talks as though her task is one of self-discovery. It is as though deep down she really is, and perhaps always has been, someone, and that she needs to discover who this person is. Perhaps she sees the study of literature as a source of ideas that will help her to articulate this vague sense of self-identity. Perhaps she sees it as a source of models of lives or selves she might adopt or a source of stimulation for her thinking.

Allen does not talk this way, but he is motivated by his sense that there is a link between the kind of person he is and teaching. He has discovered this more by active exploration than by reading and reflection. He's never said, "I am the kind of person who loves children, therefore I should teach." He has discovered his love of children and teaching by being involved with them. College can be a place for both kinds of exploration. Are there ways that you can use your college experience to explore and reflect on who you are?

2. Discovering what's worthwhile. Some things are better than others. Some things are better than others for us. We are not sure that we could argue successfully that Beethoven or Duke Ellington is really better than Snoop Doggy Dogg or Pearl Jam (although we believe they are). Nor do we think it's important for us to do so here. What is important is for you to understand that college is not only a place to find ways to satisfy your current tastes, but also to develop those tastes. Some things that people find worthwhile or enjoyable are unlikely to be experienced this way without experience and training. We are inclined to think that this is often true of the fine arts: good music, good literature, and good art. Perhaps you have had the experience of being bored by a trip through an art museum until someone was able to explain the art work to you. Perhaps you have had the experience of disliking a certain type of music until you had the opportunity to perform it. Such experiences seem commonplace. They suggest that college is an important place for change and growth. Part of this growth may involve learning to enjoy new things and appreciate new experiences. What other people have discovered about things that enhance the quality of their experience, after they have made an effort to learn them, is not an infallible guide to directions you might explore, but it is a guide.

There is always something of us in what we can enjoy. Many people find that they enjoy math, science, or engineering because they enjoy solving puzzles. Allen has given engineering a fair shot and has found that he isn't one of those people. However, he has found that he enjoys teaching. Often what allows us to experience an occupation or an art form as worthwhile is that it takes some talent or disposition that we have and extends it. We grow in ways that seem natural to us. Moreover, the activity continues to provide us with new challenges or insights. People who enjoy solving puzzles are eventually likely to enjoy chess more than tic-tac-toe. Tic-tac-toe cannot maintain interest, but the enjoyment of chess seemingly can never be exhausted. As we become more sophisticated in understanding the game, the game affords new challenges. Worthwhile activities are often like chess. They extend us and keep our interest. Thus discovering what's worthwhile is a matter of being willing to learn, change, and grow. College is a place for this.

3. Finding a place. Claudia thinks of her task as discovering an identity for herself. She feels as though she abandoned some potential self-identity when she married, and that she needs to go back to discover this abandoned self. However, this might not be the best way for her to approach her problem. She thinks taking literature courses is rather like looking in a mirror. "Perhaps," she thinks, "if I examine this character or this way of thinking, I will discover a picture of my self and I can build on that self."

This way of thinking may take the idea of discovering who one is too literally. It is almost as though Claudia has a real self lurking inside somewhere, waiting to be discovered. Allen has found out something about himself—that he enjoys working with children—but he does not talk as though he had discovered some formerly hidden person that he was all along. Perhaps Claudia needs to spend more time asking herself what she enjoys or what she finds important to do, and less time looking for her lost self.

Claudia often seems to suggest that her problem is not so much that she has lost her self as that she doesn't belong. She doesn't feel as though she belongs with her family anymore, perhaps because her children are grown and her husband doesn't need her. She doesn't feel as though she belongs in her literature class or in the college cafeteria because of the ages of the rest of the students and because of their interests. Where does she belong? How might she find out?

Answering this question is what we mean by finding a place. It may be a matter of discovering a job that employs one's talents, seems worth doing, and is enjoyable. Perhaps it is finding a cause for which to work. Perhaps it is a matter of finding something in which to believe. Perhaps it is a matter of finding like-minded or congenial people with whom to spend time.

4. Finding a vocation. Allen usually seems to think of the choice between engineering and teaching as a choice between a job that pays well and one that he enjoys, but he has also entertained the thought that teaching is what he's meant to do, his calling or vocation. At one point in Western history, the idea of a calling or vocation tended to be limited to religious roles. One was called to be a priest, but being a farmer was just a job. After the Protestant Reformation, the idea of a calling was broadened to include all work which was to be performed as something to which one was called by God and as a religious duty. This outlook makes a job into a vocation. That is, it imbues the job with a deeper purpose than just something one does for money or pleasure. Even apart from this religious context, it is possible to think of one's job as a vocation. If you think your intended work is so important that you feel urged to do it, perhaps this work is your vocation. Allen might think this way about teaching. He might want to teach not only because he enjoys it, but also because it's vitally important work that he is particularly suited to do. It's *his* work, work to which he feels a personal commitment. If he feels this way, teaching might be not only his job, but also his calling. Is there some work to which you feel a commitment? Should there be? Would your life be better if there were?

5. Resources. Allen's father may have a rather different view of the purpose of college than is expressed in components 1–4. It's quite a common view. He doesn't see Allen's college experience as an opportunity for either discovery or forming a sense of self or place, nor does he see it as a matter of discovering what's worthwhile. To him it is a chance to develop a resource base for one's life.

Of course, any kind of life requires resources. For those of us who are not born wealthy, this means getting a job that can generate an adequate income. Usually getting a job, especially a well-paying job, requires that we acquire some marketable skills. College can be a place where this happens. Few students these days need to be told this, so we won't discuss it (beyond what we've already said), nor do we plan to argue that this view of the purpose of college is wrong.

We do, however, believe that it is an incomplete view. Moreover, if all that you ask from college is that it increase your marketability, you may miss much of what the college experience can contribute to your life. What strikes us about many students, and perhaps about Allen's father, is that they are interested in using college to generate resources for their lives, but they haven't thought about using college to discover what kind of life these resources will support. Few of us are able to ignore the economic implications of college, but it is all too easy to ignore how college can help us to develop a cogent view of the goals toward which we will use these resources. It is especially important that we not miss the possibility that college can transform us.

In our culture, it is easy to assume that we know the purpose of life. It is having things: cars, compact disk players, clothes, big houses, influence, fame, power. We are told this ad nauseam on TV and everywhere else we turn. Perhaps you owe it to yourself to find out whether it is true.

To put it another way, it is easy to see college only as a means to living a life you have already conceived. You want this and that. If you become an engineer or a lawyer, you can get this and that. However, why you want these things, what kind of person you want to be, and whether you are called to some vocation, are not questions generally asked. We suggest that the real trick to getting the most out of college is to be open to change about the kind of person you want to be, what you think is worthwhile, what you want to do, and where you belong. Indeed, the trick to developing your economic potential is to apply these questions to the marketable skills you seek to acquire, as well as asking, "How much does it pay?" All students should ask themselves, "How do I wish to be transformed? To what possibilities about myself am I open?" even (especially) about their future occupations.

Questions

1. One view of higher education that emphasizes its transformative power is the liberal arts tradition. This concept of college suggests that the key to a transformative education is the study of subjects such as the arts, literature, philosophy, mathematics, and the sciences. Why should the study of philosophy be considered more liberating than the study of carpentry? What would give literature more transformative power than accounting?
2. Does the liberal arts tradition focus more on the development of rationality and taste, and less on self-discovery, than we have done? Are these goals inconsistent? Are they different? How?
3. Some people have argued that a principal goal of education is creating good citizens. Is this goal different from "getting a life?" How do you understand what it means to be a good citizen? Are there any tensions between the two goals?
4. We have suggested that part of reflecting on getting a life is authenticity, and that self-discovery is part of this, but we have cautioned against thinking of this as though there were a "real you" waiting to be discovered. We are suspicious about whether there is any "real you" at all. How does self-discovery differ from discovering a "real you?" Is a self a discovery or an invention? What else might it be?
5. Allen was unable to decide whether to be a teacher or an engineer. Thus he took an extra year of college in order to get a B.S. in engineering and a teaching certificate. He now has a job offer from a major corporation for $41,000 and an offer from a school district for $25,000. How would you advise him to think about his choice?
6. Yesterday you won the lottery. You have more than enough money for the rest of your life. How will this affect your view of your reasons for being in college?
7. Was Claudia a victim of sexism? How so?

ADDITIONAL CASES

Case 8.3: *Authenticity*

The first few months of college were difficult for Blaire in a way she'd never imagined. She'd known that going north to school would mean being far from her family and embracing new intellectual challenges, but that was exactly what she'd wanted. She had to leave home. She was tired of being treated as if her greatest glory in life would be to win a beauty contest (at age fourteen she'd placed second in the Junior Miss Southern Charm pageant, her last) and marry a millionaire. Instead, she wanted to use her mind and go where people didn't believe that girls should be beautifully helpless and graciously brainless.

However, Blaire had never imagined that up North, people would assume she was stupid, too! At home her mane of blonde hair, polished fingernails, designer clothes, and carefully made-up face looked just like everyone else's. But in the North, hardly any of the girls ("women," they were called here) wore makeup or polish, and most seemed to dress in baggy flannel shirts and ripped jeans. Blaire's appearance and her slow, soft accent seemed to spell "rich dumb Southern belle" to students and teachers alike, and she felt ostracized and humiliated. Within weeks, Blaire decided that if she wanted to fit in and be taken seriously, she would have to make herself over, lose her accent, buy "downscale" clothes, and never tell anyone about her embarrassing origins again. She'd change roommates, too, and start over with her college social life.

She worked at this personal transformation at least as hard as she worked at her classes. By the end of freshman year, Blaire had the satisfaction of seeing that her professors now treated her with respect, and her new friends believed she'd grown up as they had, in middle-class New England.

Questions

1. Do you think Blaire is correct in assuming that her accent and appearance are responsible for her not being taken seriously?
2. What other ways might Blaire have responded to the prejudices she felt she encountered?
3. Is there anything ethically dubious about remaking yourself (or your self-presentation) to fit others' expectations?
4. Does Blaire owe her new friends any true accounting of her background? Would she if she later married one of them?
5. Is she a victim of sexism or some other -ism?
6. How might Blaire's deceit, and her perception of its necessity, affect her character growth?

7. Which other ethical principles might you use in analyzing this case, and how?

Case 8.4: Divorce Aftermath

Jerry's parents divorced bitterly while he was in tenth grade. It was a wrenching experience, not least because his parents used him as the chief prize in their war with each other. Even after the divorce, they constantly pressured him to take sides, and they generally made him miserable without (apparently) meaning to. He survived by retreating from both of them, throwing himself into his schoolwork and his music, and longing for the day he could escape.

Jerry is finally living away from home in a freshman dorm, but his parents' battles seem to have followed him to college. Their latest fight is over who will pay for his college education. When Jerry was applying to schools, his dad promised to pay Jerry's tuition if he was accepted at State. Now that Jerry's made it, his dad is refusing to pay for another semester. The reason is that Jerry's mom is planning to remarry, and Jerry's father sarcastically insists that if she does, his "new dad" can foot the bill. Unfortunately, his future stepfather has made it clear that he will not pay for Jerry's college, and his mother certainly can't pay the tuition herself.

Jerry is not eligible for financial aid because he has never lived independently, and his parents' income bracket disqualifies him as their dependent. Thus it seems that Jerry will have to drop out of State. If he can afford college at all on what he can earn from a part-time job, he will have to settle for the local community college and move back in with his mom or dad. That is, unless he can get one of his notably stubborn parents to change their minds.

Questions

1. Should Jerry try to influence his father to pay for college in spite of his mother's remarriage?
2. Should his mother try to get her new husband to pay? Should she postpone her wedding so that his father will keep paying?
3. Does Jerry have an equal duty to both of his parents in this situation? How can he (or anyone) respond ethically to manipulation by loved ones?
4. What would you do if you were Jerry? Why?
5. How might the principles of relationship, character growth, and benefit maximization apply to this case?

Case 8.5: Whose Life Is It, Anyway?

Albert is trying to imagine how to break the news to his parents. For two and a half years he has dutifully majored in computer science and done reasonably well, even though he's spent many hours practicing his violin, taking lessons, and playing in musical groups on campus. Now, before it's too late, he has decided to switch to a music performance major and make computer science his minor. For some students, it would be a straightforward choice: Albert loves music and knows that he has real talent; he is only a middling computer science student, and regards a future life as a computer programmer with bored distaste. However, Albert also knows that his parents regard his dream of being a concert violinist as crazy and undutiful. He can imagine the conversation already:

His mother (in tears): "But Albert! How will you support yourself? Even if you can get into an orchestra after you graduate, you will never be able to live on what they pay you!"

His father, sternly: "You've made your mother cry! Don't you realize how much she's suffered to get to this country, and to give her children a chance at a better life than we had?"

His mother: "Albert! You can still play the violin, and have a good job as a computer programmer! Your sister earns a good living as a doctor, and she plays the piano. Please, don't throw everything away! You'll regret it when you're our age, and you have children who want to go to college."

His father: "You take your privileges for granted. You would never be able even to think of such a frivolous career if we had not slaved all our lives for your sake. Have some respect for your mother and me and all that we have done for you! When I was young, none of us would have dreamed of going against our parents' wishes."

And so on. Albert knew that his parents wouldn't listen to his side, and his sister was hardly a model he wanted to follow. She never had time to play anymore, although she had wanted to be a professional musician, too, and she had even more native ability than he did. In addition, he didn't see why he should have to give up on his dreams, just because his parents had worked like dogs. They had had to leave everything and start over when they came to the United States, putting in long hours at work they did not enjoy in order to send their children to college. Making money seemed to be everything to them, but now that they had managed to send him and his sister to college and could live comfortably, why did they need his financial "success" to vindicate their struggles?

Questions

1. In Albert's parents' culture, children are expected either to follow their parents' line of work or to obey their parents' wishes in choosing a pro-

fession. Many Americans, of course, have different expectations in this regard. Albert feels trapped between the two worlds. What kind of duty does he have to consider the wishes of his parents, who have suffered so much "for his sake?" Is it disrespectful and undutiful of him to cause his parents pain, as they believe?

2. Can you think of any arguments Albert might try with his parents to convince them to let him follow his dream of being a violinist?

3. What implications does the choice before Albert (becoming a computer programmer, as his parents wish, or defying his parents by becoming a musician) have for the growth of his character?

4. How might you use other moral principles to advise Albert?

Case 8.6: Where Do I Belong?

Bob is a scholarship student at a prestigious university. He is also the first person in his family, and his neighborhood, to go to college at all. When he returns home for the summer, everyone seems glad to see him and proud of his success, but he notices that a distance has grown between him and his old friends, and even within his family. After the first awkward greetings, no one seems to know what to say. Then one friend comments on how different he seems, and Bob is aware of a new feeling about his friends and family: embarrassment. They all seem so small-minded, shabby, and exaggeratedly ethnic. "They talk like stereotypes!" he thinks ruefully. "Did I used to sound that way, too?"

He overhears his mother defending him to a neighbor who thinks he's putting on airs: "I don't see why Bob wants to go to college anyway—none of us did, and we do just fine! That boy's head is getting turned at his fancy school. Now he thinks he's too good for us."

That's not it. Bob still loves his family and his old friends, but he just doesn't seem to fit in anymore. Unfortunately, he doesn't feel that he fits in at school, either. He always seems to be making faux pas or otherwise embarrassing himself there, and he doesn't have any close friends. It seems that he has to unlearn his entire past to make it in the academic world, because everything is different: he has to know one way to dress, talk, eat, relate to women and to authorities, and hang out at school, and completely different ways to do these things in the neighborhood. The guys at home even have a "tough" walk and "cool" street greetings that his fellow students would find ridiculous. It seems that he has to be two different people, and he's less and less sure which (if either) is really him.

It's too late for him to slip back into the neighborhood, even if he wanted to (and who could he talk to about all the new things he's learning?). However, he worries that he will never be accepted in his new world, either, and he misses the closeness and sense of being able to count on your friends that he had before.

Questions

1. Bob is living the American dream by being the first in his family to go to college, yet he seems to be struggling with his transition from a working-class background to a middle-class future. What might be the pros and cons of getting an education that will put him into a different social class than that of his family and childhood friends?
2. Countless studies have found significant differences between the college educated and those without higher education, in everything from their political beliefs and child-rearing practices to their food preferences and taste in entertainment. How might college have this tremendous effect?
3. As Bob changes his lifestyle, he is losing the strong sense of ethnic pride and blue-collar solidarity of his early life, but he doesn't yet have any new values to replace them and make him feel that he belongs to another community. How important is a feeling of belonging or community? Why?
4. What kinds of communities might middle-class college students have?
5. What can Bob do to find a sense of community at college?
6. Can he maintain his working-class connections while entering the middle class financially and educationally?
7. How should he relate to his old community of family, friends, and neighbors in light of the principles of character growth, respect for persons, and relationships?

Case 8.7: A Good Job

Sheri is very excited about her marketing internship with a major tobacco company. There's a good chance that she'll be hired when she graduates, with an excellent salary and benefits and paid business trips to the industry's annual convention in Hawaii. Sheri enjoys working with the hip, creative people in marketing who dream up new ways to "position company products" (that is, to increase young, female, and minority cigarette buyers because the older-white-male market is shrinking). She was especially proud when one of her ideas for an ad campaign was greeted enthusiastically by the head of the department during a big brainstorming meeting. "I've got to keep doing well so they'll hire me next year," she told her roommate. She thinks she has a good chance because a coworker told her that the company wants to hire young women who can help them understand how to promote products to their peers.

Her roommate, Caitlin, who plans to be an ecologist, isn't impressed. "How can you say that's a good job? The company sounds slimy to me.

Basically, they're trying to get more people, especially vulnerable people, addicted to cigarettes! How can you feel good about helping them do that?"

"No one is forcing anyone to smoke—it's the consumers' choice. You're such a '60s liberal holdover!" Sheri responds angrily. "Just because you want to save the whales doesn't mean that's what everyone has to do. And believe me, touchy-feely environmentalists have trouble finding jobs at all, much less good jobs that start at $36 grand."

Caitlin realizes that she's hurt Sheri's feelings by disapproving of her future job, but she does feel that people should choose work that makes the world a better place, although she can't think how to say this without sounding smug. "I just think that a 'good job' should be interesting for you but also good for other people and the environment," she says rather lamely.

"Well, this job is good for me and for other people," replies Sheri. "This company has factories in several poor areas. The more cigarettes we sell, the more jobs we create. And jobs are more important than the environment any day."

Caitlin disagrees, but she's starting to feel that maybe she and Sheri are on such different wavelengths that they'd better drop the whole subject.

Questions

1. Caitlin seems to think that choices about employment are not purely personal because they affect society at large. She also feels that people have a duty to improve, or at least not harm, society and the environment, and that we should choose work and lifestyles accordingly. Do you agree? In other words, is working for a (potentially) unethical or socially or environmentally harmful company acceptable if it is a "good job" that is personally beneficial?

2. If you said "yes," would you still agree if Sheri were planning to design atomic weapons for the military, create pesticides having highly toxic byproducts for a chemical company, or work for an organized crime syndicate? If her work doesn't directly harm anyone, but the company she works for or its products might, is she still ethically responsible for this potential harm? Why or why not?

3. Would you agree with Sheri or with Caitlin about the relative merits of creating jobs versus saving the environment, or can you think of some other position?

4. Would the social value of a job help determine whether or not you would take it? Assuming that you know what kind of work you want to pursue after college, what social and environmental consequences might it have?

5. How would you define a "good job" for yourself?

Case 8.8: *Working Woman*

Donna enjoys her rigorous prelaw program. She always assumed she'd be a high-powered lawyer someday like her father, older sister Cynthia, and brother-in-law Robert. However, after returning from a long visit with Cynthia and Robert, she isn't so sure. Cynthia had warned her that visiting during a work week would mean they'd have little time to hang out with her, "although it'll be great for Danielle," Donna's two-year-old niece. Still, Donna was shocked to see how little time they seemed to have for her (and each other and their daughter).

They both left the house by seven A.M. to commute to work and usually didn't get home until seven or eight at night, when Cynthia would just have time to ask the nanny how Danielle's day had been before the nanny left and they put their daughter to bed. Then they had to eat and do all the chores that had accumulated during the day before collapsing in bed.

Cynthia spent her "free" evenings running errands, walking the dog, and washing laundry and dishes, while Robert made phone calls and watched TV. They seemed to have time for each other and little Danielle only on weekends, and even then one or both of them often had to rush out for a meeting or do some research for Monday.

They both had important positions and high salaries, but life without time for family, pleasure reading, exercising, and nonbusiness socializing hardly seemed like life at all to Donna. "Of course I want interesting work, respect, and good money," Donna thought, "but does that mean I'll have to be a workaholic?" She also thought about the fact that Danielle clearly seemed to prefer her Jamaican nanny to her own parents, which wasn't surprising considering the amount of time she spent with her. "I want to have kids someday," Donna reflected. "But what's the point if someone else raises them?"

Finally, she recalled that Cynthia seemed to spend her evenings and weekends doing chores while Robert relaxed. "If I don't do this stuff, it doesn't get done," Cynthia had explained. "At least Robert takes the trash out on Thursdays." This division of labor did not seem very fair to Donna, but Cynthia seemed resigned to it.

Donna wondered, "How can I have an interesting career and still have time for my husband, my children, and myself?" When she was growing up, her father worked long hours while her mother stayed home with the children. Her mother did have time for her family and herself, but she missed the fulfillments of an outside career.

Neither her mother's life nor her sister's were models Donna wanted to follow. "It isn't fair that women have to choose between a career, a family, and personal time, and men don't!" she thought bitterly.

Questions

1. Is Donna right that women in contemporary society have to struggle to balance "a career, a family, and personal time," while men somehow do not? (See the third section of "Additional Materials," below.) If so, why does this burden fall disproportionately on women?
2. What can individual women and men, and society at large, do about it?
3. What responsibilities do you feel you and your (future) partner should each have regarding childrearing, housework, and breadwinning?
4. Do fathers and mothers have an equal duty to consider their children's needs in choosing a job, or in choosing whether or not to work outside the home? Why or why not?
5. Do you agree that jobs entailing "interesting work, respect, and good money" require "workaholic" schedules?
6. Is this a trade-off you would be willing to make, or would you have other priorities in choosing a job?
7. Do your experiences in college help prepare you to deal with the multiple demands of work, family, and personal fulfillment? If not, how might college do this?
8. How might the various ethical principles apply to these issues?

BACKGROUND READING

Studs Terkel, *The Great Divide: Second Thoughts on the American Dream* (New York: Pantheon Books, 1988).

   The Pulitzer prizewinning author interviews Americans from all walks of life about changes in American values. Pages 3–52 are particularly relevant for college students. In particular, Terkel discusses Humboldt State University's student graduation pledge "to thoroughly investigate and take into account the social and environmental consequences of any job opportunity" (p. 40 and passim); the influence of the mass media on students' education (pp. 24–27 and passim); and college students' differing views about the purposes of education (p. 44 and passim).

Robert N. Bellah et al., *Habits of the Heart: Individualism and Commitment in American Life* (New York: Harper and Row, 1985).

   This eloquent best-seller describes the isolated and beleaguered selves produced by our modern culture and suggests ways to mend the private-public split in our lives. The authors asked dozens of white, middle-class Americans the big questions: how should we live? How should we think about choosing our life paths? Who are we, as Americans? How do our individual characters relate to our society? Their analysis of the interviewees' answers is helpful to anyone pondering these questions for her- or himself.

Claudia Mills, "How Good a Person Do I Have to Be?" in *The Report from The Institute for Philosophy and Public Policy*, Winter 1988, vol. 8, no. 1, pp. 12–15. *The Report* is available from The Institute for Philosophy and Public Policy, School of Public Affairs, University of Maryland, College Park, MD 20742, (301) 405-4759.

The author humorously and philosophically discusses our "moral report cards" and what being a good person might mean in today's world.

Clark Kerr, *The Uses of the University* (Cambridge, Mass.: Harvard University Press, 1995).

The author discusses the evolution of the modern university into the multiversity and the relationships between the university and society.

ADDITIONAL MATERIALS

1. Amy Tan, *The Joy Luck Club* (New York: Putnam, 1989)

This book deals with cross-generational differences in concepts of duty, appropriate sex roles, the importance of the family versus the individual, and the purpose of education (among other themes) in women from Chinese American families. Many of the best-selling novel's basic insights apply to all immigrants who suffered tremendously before coming to the United States, and then raised offspring here who enjoy privileges they never had. To what differing ethical principles do the mothers and daughters in the book seem to appeal? If your parents (or their parents) were immigrants, is there a similar generation gap of expectations in your family? What role can college play in expanding or closing that gap?

2. Benjamin Barber, *An Aristocracy of Everyone: The Politics of Education and the Future of America* (New York: Oxford University Press, 1992), pp. 253–54.

Rutgers, the State University of New Jersey, recently created "an extended pilot program in which classroom civic education and practical community service were united in a number of bold new courses and a residence hall devoted to service learning." In particular, Rutgers developed a mandatory civic education course for all freshmen,

> *organized around [. . .] a classroom course with an academic syllabus, but also including a strong and innovative experiential learning focus utilizing group projects. [. . .] students [are] free to choose community service or non-service projects as their experiential learning group project. [. . . .] Course content [is] broad and varied, but [. . .] [covers] vital civic issues and questions, including the following: 1. The nature of the social or civic bond. [. . . .] 2. the meaning of citizenship. [. . . .] 3. the university community. [. . . .] 4. the place of ethnicity, religion, race, class, gender, and sexual ori-*

entation in a community. [. . . .] 5. the nature of service. [. . . .] 6. the na-
ture of leadership in a democracy. [. . . .] 7. cooperation and competition,
models of community interaction. [. . . .] 8. the character of civic communi-
ties, educational, local, regional, and national." (Barber, An Aristocracy of
Everyone, *pp. 256–258.)*

Does the idea of such a service-oriented course seem coercive, an en-
croachment on students' rights? Does citizenship involve duties and responsibilities as well as rights and privileges? If so, what are these duties? Is
service to others in our community a private virtue, like charity, or a public
duty that everyone needs to fulfill in order to maintain democracy and our
sense of social connectedness? How might the various ethical principles apply to these questions?

Is the idea of "mandatory service" a self-contradiction? What are the ethical implications of making service programs voluntary, versus making them
compulsory? How might participation in a service program benefit the participants? For more information, see "Chapter 7: Teaching Democracy
Through Community Service" in Barber, *An Aristocracy of Everyone*, pp.
230–261; and Robert K. Fullinwider, "Mandated Service and Moral Learning"
in *The Report from The Institute for Philosophy and Public Policy*, Summer/Fall
1992, vol. 12, no. 3/4, pp. 17–19. *The Report* is available from The Institute for
Philosophy and Public Policy, School of Public Affairs, University of Maryland, College Park, MD 20742, (301) 405-4759.

3. Until about thirty years ago, it was assumed that raising children
and making a home was full-time "women's work." Now women, especially college-educated women, have far more opportunities and pressures to work outside the home. In 1950, 23% of married women with
children under six worked; in 1986, 54% of women with young children
worked; of the mothers who worked, 67% had full-time jobs. These per-
centages have doubtless increased since 1986. Yet in families where both
parents work, women still do far more childcare and housework than
men. Thus women end up working "roughly 15 hours longer each week
than men. Over a year, they work an *extra month of twenty-four-hour days a*
year." (Ibid.; statistics taken from Arlie Hochschild with Anne Machung,
The Second Shift: Working Parents and the Revolution at Home (New York:
Viking, 1989), p. 3).

Many people see college as preparation for earning a living. Should college also help prepare students (of both sexes?) for parenting and running a
home? What kinds of courses or other experiences might do this? What
should a man and a women contribute to the family? Are ethical issues involved in how wage earning, child rearing, and housework are divided by a
couple? For more information see Hochschild and Machung, *The Second Shift;*

Kathleen Gerson, *Hard Choices: How Women Decide About Work, Career, and Motherhood* (Berkeley, Calif.: University of California Press, 1985); and Jana Singer, "Women's Work," in *The Report from The Institute for Philosophy and Public Policy*, Winter 1991, vol. 11, no. 1, pp. 1–5. *The Report* is available from The Institute for Philosophy and Public Policy, School of Public Affairs, University of Maryland, College Park, MD 20742, (301) 405-4759.

9

RELIGION, RELATIVISM, AND DIALOGUE

Before you begin to read this chapter, you might find it helpful to review the general questions raised in the "Questions" section of Chapter 1. The responses to some of those questions appear here in Chapter 9.

As you have read through this book, you have probably thought of some broad questions. Although we can't anticipate or address all of them, we want to discuss a few that may have occurred to many readers and that may be important to you as you continue to think about ethical issues.

Here are some commonly asked questions about ethics:

1. Doesn't ethics depend on religion? Can we know what is right apart from some revelation from God?
2. Are there any moral absolutes, things that are always good or bad? Aren't all ethical ideas relative to our culture? Aren't they just a matter of taste? How can we know that some ethical idea is true? "Your book," you might say, "has been full of options, dilemmas, and ambiguities, but there has been little talk about *knowing* something is right or wrong. Doesn't this make a good case for relativism?" Aren't we more likely to be tolerant if we believe in relativism?
3. When people disagree about ethical issues, how can they work it out? In order to agree, do they have to appeal to some moral absolute? Is there any way that they can discover what's right? Is there an ethics of solving ethical problems?
4. Must people agree about their ethical lives? Aren't ethical matters private? When we seek agreement, aren't we likely to end up imposing the ideas of a majority on a minority? Why not respect everyone's freedom

and let people make up their own minds? Isn't tolerance of moral diversity the most important moral concept in a free society?

By the time we have finished with our discussion, we hope you will notice the relationships among these questions. They all have something to do with ethical dialogue. In this chapter, we suggest that dialogue is an important part of ethical decision making. We have used the word *dialogue* because we want to emphasize the importance of a certain kind of moral conversation. The basic idea is that ethical issues and disagreements should be discussed. In fact, a major aim of this book has been to teach you how to have an ethical discussion.

How do these various questions relate to the idea of dialogue? First, some answers to these questions tend to make dialogue impossible or pointless. For example, if there are moral absolutes that can be received only from God, there doesn't seem to be much to discuss. We can't discover ethical truths by reasoning about them or discussing them. When we have them, we have commands from God. How can we take divine commands and treat them as topics of open discussion? Part of the idea of an open discussion is that we enter into it entertaining the possibility that we could be wrong and that we could change our minds. Can we decide that what God has commanded is wrong? If we know what is right because God has said so, our attitude toward those who disagree will apparently have to be that they are benighted or evil. Religious certainty doesn't seem conducive to open dialogue.

Curiously, ethical relativism has a similar consequence. It might seem that if we start out believing that ethical ideas are relative or simply matters of personal choice, the possibility of useful moral conversation becomes greater. After all, people will not come to a moral conversation *knowing* they are right. They will respect other people's opinions. They won't be locked into their views. They can be flexible. Unfortunately, there is more to it than this. If ethical ideas are only matters of culture or taste or personal opinion, there doesn't seem to be much to discuss. At least there doesn't seem to be much possibility of achieving a reasoned agreement about ethical matters. It's all a matter of opinion. There isn't really any right or wrong about right or wrong; therefore dialogue doesn't get us anywhere.

Notice that the idea of meaningful dialogue makes some assumptions about ethical decision making. It assumes that we don't always know what's right and wrong with any certainty. It also assumes that it is possible to have a reasoned opinion about ethics, that some ethical beliefs are more reasonable than others, and that if we work at it, we can progress toward agreement.

Meaningful dialogue thus presupposes that we view ethical questions objectively. Looking at moral issues objectively means seeking a middle ground between absolutism and relativism. Absolutism is wrong, not because there are no answers to ethical questions, but because we don't always know what the answers are before we think through and talk about the questions. Relativism is wrong because there are answers and if we work at ethical inquiry together, sometimes we can find them.

PLATO'S PROGRESS

We want to start our discussion of these questions with Plato, who, in a particularly interesting way, posed the question of whether right or wrong depend on God's commands or God's will. In his dialogue "Euthyphro," Plato lays out a dilemma that can (with a few liberties) be put this way: does what is right depend on God's commands? Neither "yes" nor "no" seem satisfactory answers, even to the religious person. If the answer is "yes," then right and wrong seem to depend arbitrarily on what God chooses. Thus, if God happened to decide that murder and theft were right, and kindness and honesty wrong, they would be.

In this view, knowing right from wrong would depend entirely on a revelation from God. There would be no way to figure it out independently. How could there be? God's decisions would be the only thing to know, and because God's decisions depend entirely on his choices, His will, there would be no way of knowing how God would choose. We could only know what was right or wrong if God told us.

This outcome seems highly unsatisfactory. Right and wrong don't feel arbitrary in this way. Although we may have to do some hard thinking to discover right or wrong in complicated cases, we don't usually have to think much to know that murder is wrong, nor do we need a revelation to decide this. It also seems hard to accept the idea that if God decided that murder were right and preserving life wrong, this would make it so. Something is wrong with the view that right and wrong depend only on God's choices. Strangely enough, such a view seems the ultimate in moral relativism. Right and wrong are arbitrary and depend only on what is chosen. However, in this case, the relativism is revealed only when we take a "God's-eye view" of ethics. It's all relative to God's will, not ours, but wasn't the point of making right and wrong depend on God to make moral knowledge absolute, not relative?

Plato suggests an alternative. Perhaps God commands us to do what is right because it is right, and forbids us from doing what is wrong because it is wrong. God's commands depend on his knowledge of right and wrong. If we say this, Plato points out, we also commit ourselves to the view that right and wrong do not depend on God's choices or God's will. What is right and what is wrong now seem matters independent of God—things God must discover himself. Even if God is all knowing, his knowledge of right and wrong is like his knowledge of physics or mathematics: it is knowledge of something independent of himself that is also independently knowable by us.

This view suggests that there is a point to moral inquiry and moral discussion. Discussion can lead us to discover something, because there may be something to discover. On the other hand, this position is equally unlikely to satisfy the religious person. Now it seems as though right and wrong have nothing to do with God.

Are there other options for the religious person? We can mention two. First, perhaps right and wrong depend not on God's will, but on his nature. Consider an analogy. Some religious philosophers believe that science is possible because the world is created by a rational and orderly God. The order of the universe reflects God's orderliness. Its intelligibility depends on God's rationality. When we come to understand the nature of space and time, we are thinking God's thoughts after him.

The same is true for ethics. The world was created by a just and good God. Justice and goodness don't depend on a capricious God's arbitrary choices. They are what they are because the created order reflects God's moral nature.

We will leave it to the reader to decide whether this is a satisfactory resolution of Plato's dilemma. What we wish to point out is that if this view is correct, right and wrong can be discovered by reflection and discussion, because what is right or wrong is, like the laws of physics, in some way part of the discoverable order of things. Inquiry has a point.

Another answer, possibly consistent with the first, is that understanding right and wrong depends on having a full vision of the nature of a good life, a vision that may depend on religion. We have already suggested something like this in our discussion of sex in Chapter 6. Some religions attach a spiritual meaning to sex. Those who are religious cannot fully understand the point of sex or develop an adequate set of sexual mores apart from their religion's understanding of sex.

If you are attracted to such a view, we think you should also ask some additional questions. One is whether there are minimal ethical standards that seem reasonable to people independently of their religious convictions or lack of them. We may need a religious outlook to see the union of a man and a woman as sacramental. But we don't need a religious outlook to know that rape, murder, and dishonesty are wrong. Such moral concepts seem commonly accepted among human beings, regardless of their religious views or lack thereof. Perhaps, then, there are basic ideas of right and wrong that can be known independently of religion. Indeed, this is just what many religions teach.

Think about your reaction to our introductory chapter. Although you may not have agreed with every detail of the moral principles we sketched there, we are willing to bet that most of our readers accepted these principles regardless of their religious views or lack of them. There is much to debate about their interpretation or application, but ideas such as respect for persons, benefit maximization, community, relationship, and personal growth seem important and commonly held. They appear in most religions. Why not view them as central to all moral conversations, even between people who may disagree about religious matters?

We aren't arguing that religion is unimportant to ethics. It may inform people's ideas about what a good life is and how they should deal with others. However, we don't think religion plays this role in a way that is inconsistent with moral dialogue between people of different faiths, or no faith. People with different religious outlooks may have a great deal in common. Although religious differences may keep them from agreeing on the deeper meaning of many activities, such as sex, they probably can agree on basic standards of morality.

ABSOLUTISM AND RELATIVISM

Are moral claims absolute, that is, are they always right or wrong? Are there moral absolutes? If not, is ethics relative?

We are reluctant to answer these questions in this simple form, not because we wish to avoid controversy or complexity, but because we think they are bad questions. Often people ask them having only a very fuzzy sense of what they mean and what might follow if there were absolutes or if ethics were relative.

In addition, some of the answers to these questions are harmful. If people believe that they possess moral absolutes, or if they believe that all moral claims are relative, they may well refuse to engage in moral dialogue, or they may engage in it in unproductive ways. Both convictions—that we know beyond doubt what is right, and that no one can know what is right—undermine moral discussion and reflection.

Perhaps we might consider the question of whether there are absolutes by looking at one of the Ten Commandments, "Thou shalt not kill." Is this an absolute? We trust you noticed that earlier we used murder as an example of something that is clearly wrong. We have no serious doubts about this.

However, the commandment doesn't exactly say, "Don't murder." It says, "Don't kill." Never? Many people who apparently accept the Ten Commandments also seem to believe that it is acceptable to kill in self-defense. Many believe that it is acceptable to kill in a just war. Some believe in capital punishment. Some believe in abortion.[1] Does this mean they don't really believe in the commandment?

---

[1] Curiously, in our culture people who object to capital punishment often accept abortion, and people who object to abortion often accept capital punishment. It seems obvious that both abortion and capital punishment are cases of killing. That either or both are acts of murder or wrongful killing requires an argument, probably a very complicated and difficult one. We are puzzled at the confidence people appear to have in their convictions on these questions. Where does such confidence come from? Are people entitled to such confidence?

Perhaps they would say that what the commandment means is "Don't murder," meaning "don't kill wrongfully," but justifiable killing isn't murder. That is a perfectly sensible thing to say, but we should notice its implications.

One implication is that we can't apply the commandment until we understand the justifications for killing. Developing such an understanding may require a difficult and complicated discussion. Religious people who devoutly believe in the commandment have produced thousands of books on topics such as the nature of a just war, or on capital punishment and abortion. Quite possibly one reason they have done so is the strength of their conviction that killing is wrong. Thus they need to be clear about the rightness of exceptions. (Probably most of us believe we should stop at red lights and that there are legitimate exceptions, but people have not filled libraries writing about what they are.)

Thus the vast majority of people who believe "Thou shalt not kill" don't see it as an absolute having no exceptions. It turns out that we can't be certain about its meaning until we have a complicated view about justifiable killing. The fact that it is a religious commandment makes no difference here. We still have to work it out, discuss it, argue about it. So the idea that religious commandments are necessarily absolutes seems untrue on closer inspection.

Many people seem to believe that religion provides us with moral absolutes, but that secular views lead to relativism. However, there are noteworthy cases of religious "relativism." St. Augustine said, "Love and do what you will." When Jesus was accused of permitting his disciples to break the Sabbath, he is credited with saying, "Man was not made for the Sabbath, but the Sabbath for man."

Are these really cases of religious relativism? Surely not if relativism means that moral judgments are nothing but matters of taste or opinion. Neither are they absolutes, if that means commandments that must be followed, independently of context or any understanding of the good to be achieved by following them. Both Augustine and Jesus implied that the right action is relative to the good to be accomplished. In Augustine's case we should look to the good of the beloved in our actions. In Jesus' case we are to look to the needs of those for whom the Sabbath was made. Moral acts are relative to the goods to be achieved and their context. Are they still absolutes? What is gained by describing them so?

We should also note cases of what might be called secular absolutists. The philosopher Emmanuel Kant believed that moral maxims such as "Don't lie" have no exceptions, even when acting on them will have bad consequences.

Utilitarian philosophers such as John Stuart Mill believe in the greatest good for the greatest number. Is this a case of absolutism or relativism? Well, utilitarians may claim that this principle is completely general, universal, and without exceptions. It is the one moral principle from which all others follow.

However, if this is true, we must judge all other moral claims by their implications for the greatest good for the greatest number. Is lying wrong? It is if its consequences are bad, but they aren't always bad. Perhaps we should lie to preserve a life or to prevent some other, greater harm.

Similarly, the way we apply the utilitarian principle depends on our understanding of the goods to be achieved and the bads to be minimized. We can't use utilitarianism to decide on the best course of action without knowing the consequences, because we must judge actions by their outcomes (the greatest good for the greatest number). Relativism or absolutism? It's hard to tell. Is there some sense in which utilitarians are relativists and Jesus and Augustine are not?

Let's think about relativism for a while. One thing that relativism might mean is that we need to consider moral judgments in their context. It might be right to do something in some situations but not in others. It might mean that some moral claims are relative to others, in the way that keeping the Sabbath might be relative to other, higher, human goods. However, as we have argued above, if this is all that relativism means, it is hard to see why anyone would object to it. Reasonable people, religious or not, must sometimes consider circumstances or higher principles and goods in deciding what's right. If this is what relativism means, we are all relativists. Moreover, this kind of relativism is perfectly consistent with moral objectivity.

A more interesting kind of relativism is sometimes called cultural relativism. In this kind of relativism, moral judgments are viewed as valid only within a particular culture. Different cultures have different values. Although it is possible to judge the rightness or wrongness of ethical questions within a culture, it is impossible to make universal judgments between cultures.

Consider a plausible example. In some cultures it is considered rude to belch at the dinner table, especially for a guest, but in other cultures, guests belch to show the host their satisfaction with the meal. In these cultures belching is actually polite. Can we decide across cultures whether belching is "really" rude?

It is also important to notice that many people are motivated to believe in cultural relativism because they believe in the importance of tolerance. A culture that tries to impose its values on another is intolerant. Anti-belching cultures, they would say, have no right to impose their views on belching cultures.

We are willing to be cultural relativists about belching. Different belching customs are no more right or wrong than are different languages. However, we do not believe that this example can be generalized to most moral issues. In fact, the example is terribly misleading.

First, notice that in both belching and anti-belching cultures, it is considered desirable to be polite. One should express appreciation to one's host at a dinner party. The difference between the belchers and the anti-belchers doesn't have to do with politeness itself. It concerns how politeness is expressed. Suppose, instead, that one culture valued politeness and another rudeness. Should we be culturally relative about this?

If you think so, consider another case. Let's imagine two cultures in two neighboring states. One group we will call the Talls; they live in Tallvania. The other group, the Shorts, live in Shortland. Now the Talls and the Shorts do not differ in their average heights. Each culture has people of various heights. However, they differ in how they regard height. The Talls consider tallness attractive and shortness ugly. The Shorts find shortness attractive and height ugly.

They also disagree about the significance of these differences. The Shorts are absolutists about their tastes. They believe that tallness is objectively bad, and therefore they actively discriminate against tall people. They prevent them from holding good jobs. They restrict them to ghettos and poor housing. They deny them proper health care and good educations. No one whose height exceeds six feet is permitted to continue in school. In fact, the Shorts are so aggressive about their beliefs that, whenever they can, they insist that others practice them. When they trade with other states, they refuse to deal with tall people. Indeed, many Shorts want to make shortness central to their foreign policy and to fight against those benighted societies that value tallness.

In contrast, the Talls regard their preference for height as a social convention. Although tall people are in fashion and on that account may have better chances for good jobs, short people do not experience active discrimination. Indeed, such discrimination is illegal. The Talls recognize that their preference for height can injure short people. They seek to prevent this as best they can. Their attitude toward tallness is a bit like ours toward what our culture considers beautiful. In fact, many Talls regard the preference of their society for height as undesirable because of the harm it can do to short people. Among them "tallism" is considered unethical.

Are the Talls relativists? And are they tolerant because they are relativists? Before you say yes, ask yourself how the Talls should feel about the beliefs of the Shorts.

Suppose the Talls are consistent and tolerant cultural relativists. In this case, they should conclude that values can be judged only within a culture, so they have a duty to respect and tolerate the values of other cultures when the values conflict with their own. Unfortunately this puts the Talls in an untenable situation with the Shorts, for they must now conclude some unpleasant things. First, the Shorts' views about tall people are "right for them." The Talls must respect the Shorts' absolutism about Shortness. Indeed, the Talls must even tolerate the Shorts' aggression toward them. After all, such absolutism and aggression are right within the context of Short culture. Ironically the Talls must accept the rightness of the Shorts' views for the Shorts, simply because the Shorts happen to hold them.

Most seriously, the consistent cultural relativist must be a relativist about tolerance. Tolerance is therefore a moral requirement only within cultures that happen to value it. It cannot be used where it seems most necessary—against the intolerant Shorts. If the Talls are consistent cultural relativists, they must not only see their preference for height as relative to their culture, but they must also see their preference for tolerance of shortness as similarly relative. Cultural relativists have to treat tolerance as only a relative good, and accept intolerant cultures without moral criticism.

Note that cultural relativists can, with equal consistency, value intolerance. Many Nazis were cultural relativists. They accepted the variableness of human cultures and their own lack of objectivity. They also asserted their right to impose their will on others. How would a cultural relativist criticize Nazis? Were they objectively wrong? Was their intolerance right for them?

These considerations suggest that the idea that tolerance rests on relativism is a deeply confused view. Tolerance itself is a moral commitment. It can be justified, perhaps, by appealing to such principles as respect for persons. To root it in relativism robs tolerance of any moral force regarding the intolerant. Indeed, the main consequence of justifying tolerance in terms of relativism is to require that those who accept the value of tolerance put up with the intolerance of those who do not. What could possibly be more unacceptable? Paradoxically, we can best affirm tolerance if we regard it as an objective moral requirement.

What should we conclude about relativism and absolutism? These examples suggest several important things. First, contrary to much popular sentiment, it is not true that religion tends to support the view that there are absolutes, and nonreligion leads to relativism. The history of religious and secular moral theories offers little support for this view. Second, the terms themselves are unclear. It's not even clear what we want to say when we talk about "absolutes" or "relativism."

Third, both relativism and absolutism undercut necessary moral discussion. Absolutism does so by creating the illusion of moral certainty where there is none, and relativism by undermining the possibility of discussion and criticism, especially when it is most needed, in dealing with intolerance. In fact, no matter what view we take, we still need moral discussion. If we believe in absolutes, we still have to interpret or define them. Probably when we discuss them we'll raise the same kinds of issues, face the same kinds of problems, and appeal to the same kinds of evidence to which relativists appeal. Often we will end up talking about respect for persons, benefit maximization, relationships, community, and character growth. Talk about absolutism and relativism unnecessarily polarizes discussion while shedding little real light on how we should behave. We must take the stance of objectivity.

TOLERANCE AND DIALOGUE

Why should we be tolerant? What should we tolerate? A reasonable view of tolerance must answer both of these questions. Tolerance, we have argued, doesn't depend on relativism; on what does it depend, then? Can we give reasons for tolerance? Also, a sensible view will reflect tolerance of some things but not others. Any concept of tolerance requiring that we accept murder and theft, but not religious differences or differing food preferences would be highly suspicious.

Let's consider tolerance instead as an implication of the principle of *equal respect for persons*. What follows from this idea?

1. Because people are of equal worth, they are entitled to equal treatment and equal rights. Minimally, this requires that we treat people equally and fairly regardless of their differences. We cannot discriminate against people because of such characteristics as their race, religion, or gender. Thus we must tolerate these forms of diversity.

2. Respect for persons requires that we respect people's choices and viewpoints. Respecting people partly means accepting that they are moral agents who are responsible for their own decisions and welfare. If we respect people as moral agents, we must respect their choices, convictions, and decisions.

This might mean at least two things. First, the fact that someone chooses to want something, believe something, or do something is a reason to respect that choice. If we view others as moral agents, we must see them as responsible for their decisions. We do not have the right to interfere because we disagree or would have decided otherwise. Second, we have to recognize that we hurt others in a particularly serious way when we seek to override their basic convictions. For example, to prevent people from worshiping God as they see fit, or to compel them to worship God when they are not believers, is to cause them to violate their deepest and most central obligations. Responsible moral agents will view this as an especially serious offense.

3. Respecting people's choices or convictions does not mean agreeing with them. It means that we accept an obligation not to interfere with them. Consider freedom of religion. To respect the religion of other people does not mean that we must regard one religion as equal to another, or all religions as equally true. People may continue to view their own religion as true and those of others as false. They may consider all religions untrue. Nevertheless, respecting the religious liberty of others requires that we not view the truth of our religion or the error of others as a reason for coercion. Here, as elsewhere, tolerance depends not on relativism, but on equal respect.

4. Respecting other people's choices does not mean that we should permit people to violate the rights of others, but if we must respect others' choices, what reasons can there be for not tolerating particular conduct? Again we can use religion to illustrate. Suppose some religion teaches that coercing others to the true faith is permissible, good, or even obligatory. Clearly, tolerating people who act on such a belief is inconsistent with the belief that everyone has an equal right to freedom of religion. Thus the limits on tolerance are set by the conviction that whatever rights people have, they must have them equally. If we accept this, we cannot tolerate practices that permit some to act so as to deny equal rights to others. We can criticize intolerance because it is objectively wrong, and we can prevent people from acting intolerantly when their behavior interferes with the freedom of others.

Philosopher John Rawls [1971: 60] argues that people are entitled to the greatest possible liberty consistent with an equal liberty for others. In his view, tolerance is an objective moral principle; he does not associate tolerance with relativism or moral skepticism. We ought to be tolerant because the principle of *equal respect* requires it of us. (Question: Can arguments be made for tolerance from other moral principles, such as benefit maximization or community? What would such arguments look like?)

Consider how this idea might be applied to the Talls and the Shorts. Rawls's way of looking at tolerance allows the Talls to avoid the trap of cultural relativism. They do not have to accept the views of the Shorts as "right for them" simply because the Shorts have these views, nor do they need to see their tolerance as relative to their own culture. The Talls may believe that the Shorts are wrong because their views are intolerant. They may criticize the Shorts for their views and urge them to be more tolerant. They may object to the Shorts' treatment of tall people in their society and may even take action to oppose this injustice.

Of course, this doesn't mean that there aren't some hard questions to be answered about tolerance. Must the Talls tolerate the Shorts' beliefs? Quite possibly; see the discussion of hate speech in Chapter 3. However, we need to be clear that tolerating the Shorts' views does not mean that the Talls have to agree with them or to see them as true for the Shorts. It means the Talls have to believe that they have no right to try to coerce the Shorts to change their beliefs. The difference between ideas and actions is important here. The Talls might reasonably believe that they should tolerate the Shorts' convictions, and also resist the Shorts' attempts to act on them.

It is important also to remember that we described the Talls and the Shorts as members of different countries. Presumably, unless they resort to economic sanctions or military invasions, the Talls have little ability to coerce the Shorts. (Question: Would the Talls have a right to seek to protect tall people in Shortland?) Suppose, however, that the Talls and the Shorts were different groups in the same society. Does this change things? How?

If the two groups were in the same country, the Talls might (as we have described them doing) pass laws to protect people from discrimination on the basis of height. They might also teach their children tolerance. Notice again that these affirmative steps to secure tolerance make sense only if we believe that tolerance is an objective moral principle binding us all.

DIALOGUE

One of our objectives in this chapter is to persuade you that moral dialogue is important. It is our principal means for settling ethical disputes and for gaining moral knowledge. To demonstrate this, we've had to discuss topics such as the relationship between religion and ethics, the ideas of absolutism and relativism, and the nature of tolerance. To talk about dialogue, we've had to defend the possibility of moral inquiry against two incompatible ideas. The first view, absolutism, says that moral inquiry is unnecessary because the moral truth is known. The second, relativism, says that moral inquiry is impossible because there is nothing to find out.

Against the first view, we have argued that people of faith are not necessarily committed to moral absolutism. Against the second, we have argued that relativism does not promote tolerance. In fact tolerance seems to require a belief in moral objectivity. To believe that ethical dialogue has a point, we must believe both in the possibility of objective moral truth and in our own fallibility.

Perhaps you have noted that neither of these arguments makes a decisive case for moral objectivity or the usefulness of moral dialogue. You might, for example, accept that tolerance requires a belief in moral objectivity and conclude, "Too bad for tolerance." You might ask, "Can you prove that moral objectivity and moral dialogue are good and necessary things?"

We cannot prove this decisively. Instead we're inclined to rest our case on two kinds of experience that we believe almost everyone has had. The first is that some moral claims seem strong enough (if not certain) that we accept them without argument. For example, everyone who reads this will probably agree that it's wrong to cause gratuitous pain to others, or to abuse children. Such strong moral intuitions seem to require little defense. We become skeptical about them only if we're motivated by some philosophical theory; in real life, no sane person doubts them. In addition, such moral intuitions often can be used to judge other moral claims. We can be reasonably sure, for instance, that any moral theory that says it's acceptable to inflict gratuitous pain or to abuse children is wrong for that reason.

We also believe that most people have numerous experiences with successful moral arguments. Perhaps you've had some with this book. For instance, many students believe that cheating is a victimless crime, but they usually can be persuaded that it isn't. Moral arguments often persuade us be-cause they help us see more clearly what's involved in some conduct or be-lief. We are persuaded because we see that harm is done or respect denied or relationships or community broken, whereas before we didn't see that. Therefore, the best evidence we can give you for the value of moral dialogue is that sometimes it succeeds in changing people's minds for good reasons.

We don't mean to deny that often ethics are ambiguous and life has tragic elements. Sometimes we must choose between conflicting goods or conflict-ing bads, and there is little to guide us. However, even here, when moral ar-gument may not resolve an issue clearly, it can help us be clear about the nature of the issues. For example, moral dialogue may not (as yet) have set-tled the abortion debate. Perhaps it cannot. But it can help us understand more clearly the conflicting values involved. Wanting all children to be loved, respecting life, and respecting privacy all count! (We suspect that people who find the proper conclusion about abortion obvious or easy have missed something in the debate.) Even when moral discussion fails, it may help us to see our opponents in the debate as good people who are wrong about some-thing, instead of seeing them as evil. There are evil people in the world, and there are occasions when we must oppose them, not argue with them. How-ever, such a judgment about others usually should be earned by an attempt at conversation. It's a rare occasion when moral dialogue has no point.

Up to this point, we haven't distinguished much between moral reflec-tion and moral dialogue. You might think, "OK, I accept that I should reflect on ethical issues, but why should I try to get others to reflect, too? Why dia-logue?"

One reason is that a willingness to dialogue recognizes our fallibility and our limitations. To engage in a dialogue, we must accept that we might be wrong, and also remember that we have much to learn from others. Recall the views of John Stuart Mill that we quoted and discussed in Chapter 3. Mill notes that when we refuse to dialogue and seek to enforce our views instead, we assume that we're infallible. Additionally, free and open debate is some-thing from which we can profit. Dialogue lets us test our views by having to defend them; we grow and learn from the process. If we repress the views of others, we are presuming that we never make mistakes; if we refuse to dis-cuss things, we are presuming that we have nothing to learn. We must dia-logue because we are not self-sufficient in this way.

There are other reasons to dialogue. Mill's arguments bid us to view other people as sources of ideas, information, and argument. People are also objects of respect. Thus when we propose to act in a way that affects others, we should also view them as having a right to participate in decision mak-ing and to have opinions. That is one way in which respect for others is shown. Recall the opening cases in our discussion of privacy in Chapter 4. In one case, Bill and Fred were in conflict about the use of their room. In the other, Judy and Rachel had become unhappy with each other over how Rachel's mother treated Judy. There is something to learn about dialogue from each of these cases.

Recall that we criticized Fred not only because he treated Bill badly, but also because he refused to discuss the matter with Bill. The basis of our criticism here isn't that Fred might learn something from Bill. It is that Bill has a right to a vote about the use of the room. In refusing to discuss the matter, Fred is not only saying that he doesn't care about Bill's ideas. He is also saying that Bill has no rights concerning the room.

Another issue is involved here. Although we think that Bill and Fred can profitably discuss the use of their room, we don't have such a high regard for moral dialogue that we believe there is only one fair way to use the room. There may be some clearly wrong ways, in which the interests of one party dominate the other. There also may be many reasonable outcomes. Within this range of plausible outcomes, what may make one result the right one is that Bill and Fred freely agree to it as the result of an open discussion.

The case of Judy and Rachel can help us see one further point. Judy and Rachel both believe that it is important to be polite and to avoid being rude to others. Neither wants to cause pain. However, their two families have different views about what counts as showing respect for others. Judy's family links respect to privacy, Rachel's to openness. Is one wrong and the other right? Perhaps. That, itself, requires a discussion. We should recognize that these different views share common ground in at least two ways.

First, regardless of what might be the "right" way to show respect, both Judy and Rachel did intend to show respect; they understood the concept differently. Neither will understand this without dialogue. They need a discussion to see respect from the other's point of view.

Second, perhaps people have a right to define what counts as showing respect in their own way, consistent with their own cultural traditions or their own preferences. This right may be a consequence of the idea that respect for persons requires tolerance. However, we need to be careful here. If some people tell us that they prefer to be shown respect by having us give them our paycheck every week, or wash their windows, we are quite unlikely to accept their interpretation of respect. Nevertheless, one significant way to oppress people is to insist on treating them according to our definition of what counts as satisfactory treatment. To respect others, first of all we must understand what they mean by being respected. We should reject their understanding of respect only for good reasons; we cannot simply assume that what we mean is what they ought to mean. (Question: Can you think of some examples in which what counts as respect is understood differently by members of different cultures?)

Why dialogue? We have provided four reasons. In summary they are as follows:

1. Dialogue makes moral judgments more reasonable by bringing evidence and argument to bear on our opinions.
2. Dialogue is a way of affirming the equal right of people to participate in decisions that affect them.
3. Dialogue recognizes that sometimes what counts as the right thing to do is the product of an open and uncoerced agreement, a contract.
4. Dialogue accepts people's right to their own understanding of the meaning of respect and helps us to understand one another.

Implied in these views is an ethic of moral dialogue. Its features are as follows:

1. Dialogue involves respect for argument and evidence.
2. Dialogue respects the right of people to have a voice in matters that affect them.
3. Dialogue seeks agreements that result from the better argument rather than from superior power or social position.
4. Dialogue recognizes individuals' right to define their own understanding of the conditions of respect.

Dialogue requires and shows a certain moral stance toward the world. It expresses our rationality and our fallibility, our limitations and our willingness to recognize that others have a value equal to our own.

A final thought: dialogue can be understood as part of moral growth. At the beginning of this book, we noted that decisions not only produce actions, they also produce character. We become the kinds of people who do what we choose to do. There is an analogous point to be made about dialogue. Dialogue requires not only that we be able to argue, but also that we be willing and able to listen. Listening is a matter of both will and discernment. We must want to hear, but we must be able to hear what others want to say. When we refuse to listen, when we refuse to consider the other's position or the other's pain, we gradually make ourselves into the kinds of people who don't count others' interests and who can't hear others' pain. We make ourselves morally deaf. Fred, who will not talk with Bill; Percy, who hates African Americans; and Peter, who seduces unwilling women, are not only selfish. They are doing themselves moral harm from which they may have difficuly recovering. They have dulled their capacity to hear others' pain, to see the world from others' point of view, to listen, to understand, to care.

Sometimes others are hard to hear and easy to misunderstand, for example, if they come from a world quite different from our own. However, that is not true in these cases. Fred, Percy, and Peter have refused to hear. They have dulled their consciences and blunted their capacity for moral judgment. They have diminished their capacity for seeking their own good in their relationships with others. They enjoy what is base and harmful. They may be putting themselves beyond the reach of moral discourse. They are becoming lost.

Why dialogue? Your character depends on it.

BIBLIOGRAPHY

James Hunter, *Culture Wars* (New York: Basic Books, 1991). Hunter argues that disputes in America are increasingly between moral absolutists and relativists who are unable to dialogue or find acceptable accommodation.

John Stuart Mill, *On Liberty* (1859; edited and with an introduction by Gertrude Himmelfarb, New York: Viking Penguin, 1987). For a description of this work, see Chapters 1 and 3.

John Rawls, *Theory of Justice* (Cambridge, Mass.: Belknap Press of Harvard University Press, 1971). For a description of this work, see the references in Chapter 1.

10

FOR FURTHER REFLECTION: ADDITIONAL CASES

Case 10.1: Out with the Old

Ralph and Jessica were an inseparable couple throughout their junior and senior years of high school, and they've promised each other to continue their commitment when they go to college. Freshman year finds Ralph living at home with his mother and attending Stonebridge Community College, while Jessica has gone off to Rockford College, two states away. Jessica seems unable to come home for a visit, so Ralph arranges to visit her school one weekend in mid-November. Jessica hasn't been very good about answering his letters, and he can't afford to call her long distance as often as he'd like, so this will be their first opportunity to really talk and be together in two months. Ralph is thrilled.

However, when he finally sees Jessica again, things seem all wrong between them, although Jessica won't admit it. Her obvious embarrassment over him deeply hurts Ralph's feelings and offends his pride. After a particularly humiliating evening at a dance (Jessica all but ignored him and introduced him to only one of her friends, and then merely as "a friend from high school"), Ralph said, "I don't think I'm so bad, but you're clearly ashamed of me. What's changed? Why'd you let me come?"

Jessica doesn't know what to say. The fact is, Ralph now seems hopelessly awkward, unattractive, and uncool compared to her new sophisticated college friends. In addition, she really likes one of the boys in her crowd and doesn't want him or his friends to think she already has a boyfriend, especially such a dork as Ralph. She hadn't realized until she saw Ralph again how little he fit into her new life. Now she doesn't want to hurt his feelings by telling him. She knows he really cares about her, and he has helped her a lot in the past when she had trouble with her family. The least she can do is be nice to him and spare him as much pain as possible, for old times' sake. But how to get him to be "just friends"?

Questions

1. There's an old saying, "It's cruel to be kind," for such a situation. What would be the ethical thing for Jessica to do regarding Ralph?
2. Was it wrong or stupid of Ralph and Jessica to promise each other to continue their commitment when they went off to separate colleges? Are they now morally obliged to honor such a commitment?
3. Is it reasonable or fair for Jessica to expect Ralph to move from being her boyfriend to "just a friend"? What should Ralph do?
4. Jessica's feelings for Ralph seem to have changed at least in part because of her desire to be accepted by her new friends. Is this an ethically dubious motive for changing her feelings? Why or why not?
5. Do we owe loyalty to people who have been helpful or kind to us in the past but no longer are useful to us? Why or why not?
6. If we do owe this loyalty, how should it be expressed?
7. Do we owe something to people who care about us, even if we don't care about them? What?
8. How might the principles of relationships, personal growth, and respect for persons apply to this case?

Case 10.2: Overloaded

Brad, a freshman at State University, is close to panic. There is just no way he can juggle his current load of schoolwork with his part-time work-study job, his swimming team responsibilities, and his romance with his girlfriend, Melissa. A crisis is coming because he has three midterm exams the week after his six-month anniversary with Melissa (who has made reservations at a nearby ski resort for a romantic weekend, for which she has planned and saved for more than two months).

He also has newly increased responsibilities and hours at his job in the undergraduate library, and the swimming team has two away meets during the same week. He can't study for his exams and do everything else—in fact, he's not even sure how he can juggle his new work hours and his meets and practices, much less fit in the promised trip with Melissa. Something, in fact several things, have to give. But what?

Brad thinks over his choices. He can ask some friends for help with the test material. For example, maybe he can get one of them to tell him enough about the long novel he should have finished for his English class so that he can at least pass without reading the rest of it. He might try asking Abdul to cover some of his library shifts for the next week. Although Abdul seems pretty overworked as it is, Brad knows that he likes him and might do him one more favor. He can try to get Melissa to celebrate their anniversary a couple of weeks later. Of course she'd feel disappointed and probably angry about losing her deposit, and she would be hurt (understandably) that he'd waited until the last minute to upset their long-standing plans. He can pretend to be injured or sick so that he'll miss that week's swim practices and meets. None of these options really appeal to Brad—they all involve imposing on or disappointing people he cares about.

Questions

1. Brad's options all seem to involving cheating or manipulating others in order to meet his responsibilities. Which choice or choices seem the least egregious ethically? Why?
2. How would you advise Brad to prioritize his commitments? Why?
3. Would different moral principles suggest different orderings of his responsibilities?
4. Do you see a moral issue in Brad's dilemma, or is it just a matter of his fitting a large number of commitments into a limited amount of time?
5. Does the university have a duty to regulate the level of time conflicts students might experience, for example, by forbidding away meets or games before or during midterms, or is this the individual student's responsibility?
6. What can Brad do to avoid similar crises in the future?

Case 10.3: Performance Anxiety

Alice enjoys singing in the Heptones, the college's highly selective a capella sextet. The repertoire is enjoyable and challenging, and being in such a small group allows Alice plenty of opportunities to shine. Normally Alice doesn't mind the Heptones' busy concert schedule. She's used to performing regularly around campus and in the nearby town of Red Springs, and occasionally traveling to bigger towns upstate. In fact, Alice is looking forward to their big spring concert; it's always one of the highlights of the Heptones' semester.

Alice and her mother have been arguing a lot on the phone lately. Alice realizes that most of the trouble has been her fault, and she'd like to apologize in some way. After all, her mom has had a hard time ever since the divorce, and she sounds kind of lonely now that Alice is out of the house. Alice decides that it would do a lot to patch up their relationship and cheer up her mother if she made a surprise visit home on her mom's upcoming birthday, and it just so happens that she's noticed a sign on the Ride

Board offering a cheap ride to her hometown just in time for her mom's birthday. Unfortunately it means that she will miss the spring concert.

There isn't much time before the weekend, and Alice makes a quick decision. She leaves a message with Professor Bell, the Heptones' director, that she won't be able to make the concert, and then she packs up her backpack and catches the ride home. She realizes that her last-minute decision might leave the other Heptones in a lurch, but she feels that her relationship with her mother is more important. And at least she's giving them a couple of days' warning so they can perhaps hire someone to replace her, or give her solos to someone else.

It isn't until she returns and goes to the next Heptones rehearsal that Alice realizes how angry the director and other performers are. "Your behavior was completely irresponsible. We couldn't get a replacement for the concert; no one could learn all of the parts we've worked on for months in two days. So now we are auditioning for your permanent replacement," she is frostily informed by Professor Bell. "You are simply too unreliable."

Alice is flabbergasted—she has never even missed a rehearsal before, so this punishment seems rather extreme. She had believed that she was irreplaceable, anyway, especially this late in the year. Besides, she thought they would understand why she had to miss the concert. "You don't get replaced if you miss a concert because you're sick!" she complained. "So why am I getting booted out because I did something nice for my mom?"

Questions

1. Alice feels a conflict between her obligations to her mother and her music group duties. Where should her first responsibility lie? Why?
2. How could Alice better juggle her obligations?
3. Why might the Heptones feel more lenient toward a member who misses a concert commitment out of sickness than toward Alice's "personal" reason? Should they?
4. Professional performers, whether in the arts or sports, often feel that their first duty is to their performance. "The show must go on," and so do they, despite minor injuries, sickness, or private problems. Is this an unreasonable expectation for amateur college athletes, musicians, or actors? Do different ethical standards apply to student amateurs and professionals? Why or why not?
5. How might the ethical principles discussed throughout this book apply to this case?

Case 10.4: What Was That Again?

Wei Jie Chan is a graduate student in chemistry and one of the section leaders for Chemistry 205. He is friendly, but unfortunately his command of spoken English seems to be minimal, and it is further hindered by a heavy accent. The students in his section often cannot make head or tail of his lab presentations or explanations of the professor's lectures, although his written comments on their lab reports and quizzes are clearer. He tries to answer their questions, but his replies usually leave them more confused than before (if not giggling at a completely incomprehensible sentence).

The students often meet after lab to compare notes and see if they can piece together something that makes sense. However, this takes extra time that many of them begrudge, and their quiz grades are suffering. After several weeks, they deputize two of their number, Juan and Lynn, to talk to the professor about either getting rid of Wei Jie Chan or splitting up the members of their section among the five other section instructors.

Juan and Lynn are surprised to find that Professor Black already knows about Wei Jie's trouble in speaking English, although he doesn't seem to think the problem is as bad as they do. However, Professor Black explains, the students can't go into other sections, because they're already full. The chemistry department has no intention of getting rid of Wei Jie as an instructor, because all graduate students are expected to teach as part of their professional training. Furthermore, Wei Jie is a very promising chemist. His written English is fine (as proven by the fact that he passed his English as a Foreign Language exam in order to enter the University), and his spoken English "will no doubt improve rapidly as he teaches."

"But," protests Lynn, "we're getting graded on what he doesn't teach us, right now! We can't wait until he 'gets better.'"

Professor Black replies, "You can certainly come to me with any questions you have. Try to be patient with Wei Jie; it's very difficult to teach in a second language, and he's working hard."

Clearly this is supposed to end the discussion. Lynn and Juan, and the other students in their section, are very discouraged. It seems completely impractical to talk to the professor whenever they have "any questions," because they have questions about almost everything Wei Jie Chan says. Furthermore, they don't see why they should feel pity for Wei Jie, when he's the one grading them!

Questions

1. After meeting with this discouragement, should the students in Wei Jie's section just forget about the class, or should they continue trying to learn the material partly on their own? What else could they do?
2. Might it be their duty to try to help Wei Jie improve his spoken English so that he can teach them better? If not, whose job is it? If so, how could they help?

3. Whose responsibility is it that the students learn the course material?

4. Should the fact that they are being graded change the students' ethical obligations toward Wei Jie? In other words, does the principle of respect for persons require that they show Wei Jie as much patience or sympathy as they would a struggling peer who doesn't have power over them? Why or why not?

5. Should they try to warn future students away from Wei Jie, given that he's just beginning several years of required teaching? How?

6. Professor Black and the chemistry department seem to feel a greater obligation to (or perhaps interest in) graduate students such as Wei Jie Chan than to undergraduates taking their courses. How might they better balance the needs of both Wei Jie and his undergraduate students?

Case 10.5: Special Treatment

Although both of her parents were born in the United States, Juliet Fuentes's grandparents originally came from Argentina. Her family was quite cultured and well-to-do, and she grew up in a sheltered world of prep schools and country clubs. When Juliet was ready to apply to college, her parents realized that her Hispanic surname and Latin American background could be valuable assets in the application process, and they encouraged her to apply for any available minority fellowships or special programs for Hispanic students.

"Colleges, especially the good ones, really want to increase their student diversity," Juliet's father told her. "With your good grades and Hispanic background, you should have no trouble getting in wherever you want to go." Her father also helped her modify her applications to emphasize her ethnicity and disadvantaged status, "so you're more like what they're looking for."

Juliet was overjoyed when she got into her first choice, an Ivy League school, and received a fellowship reserved for minority students as well. She was a bit worried, however, that the college would find out that she wasn't really disadvantaged and kick her out, or at least revoke the fellowship. Her father reassured her. "It's not really a need-based fellowship. They just want to improve the diversity of their student body. You're exactly what they want: a bright, hardworking Hispanic girl."

Juliet chuckled at this description of herself, because she didn't usually think of herself as "Hispanic" (and no one else did, either; she knew only a few phrases of Spanish and had dark-blonde hair and blue eyes). Then she realized that perhaps her getting the fellowship might mean that some poorer, really "Hispanic" (whatever that meant) student wouldn't be able to go to the college.

"Don't worry, honey," her father said with a hug. "Everyone pulls whatever levers they can. Just work hard and have a great time!"

Questions

1. Does Juliet "deserve" a minority fellowship or special consideration because of her Hispanic background? Why or why not?
2. Does someone like Juliet really add to the diversity of an Ivy League college's student body?
3. Many students try to modify their college applications and essays to fit the image of the person they think the college is seeking. Others mildly pad their resumes, for example, by exaggerating the importance of an achievement, or including in their list of high school activities a club they attended for only a month. Are such modifications or padding unethical lies, or are they simply common sense in the college application competition?
4. Has Juliet's father encouraged her to do something immoral? If so, exactly what was unethical about it? If not, what kinds of modifications or padding would you consider immoral on a resume or application?
5. What's wrong with presenting a (slightly) misleading image of yourself when applying for college, a fellowship, or a job?
6. What do you think of Juliet's father's comment that "everyone pulls whatever levers they can"?

Case 10.6: It Isn't Really Stealing

In Tom's otherwise shabby student apartment, one piece of furniture stands out: a large, glass-doored, wooden display case, which he has filled with his sizable collection of animal skulls and unusual rock samples. Tom prides himself on being a naturalist, and he has carefully labeled each item in his collection. As many of his friends have told him, the cabinet and its contents look as though they belong in a museum.

Tom is very proud of this elegant piece. He has carefully waxed and polished all of the wooden surfaces of the case, as well as re-glued some of its loose moldings. His friend Grace, who has taken a number of woodworking courses, is impressed with it. "How much do you think it's worth?" Tom asks casually.

"Wow—maybe $800, or $1000? It has that expensive nonreflecting glass, and everything's beautifully dovetailed. The wood looks like really nice cherry, too. It's beautiful! Where'd you get it?"

Tom is used to his visitors' remarking on the handsome case, and he has often told the story of how he acquired it:

"Last summer I worked as a lab assistant for Professor Costello over in the biology department. It wasn't a very exciting job, because I was mainly washing glassware, but I did get access to the entire storage area of the department. Every time I went into that basement, I saw this beautiful old case and two others just like it—covered with dust. They looked as though they hadn't been used since the building opened. It was such a waste, and I finally decided to take one home. So here it is! They've never missed it. And after a little work, it was better than new. Hey, if I slave for Costello again this summer, maybe I can fix up one of the other ones! My collection is still expanding."

Questions

1. How would you react to Tom's story if you were Grace?
2. Is anyone hurt by this kind of stealing? Tom seems to feel that he has a right to the display case for several reasons: no one seemed to be using it, or even to remember it; he needed it; he has fixed it up; and it wasn't being appreciated or taken care of the way he appreciates it and takes care of it. Do any of these reasons lend legitimacy to his claims on the case?
3. Is it somehow less hurtful to steal something from a large organization or institution rather than from an individual?
4. How might the principles of benefit maximization, character growth, relationships, and community apply to this case?

Case 10.7: Fender Bender

Michiko was preoccupied as she drove to Meadowland Community College on Thursday afternoon. She was running late for her statistics exam because she had been studying her notes and had forgotten to leave as early as she'd planned. Not only that, but she'd also quarreled with her father that morning, and she still couldn't get some of his biting remarks out of her mind. "I have to concentrate for the test!" she told herself sternly. "And I have to hurry!"

Just then the light changed to green. Without thinking, Michiko stepped on the gas. Unfortunately there was a Honda in front of her that was slow to accelerate. Michiko's heavy old Ford hit the Honda with a jolt. Because she'd been going only about ten miles an hour, the damage was slight—her Ford's higher bumper missed the Honda's bumper and shattered its rear brake lights. There was no damage to Michiko's car.

An elderly man slowly got out of the Honda, rubbing his neck. Her heart pounding, Michiko jumped out of the car. "Are you OK?" she asked.

"I think so," the man replied. He seemed a bit dazed, but maybe he was always like that.

"I'm really sorry," Michiko explained. "I'm late for a test at the college, and I guess I jumped the gun."

"Well, it doesn't look too bad. We'll just see what the police say when they turn up," the man said.

"Oh please!" Michiko begged. "I'll miss my exam! Let me give you my phone number. I'll pay for the damage, but I can't wait for the police to arrive!" Then she hurriedly wrote down her name and phone number, jumped back in her car, and rushed the rest of the way to school.

The whole accident set Michiko back only about five minutes, and she got to class just as the professor was handing out the exam. She calmed herself as well as she could and concentrated. Afterward, Michiko reflected that it was a good thing she hadn't waited around for the police for another reason—now her insurance wouldn't go up. She'd call that old man as soon as she got home to make sure he was all right. Then, with a shock, she realized that she hadn't gotten his name or number. If he lost hers (and he did seem kind of foggy), how would she pay for the damage she'd caused? And what if he were acting dazed because he'd hurt his head? She'd never know or be able to make amends!

Questions

1. Leaving the scene of an accident is against the law, but if both parties agree to do so, is there anything ethically wrong with this?
2. Was Michiko's treatment of the accident victim unethical in some way? If so, how? If not, are her guilt feelings unjustified?
3. Because she made a good-faith effort to be responsible, is she morally obligated to do anything else?
4. If the man never calls her, what can, or should, she do?
5. How might the principles of character growth and respect for persons apply to this case?

Case 10.8: The Hacker

Larry is a computer hacker and proud of it. When he's not doing his course work, he spends many hours figuring out how to break into his community college's student record files. Finally he succeeds, and, chuckling to himself, programs a simple worm to add the words "here today, gone tomorrow" randomly to the records. He also downloads some records he's curious about—his own, those of his friends, and those of a girl he likes but doesn't know well. The records contain all kinds of interesting information, including grades, recommendations, and medical and psychological information.

The college's computer experts track him down a few days later. Larry claims that he wasn't trying to cause trouble, that in fact the whole exercise was intended to demonstrate how vulnerable student records are to such a break-in. "You guys have a security risk there!" he says. "I just wanted to show you that. That's why I left the worm instead of just downloading the files I wanted. And I didn't take any illegal information. Students are allowed to see what's in their files, according to federal law. I just got my friends' files for them."

Larry is being a bit disingenuous, of course. He looked at all the information first, and he didn't tell the girl he likes that he has her file. His friends can ask for their files directly from the Student Records Office if they want to see them. At any rate, the college does not appreciate Larry's little object lesson. In fact, they intend to prosecute him to the fullest extent possible in order to discourage other potential computer vandals and information thieves. They also tell him he was lucky his hastily written virus didn't replicate in unforeseen ways and cause serious damage.

"It wasn't luck, it was skill!" Larry defends himself cockily. The college officials do not seem impressed.

Questions

1. The federal law that Larry mentioned, the Buckley Amendment, guarantees students access to (most of) their own records and limits others' access to this information. (See Chapter 4 for more details.) Is there anything unethical about what Larry did? Are there moral distinctions between his taking his own file, his friends' files, and the file of the girl he likes?
2. Is stealing information morally different from stealing possessions?
3. Can Larry steal information to which he has legal access anyway, such as his own file?
4. Because the college probably will learn from Larry's "lesson" and tighten their computer security, shouldn't the administration feel grateful toward him rather than attempting to punish him as severely as they can?
5. How might the ethical principles of respect for persons and community apply to this case?

Case 10.9: Fit to Print

Heather is a student reporter for the campus newspaper, *The Daily Sun*. Because there is a lot of debate on campus currently about the advisability of having separate dorms for minority groups such as gay students or African Americans, her editor asked her to write a color piece about life in the college's Third World Residence Hall. The Third, as it's known, is mainly inhabited by black and Hispanic students, with a smattering of East Indians and an occasional Caucasian. Students in other dorms sometimes refer to it disparagingly as "the Peace Corps dorm." Most of the college's white students (and faculty) assume that the Third's residents are at best cliquish, and at worst outright hostile to others on campus. Therefore a piece on life in the Third by a white student promises to have a large readership in *The Daily Sun*.

Heather was surprised to find how open people in the Third were to being interviewed. Everyone was so friendly that she decided to share a room with a resident for a week, to really get the flavor of the place. She told everyone she met in the Third that she'd be writing about their daily life. However, she didn't go into detail about what would be in the article; she wouldn't know that until she wrote it.

Heather did some formal interviews, and then she decided that the bulk of her story would be based on her observations. She took copious notes on everything she saw. She asked all of her possible subjects whether they wanted their names changed in the article. Everyone said, "I have nothing to hide! Go ahead and use my name." In fact, they seemed flattered about being the subjects of a *Daily Sun* story. Many students confided in Heather over the course of the week she spent with them, and they all seemed to forget that they were being observed by a reporter. In fact they seemed to consider Heather their friend.

When Heather's long article finally came out, she was surprised and upset about her new friends' reactions. A number of Third residents approached her to tell her how angry they were about the story. Many felt that their privacy had been invaded, even though Heather thought she'd presented them sympathetically. "I didn't realize you'd tell the whole campus I had a hair weave!" one woman said bitterly.

Another student was angry that Heather had printed some of his nonflattering comments about a certain professor. "I told you that stuff in confidence! How am I supposed to face my prof. now?!"

A third student, Kim, practically spit in Heather's face as she yelled, "That guy you described as my boyfriend was only a friend! Now my real boyfriend wants to break up with me. You really messed up my life!"

Others seemed outraged at how Heather pictured them, not so much because she'd made mistakes or said negative things, but because her descriptions didn't match their self-images. Also they didn't appreciate being pointed out by other students as "Aren't you the one who . . . ?"

That was not all. Heather's article generated numerous letters to the editor of the *Daily Sun*. One anonymous Third resident wrote, "A lot of us think your reporter misled us. We hadn't realized her story would be so much about the people who live in the Third. We thought it was going to be more about our residence hall programs and how the Third is set up. We feel humiliated that she printed private details from our personal lives, along with our real names. This is irresponsible journalism." Another wrote that "Heather Mifflin used us to make political points in the campus debate over housing. What she wrote doesn't necessarily represent our views. Her interpretations and conclusions are way off base."

Heather thinks these criticisms are largely unfair. Her subjects seem to have willfully misunderstood or forgotten what she told them in advance. She doesn't think she misrepresented what they said, and she has her notes to back her up, but she does feel sorry that so many of them are upset. Kim, the Third resident whose boyfriend split up with her after the article came out, is even talking about suing Heather and the newspaper. It's not clear what grounds for a suit Kim has, and Heather doesn't have much money, but she wonders whether she should give Kim some of the money she's saved from her summer job. "Maybe I did do something wrong," she thinks to herself. "And even if I didn't, maybe I owe her something because she's so upset."

Questions

1. Is the very idea of having a white student write about a nonwhite residence hall suspect? Why or why not?
2. Who is responsible for the unpleasant results of the article—Heather, *The Daily Sun* editor, or the Third residents themselves? Why?
3. How might such a problem be avoided in the future?
4. To whom or what does Heather have a primary duty: The truth as she sees it and journalistic standards (she considers herself a serious, aspiring journalist)? The subjects of her piece (should she protect their privacy first and foremost)? The college community's "right to know" about a rather closed society in their midst? Or to something else?
5. Would your answers change if the article had been about a campus crime?
6. What kind of recompense, if any, should Heather (and/or *The Daily Sun*) make to the irate subjects of the article?
7. Heather has read that inexperienced interviewees often come to trust reporters and forget that their words will be published. Is there anything Heather could or should do to help ensure that her future subjects won't be embarrassed about what she prints? Or is it a reporter's job to get people to reveal things they don't want to reveal?
8. Which ethical principles might apply to this case, and how?

Case 10.10: Rent Battle

Gail and Diane share an off-campus, two-bedroom apartment in a desirable location with few vacancies. Gail has lived there since the previous year and holds the rental contract in her name alone. She recruited Diane through an acquaintance to fill the vacant room; they didn't know each other before Diane moved in.

One day Diane sees a letter in their mailbox from their landlord. Even though it is addressed to Gail, Diane opens it because Gail is gone for the weekend and she'd mentioned that the landlord was talking about raising the rent. Diane is curious about what the new rent will be. She can barely afford the current rate. She is shocked then to find out that she and Gail aren't splitting the rent evenly. In fact Diane is paying almost three quarters of the cost of renting the entire apartment, even though she has the smaller bedroom.

Diane confronts Gail with her outrageous unfairness when she returns. Gail, however, is not easily intimidated. Her attitude is, "I found this apartment first. The rent I told you is the going rate and a price you were perfectly happy to pay for your room. Just because I got a good deal on the rent doesn't mean I have to pass the bargain on to you. You can like it or lump it. And how dare you go through my mail!"

Diane replies that she hadn't suspected anything unequal about their rent payments, so she hadn't thought Gail would mind her opening the landlord's letter. "It never occurred to me that you had something to hide. How could you be so slimy?"

Questions

1. Does Gail have an ethical duty to split the rent equally? Why or why not?
2. Exactly what is wrong (aside from the fact that it's illegal) with opening someone else's mail if your motives are not malicious?
3. Are Diane's and Gail's misdeeds (reading another's mail, making a profit from a roommate) equally dubious ethically?
4. If Gail refuses to split the rent more equitably, Diane has no legal way to force her to do so. What should Diane do then?
5. Should landlords, colleges, or other authorities have the power to insist that roommates split the cost of rent equally?
6. What effect do you think Gail's arguments might have on the growth of her character?
7. Are other ethical principles involved in this case?

Case 10.11: Suicidal?

Several students are talking about whether Jeff, an apparently suicidal student, is "really serious." He certainly seems rather depressed; he doesn't seem to have any close friends, and he talks a lot about dying. However, it's hard to know what he really feels. He has a dark and sarcastic sense of humor, and all his talk about death may just be posing for effect.

"I think he's just trying to get attention, being dramatic," says Ping Li.

"The guy's kind of a creep," agrees Leslie. "Who cares about him?"

Fernando, who's taken some psychology courses and has read that talk of suicide should always be taken seriously, feels that he should get involved to stop Jeff from hurting himself. So Fernando decides to sound Jeff out about whether he's really suicidal. It isn't too hard to get Jeff talking about how everything is terrible and life's not worth living.

"Do you ever, you know, think about ending it all?" Fernando asks him.

Jeff gives him a funny look. "All the time, man."

"I mean, have you ever tried?"

"Yeah; see these scars on my wrists? That was from one time in high school. But that's not it for me. I haven't figured out the best way yet. You got any suggestions?" Jeff adds with a half smile.

"Maybe you should go to counseling," Fernando responds nervously.

"Therapists suck. My parents made me go to some jerk after I tried to kill myself in high school. She was a real bozo. So nooo thanks."

Fernando isn't sure what to say. "Maybe you could give it another try. The people at the Health Center are supposed to be good."

"What, have you tried to talk to them about suicide? Therapists don't know crap. What's it to you, anyway?"

Jeff seems to resent Fernando's awkward interference, so Fernando backs off, defeated.

Questions

1. Fernando made an effort to advise Jeff, and Jeff seemed to resent his well-meaning efforts. Should Fernando just leave him alone? Is there something else he could or should do to help Jeff?
2. The two students hardly know each other. Do we have a duty to help people we don't really know, or people who say they don't want our help? Or are people who interfere in such situations just busybodies?
3. Is Fernando's behavior morally superior to Ping Li's and Leslie's, or is it just that some people are more outgoing and willing to get involved than others?
4. What ethical principles might inform Fernando's concern for Jeff and help him make a decision about what to do?
5. Because Jeff talks about suicide all the time, do you think he's actually less likely to try to kill himself than he would be if he didn't discuss it?
6. What if he does try—doesn't he have a right to die if he wants to? Why should others interfere?

Case 10.12: With Charity toward All

The Green College Student Service Organization recently conducted two different fund-raising campaigns. One was to raise money for a local homeless shelter, and the other was to contribute to the national campaign of Help the Children, a charity benefitting sick children. GCSSO's Help the Children drive was much more successful than the one for the homeless shelter, perhaps because the Help the Children organization had advertised in national magazines and television to support local fund-raising efforts during their drive. No group except the GCSSO had advertised the homeless shelter campaign.

Now the GCSSO officers are meeting to decide what to do with the money raised. The problem is that the director of the local homeless shelter recently talked to several GCSSO members, thanking them for their efforts but commenting that with recent cuts in state aid, they might well have to close. Even though the shelter operates on a shoestring, they won't be able to stay open unless they can raise almost double the amount they had originally targeted in their fund-raising drive. "So, should we divert money people donated for Help the Children to the shelter?" GCSSO Chair Kelly asks her fellow officers. A vigorous debate follows.

Questions
1. Should the final decision be made by the GCSSO officers, or by the entire membership?
2. Should they try to get opinions from the donors, perhaps through a local newspaper ad or letter to the editor? Why or why not?
3. The managers of the homeless shelter will never know that much of the donated money was originally intended for another cause if GCSSO doesn't tell them. Likewise GCSSO can easily doctor their records to show the Help the Children organization that a much smaller amount was donated to them than was actually the case. Should these facts influence the group's decision?
4. Would such acts be unethical? Is one worse than the other?
5. Is giving extra money to the homeless shelter, which may have to close anyway, just throwing good money after bad?
6. Should the fact that Help the Children has a far bigger budget than does the homeless shelter affect the GCSSO's thinking? If so, how?
7. Which ethical principles could be involved in this case? How might the GCSSO use them to reach a decision?

Case 10.13: Contemporary Social Problems: Who Cares?

Springview College requires that students take a one-credit interdisciplinary course on "Contemporary Social Problems" during their freshman year. The intent is to raise the mostly affluent students' consciousness about the harsh realities of hunger, poverty, and disease facing many in America and in the rest of the world, and to use these issues to introduce students to critical thinking in the social sciences and humanities. Among other topics, the course includes lectures on poverty, AIDS, and hunger, illustrated by slides of starving people, AIDS sufferers, and the desperate poor in American inner cities and in the Third World.

Neil Benjamin, who teaches a section of the course, is disappointed by the students' reactions to it. He's noticed that several students sleep though the lectures. The rest, while polite, seem unenthusiastic. Indeed, a number of students walked out partway through the AIDS lecture, when some rather horrific slides of lesions on AIDS sufferers were shown. There is little participation in the "dialogues" at the end of each class. The few students who do ask questions and appear engaged during discussions are treated as irritants by the others, who roll their eyes and make every sign of wanting to leave early.

Professor Benjamin would be more than disappointed to overhear the following postclass conversation. Sarah, Amy, and Phil are discussing the class in the cafeteria. "What a total waste of time it is; it's so boring," says Sarah. "Who cares about that stuff? I've slept through most of the classes, except for the time they had those gross-out AIDS pictures. We should get people to boycott the classes if they have them again next year."

Amy notes, "It's so irritating how a few people go on and on asking dumb questions at the end of class. We could be out of there a lot sooner if they would just shut up. They're so obviously trying to suck up that it's disgusting."

Phil mentions that his friends laugh about the course, calling it "sentimental liberal crap." "The worst part is," he adds, "we could have more time for other courses if we didn't have to waste time on that stuff."

"Or just spend some time relaxing!" says Amy. "It's scheduled during my favorite soap, and I hate having so many stupid requirements. I hardly have any free time."

Questions

1. Why would the college administration think this mandatory course is a good idea? Do you agree? Why or why not?
2. What does the students' apparent rejection of the course say about their values?
3. How can students become aware of the suffering of others?
4. Should such a course be mandatory for all Springview College freshmen, regardless of their interests or backgrounds? Is awareness of the plight of the poor and other social problems something colleges should try to instill in their students?

5. Might there be other more effective ways of getting students to empathize with the less fortunate?
6. Do institutions such as colleges, as well as individuals, have a responsibility to alleviate suffering in the world? If so, how might they best do this?
7. Is there something unethical about embracing ignorance about social problems and deciding not to get involved, or is this just a matter of personal preference? Why might these students seem so apathetic?
8. Which moral principles might apply here, and how?

Case 10.14: Freedom of Religion?

The Coldwater College community is almost notoriously liberal, yet it seems quite intolerant toward the few Muslim students on campus. There are seven Muslim foreign exchange students, two of whom are women, who stand out in their head scarves and long, baggy garments.

Many American students, particularly those who consider themselves feminists, shun the Muslim men as "sexist and intolerant" because of their supposed attitude toward women. They are no friendlier toward the Muslim women, because the Americans cannot understand "why they would put up with the way they're treated in Muslim society. Just look at the way they have to dress, even here!"

Perhaps unspoken prejudices about the Middle East's supposed fanaticism and propensity for terrorism also play a role in the Americans' hostility toward the Muslim students. Or perhaps they are simply uncomfortable with the unfamiliar.

At any rate, the American students' intolerance seems to come to a head when the college offers an assistant professorship in economics to an Arab American man who is known to be a practicing Muslim. A number of students protest his hiring even before he has taught a course, because of his supposed belief in the inferiority of women. As one of the protesters put it, "How can you expect someone whose religion says women are inferior to be fair to the women in his class?"

Questions

1. The protesting students' knowledge of the Muslim religion seems to be based on hearsay and prejudice. Do they have a moral duty to learn more about Islam before they reject it or its practitioners?
2. Do people with one world view (such as Western feminists) have a right to criticize people holding different world views (such as Muslims)?
3. If individuals find the behavior of a religious group offensive, are they ethically entitled to shun them or more actively express their distaste?
4. Are a professor's religious views any business of his students?

5. Should colleges be particularly open to religious diversity, or should they attempt to keep all religious debate off campus? Why?
6. What might Coldwater College do to smooth relations between the non-Muslim student majority and the Muslim students?

For more information about the role of women in Islam as seen by a relatively sympathetic western feminist, see Geraldine Brooks, *Nine Parts of Desire: The Hidden World of Islamic Women* (New York: Anchor Books/Doubleday, 1995).

Case 10.15: Yes, Master

Professor Beatty, an instructor in Southeast University's freshman writing program, is disturbed and exasperated by what she considers her students' unhealthy deference to authority and unwillingness to engage in independent moral thinking. She devises a trick writing assignment to test their obedience to authority. First she sends Ingrid, a warm and friendly girl who seems to be the kindest student in the class, out of the room. Then she tells the rest of the class to write the nastiest character assassination of Ingrid that they can. "I want it to be really mean—critique her looks, her behavior, her morals, everything. The worse it is, the better your grades will be. When you're finished, the two best essays, that is, the two most crushing ones, will be read out loud to Ingrid. Any questions?"

Professor Beatty is shocked when the students have no questions about obeying this assignment and are ready to get to work. She asks them why they would be willing to do this.

Jake says, "I want to get a good grade, and I don't have to take this class again."

Nancy adds, "I don't know Ingrid, and I'll probably never see her again. So it doesn't matter what I write."

Most of the class doesn't volunteer any reasons for their willingness to do the assignment; they seem apathetic. Then the professor lambasts the class, saying, "This wasn't a real assignment, but a test of your moral fiber! I'm shocked that none of you said, 'It would make this girl feel too humiliated; my grade isn't worth that much, so go jump in a lake.' You shouldn't just do whatever you're told to by an authority figure—what if I told you to do something really evil, or stupid? You have to think for yourselves!"

The students look sullen and confused under her outburst. Bewildered, Ed says, "But you're the teacher. If you think this is a bad idea, why did you assign it?"

Jake asks angrily, "What do you want from us? We were just going to do what you told us. Since when is it a crime to do what the professor tells you to do?"

The professor wants to throw up her hands in despair. The class has proved her point all too well.

Questions

1. How would you respond to Professor Beatty's assignment?
2. Is it unethical of her to give out trick assignments in order to morally test her students? Can trick assignments be justified for some other purpose, such as to show students the impossibility of performing a seemingly simple task, or the complexity of an apparently straightforward concept?
3. Do students have a duty to consider the moral implications of their assignments, lectures, and readings, and to resist anything they find ethically suspect?
4. Whose responsibility is it to ensure that the moral dimension of a subject is not overlooked?
5. Should students be ready to question their professors' authority or integrity? Is this something you can see yourself doing?

Case 10.16: *What's Wrong with This Girl?*

Vanessa, Rasheeda, and Jennifer are all transfer students, and all were assigned to the same student apartment at the beginning of their junior year. Vanessa and Rasheeda have become good friends, although they both find Jennifer harder to like. However, they're friendly to her because she seems otherwise friendless.

Jen often seems strangely secretive and even dishonest about petty things, such as the number of pairs of shoes she owns (Vanessa and Rasheeda are amazed that they rarely see her wear the same pair) or the grade she got on a midterm, although as Vanessa said, "It's not like I really care!" Her lies seem to be connected to her excessive concern with status: popular So-and-So has asked her out, or her fabulously wealthy parents are buying her not one, but two sports cars. Rasheeda and Vanessa have gradually realized that she can be quite manipulative, telling Vanessa something bad about Rasheeda, and then turning around and pretending to Rasheeda that she likes her better than she likes Vanessa.

Jennifer's strangest behavior involves food. Many a time Rasheeda or Vanessa have left part of a carton of ice cream or some take-out Chinese food in the refrigerator, only to find it disappear in such a way that only Jen could have taken it. She always denies stealing the food, even though Vanessa has told her, "I don't mind so much if you eat something of mine once in a while—but tell me, so I know not to count on it being there!" Her roommates have also noticed that Jennifer will pig out on several gallons of ice cream and a couple of bags of cookies during the middle of the night (the telltale evidence being in the trash can the next morning), even though she's always talking about her weight and trying various diets (she doesn't look fat to them). Perhaps most troubling of all is the disgusting vomit smell that lingers after Jennifer has been in the bathroom, although she never admits to being sick.

Rasheeda and Vanessa describe their weird roommate to a friend, who promptly says, "That girl's got bulimia! I know because my sister was bulimic for a while, and she was just the same—stealing food, lying, trying to manipulate everyone, making herself puke to keep thin. It's an eating disorder, and it can be pretty serious, even life threatening for her, not to mention a pain for anyone living with her."

Vanessa and Rasheeda confront Jennifer with this diagnosis. Amazingly, Jen confesses to years of therapy throughout high school for bulimia, but she asserts, "It's under control now; my last therapist cured me."

Questions

1. Jennifer won't admit to any problems, and the irritating things she does (stealing food, lying, and the smell in bathroom) seem too minor to justify a formal complaint to the authorities. Vanessa and Rasheeda can deal with the bother Jennifer causes fairly easily: never leave your leftovers in the fridge; always open the bathroom window after Jen's been in there, no matter what the weather; and don't believe anything she says. They've already decided to move out together at the earliest opportunity.
2. What should Vanessa and Rasheeda do about Jennifer's antisocial behavior? Do Vanessa and Rasheeda have a duty to try to get Jen counseling or other help with her problem, even though they don't particularly like her? Is her private eating problem really any of their business?
3. How might they use the various ethical principles in deciding what to do?

Case 10.17: A Second Chance?

It was not surprising that out of eighteen thousand applicants, Gina Grant was one of the two thousand students admitted to Harvard for the class of 1995. Gina was a bright, popular, talented, and pretty student who had been the first female student-body president of her middle school, served as co-captain of her high school tennis team, tutored underprivileged children, and graduated near the top of her class at a well-regarded high school.

Before she could attend Harvard, on April 3, 1995, the college's admissions committee held a rare emergency meeting and voted to revoke

Gina Grant's acceptance. The reason was that someone had anonymously tipped them off that Gina was hiding a terrible secret—she had brutally murdered her abusive mother when she was fourteen years old. Because she was a minor at the time, Gina had served only a brief prison sentence, and her court records had been sealed.

She expected to be able to start over again, and she had tried hard to pick up the pieces of her life. Being accepted at Harvard was the high point of her amazing turnaround. However, now that her secret was out, Harvard declined to give her a second chance on the grounds that she had lied about her past. (It seemed likely that Harvard would never have admitted her if she had *not* hidden her past.)

Questions

1. We have said about the principle of character growth that you are to a large extent what your choices have made you; your ethical decisions make you into the kind of person who will continue to decide in similar ways. (See Chapters 1 and 2.) Does this view preclude the possibility of redemption and forgiveness? Specifically, has Gina's matricide made her unfit to be given a second chance, no matter how "reformed" she might appear?

2. Should we (personally, and as a society) be willing to forgive any deed, no matter how heinous, so long as the perpetrator sincerely regrets it and has "reformed"? If not, where would you draw the line, and why?

3. Should Gina's actions as a juvenile have any effect on her college career? Why or why not?

4. If it turned out that Gina had good reasons for killing her mother, should Harvard (or any other institution or person) trust her not to kill again?

5. How does forgiveness differ from trust?

6. Gina is not the only Harvard applicant to have been convicted of murder, although other murderers have been admitted to the school without incident. General Héctor Gramajo, a Guatemalan officer who supervised the extermination of 100,000 Maya Indians in the 1980s, was later admitted as a Mason fellow at Harvard's Kennedy School of Government. Carlos Salinas de Gortari, the former president of Mexico who murdered a family servant as a youth, received his masters and Ph.D. degrees from the Kennedy School. Is it inconsistent of Harvard to forgive and forget some murders and not others in its applicants' pasts? Is there some ethical distinction between these killings that makes the two men more deserving of a second chance than Gina Grant?

7. Which ethical principles might apply to this case, and how?

For more information, see Jane Mayer, "The Justice File: Rejecting Gina" in *The New Yorker*, 5 June 1995, vol. LXXI, no. 15, pp. 43–51; Joe Mathews, "Should Harvard

Accept a Student Who Killed?" in *The Los Angeles Times*, 16 April 1995, sec. M, p. 3, col. 3; Ellen Goodman, "A Promising Student, An Unclean Slate" in *The Boston Globe*, 16 April 1995, sec. A, p. 7, col. 2; Cynthia Tucker, "Saving All the Ones Who Can Be Saved" in *The Atlanta Journal and Atlanta Constitution*, 16 April 1995, sec. B, p. 7, col. 2; Alice Dembner, "Judge, Others Back Student's Right to Conceal Past" in *The Boston Globe*, 8 April 1995, p. 1, col. 3; Alexander Cockburn, "Harvard and Murder: The Case of Carlos Salinas" in *The Nation*, 29 May 1995, vol. 260, no. 21, pp. 747–48.